My Dear Father and Mother

The Personal Letters of Livingston N. Clinard
Correspondence From Family and Friends
1871-1880

REMINISCING
BOOKS

Compiled and edited by
Karen L. Clinard and Richard Russell

Published by Reminiscing Books
Asheville, North Carolina
Library of Congress Control Number 2007923812
ISBN-13: 978-0-9793961-6-8
ISBN-10: 0-9793961-6-6

Printed in The United States of America by
Edwards Brothers, Incorporated

Direct all correspondence to:
Reminiscing Books
1070-1 Tunnel Rd
Suite 10, Box 326
Asheville, NC 28805

info@reminiscingbooks.com
ReminiscingBooks.Com

On the cover: Hickory, North Carolina circa 1906. Photo courtesy of
Catawba County Historical Association

This work is dedicated to
Livingston N. Clinard, his wife, family and close friends.
Without their devotion to each other and their commitment to written
communication, the hopes and joys they experienced and the hardships
they endured would never have been known by those who followed.

The L. N. Clinard Papers courtesy of
The North Carolina Office of Archives and History
Raleigh, North Carolina.
Originally donated by Miss Helen Vogler, biennial years 1930-1932.

Memoirs of Livingston N. Clinard, Charlotte Elisabeth Shultz Clinard
and Mary Emmeline Butner Clinard were reproduced courtesy of
The Moravian Church Archives Southern Province,
Winston-Salem, North Carolina.

Special Thanks To:
Martha Rowe; Old Salem Museums and Gardens
Jason Toney; Catawba County Historical Association
Alex Floyd; Catawba Country Public Library
Leslie Keller and Patrick Daily; Hickory Landmarks Society
Molly Rawls, Forsyth County Public Library
Stuart Clinard, Jerry Loafman, Christina Carlton
Larry Clinard, Charles C. Clinard, June Clinard

iv

Introduction

Housed in the North Carolina Office of Archives and History in Raleigh, North Carolina are the L. N. Clinard Papers, a collection of letters written in the mid-1800's to Livingston Clinard of Salem, North Carolina by family, friends and business associates. The letters, surviving for over half a century, were donated in the early 1930's to the Archives where they are officially known and described as the:

> *"Papers of Livingston N. Clinard, storekeeper for Patterson and Company, Salem, especially letters from son Francis A. Clinard, employee of J. G. Hall and R. L. Patterson (later Hall Brothers) in Hickory, dealers in merchandise and produce. Letters describe purchase of produce from Watauga Co. area and its shipment from Hickory; towns of Hickory, Lenoir and Statesville; funeral procession of Gov Tod R Caldwell; elections of 1874-1876; and fairs, balls, temperance meetings, Sunday school and Masonic picnics, concerts and other entertainment in Hickory. Other letters concern the hotel business in Athens, Ga.; the Centennial Exposition in Philadelphia (1876); and medications from World's Dispensary Medical Association (1879-1880)."*

But these letters are much more than the above suggests, and were destined for a larger audience than those who by chance or through research might discover them in Raleigh. The mid to late 1800's was a time when the written word was the primary mode of long distance communication. For those adventurous men and women who left to pioneer a new life and for those who remained "home", receiving a letter was a highly anticipated event. The letters they received were where the stories of their lives would unfold. They provide an eyewitness account of living in the post-Civil War era, describe beginning business practices of a small town, and reveal the personal relationships of a close knit family. They depict a life of hard work, of realized and unrealized dreams, of triumphs and defeats, the joy of birth and the sorrow of death.

Livingston N. Clinard, son of early German settlers Andrew D. and Lydia Brown Clinard, began life September 6th, 1828 in Davidson County, North Carolina. After working as an eighteen year old store clerk in Guilford County, he moved at age twenty-three to the nearby village known as

Salem, where he was employed at the store of Boner and Crist. A short time later he was officially admitted to the Moravian community, and it was in Salem that he would begin his business activities. Moravian Church Archive records state:

> *12 Jan.1852 "Br. Thomas Boner asked to announce that he plans to open a store with the single Livingston Clinard. He applied for permission for the construction of a two-storied frame building on the lot of his brother Will(iam) on Main Street. The house is to measure 23 feet front and 40 feet depth. In this connection Br. Clinard asked for permission to run his business. Since his application for admission to the community dates back a whole year, we do not believe that it is in connection with his present plan, and therefore replies to Br. Boner that the Collegium does not object to his plan, as soon as L. Clinard will be admitted to the community."*

In 1853 Livingston Clinard would marry Charlotte Elisabeth Shultz, daughter of Jacob and Johanna Vierling Shultz, with whom he had two sons, Francis Augustus and Edward Clifton. Following the passing of Charlotte he was married a second time in 1870 to Mary Emmeline Butner, daughter of John and Mahala Ray Butner. In 1875 Livingston and Mary built a two story home which still stands today near Old Salem.

It seems evident from correspondence received by Mr. Clinard that letter writing must have been a weekly or perhaps a daily ritual for him and for his family. It is not known by the compilers of this book whether any of the hundreds of letters Livingston surely must have written survived (we have only one).

The letters transcribed here characterize Livingston Clinard as a man who apparently was well respected and loved… *"You were truly a brother to me and done more than one of my own brothers would."* Livingston also exhibited a strict disciplinary presence to his children… *"I have not been to a dance since Father wrote me about dancing."* The reader of these letters will see Livingston Clinard through the eyes of his family and friends.

The passing of Livingston Clinard was noted by Rev. Edward Rondthaler,[1] Pastor of the Salem Congregation of the Moravian Church. Speaking of the departures for 1896, he stated "Most of them have left us unexpectedly, in some instances very suddenly. One Brother passed into eternity on his way home from his store."

---

[1]"The Memorabilia of Fifty Years, 1877-1927", page 154

Introduction

In 1873, Francis Augustus "Frank" Clinard, son of Livingston and Charlotte Shultz Clinard, and author of the majority of letters in this volume, left the structured Moravian life he had known in Salem to become a store clerk in the small town of Hickory, North Carolina. After a period of adjustment, *"Give me half a chance and I will make my way through this veil of tears"*, it was here that he would spend most of his life and become an outstanding and prominent citizen, businessman, socialite, political activist and lifelong Freemason. He was described as always smiling and was *"never seen without a flower in his buttonhole."*

Frank and Gertrude "Gertie" Jones became the first couple to be married in a Hickory church, and their son, William, the first to be baptized there. Frank's letters show the personal growth of a hard-working young man from one whose attention and interest was focused on learning the *"fancy dances"*, to a mature and dedicated husband, father and businessman, whose life and thoughts were devoted to providing for his wife and children.

———————

In the early days Hickory seemed to be a community searching for an identity... *"Please drop the Tavern in backing letters to me, as we are all trying to stop it being called Hickory Tavern"*, but was soon to become a thriving hub for local and mountain people to sell and trade their produce and other goods... *"We have shipped about 800,000 lbs dried fruit and berries, think we will reach 1,000,000 lbs.,"* states Frank. New businesses were opening and new buildings being constructed. The roads and railroad were expanding to accommodate this influx... *"Hickory is on the upward tide, several families have moved here recently & more coming. There are several Tobacco Factories to be opened here shortly. There are six or eight new houses being built at present"*.

———————

These courageous, persevering and industrious people have long since passed from this earth, but the essence and spirit of who they were will continue to live through the words they wrote so long ago. "My Dear Father and Mother" forever presents those words for all to read and enjoy.

———————

To preserve authenticity most of the original spelling was left intact.

"Study the past if you would define the future."
-Confucius

Table of Contents

"Salem From the Northwest", 1856 Alexander C. Meinung watercolor
Private Collection; Photograph Courtesy of Old Salem Museums and Gardens

Personal Letters of L. N. Clinard 1871-1872

A. D. Clinard[2] to Livingston N. Clinard

Newton House
Athens, Ga
Nov 16th 1871

Dear Brother,
 Mr. Scales from Winston is here tonight. He says you have written two letters to me and received no reply. I have replied to all your letters except the last. Would have replied to that but had written just previous to receiving it. I am glad to learn from Mr. Scales that all are well. I am very well. My wife is still feble. Blanche[3] is not very well, has staid at home from school two days suffering with severe cold. Hope she will be well in a few days.
 Dear Bro., I have nothing of interest to write you. We will keep the hotel next year. We have made nothing yet, but hope to do better next year. All business has been light this year. I must close. Write soon. Convey our love to your family.
As ever,
A. D. Clinard

A. D. Clinard to Livingston N. Clinard

Newton House
Athens, Ga
Jan 16th 1872

Dear Brother,
 Your welcome letter of recent date came duely to hand. We were delighted to hear from you and to learn that all were well. My wife's health is

---

[2] Andrew D. Clinard, son of Andrew D. Clinard, Sr. and Lydia Brown, brother of Livingston N. Clinard. Married Mary "Molly" Wharton. Operated boarding hotels in Athens, Georgia. Reported to have committed suicide in Rome, Georgia, in 1887 by throwing himself in the river
[3] Blanche Clinard, daughter of Andrew D. Clinard and Mary "Molly" Wharton

still bad. Blanche is well. I have a severe cold. The weather has been very changeable here this winter.

Business has been very well this winter and the prospect is good for it continuing so. We are keeping the hotel this year again. We have not made any clear money at the business yet, but see nothing that we can do any better at without capital. All join in love to you & family. Write soon.

As ever,

A. D. Clinard

Write soon

Carrie S. Grier[4] to Livingston N. Clinard

East Point
Jan 21st 1872

Dear Brother,

I received yours of the 18th of Dec. with $6.00 enclosed. It found us all well. I have received two letters from Frank.[5] I confess it is a shame that I have not answered them, but must beg him to have patience with me. I do not think any the less of him or any of you by my neglect in writing.

It would be a great pleasure to me to see you all and many of my friends in Salem. Mary and I have a lonesome time. John is about 20 miles from here at work—will be gone 4 or 5 weeks. I feel lonely today. Mary is so much company—is a "real Frank," when he was her age. It pleases her greatly when we receive letters with a "kiss" for Mary. "The other baby" you spoke of is not at our house. Mary is the only one and is a great pet, especially with her Pappa.

John has sold his land and we are now living on his nephew's land. I would not have lived where we did if the place had been given us. The land and situation was good but neighbors too near and such as we did not like. I would not be compelled to raise my child in such a neighborhood for anything in this world. That is one thing that causes me a good deal of trouble, to think if she lives her advantages will not be such as mine were in my childhood. But if we are spared it is our determination, (with the help of God) to do all we can to train her aright.

---

[4] Caroline Shultz Grier, sister of Charlotte Elisabeth Shultz (first wife of L. N. Clinard)
[5] Francis Augustus (Frank) Clinard, first son of L. N. Clinard and Charlotte Elisabeth Shultz, and nephew of Carrie Greer

John joined the Methodist Church South on Christmas Day. I also intend to unite with that Church, as I do not think I will ever live where I can enjoy the privilege of the Moravians. I feel it is my duty to belong to some branch of the church, and the M.E.C. suits me better than any other.

I should be so glad to see Auntie and Mother. Give my love to them and tell them not many days pass that I do not think of them. I would write to each of them but my chances for writing are not so good as they formerly were. I received a letter from Bro Gideon[6] not long since they were well when he wrote.

We have had a cold, disagreeable winter—several snows, but none of much depth. The ground was covered this morning, and has been snowing some all day. I never saw a more beautiful fall season than we had last.

John was away from home about four months working at his trade. Mary and I had a lonely time, we staid alone excepting Saturday night and Sunday when he came home. John's brother Sam has gone to N.C. It may be he will pass through Salem. He went with another man to take a drove of horses South. We have not heard from Mother and the Caldwell friends for some time.

Frank you must take your share of this letter, I want to see you and Eddie,[7] and hope someday to have that pleasure. We often speak of you and wish we could see you. I would like to see that pretty girl you spoke of. I wish you could see your little cousin Mary, you could have some great romps with her. She is now standing in the door talking to her chickens— she is so fleshy—that I have to be careful with her, and keep her closely housed this snowy weather. I fear croup with her. I am fleshier than I ever have been and my health is very good—this is a healthy portion of the country.

I asked Mary just now what I must tell you. She says, "tell him I kissed you today for him." If you see Cousin Charlie or Mina give my love to them, and tell Mina I want to see her to talk with her and tell her some of my life since I last saw her—tell her I have got the best old man, and the dearest little girl I ever saw. Eddie ought to write to me and tell me what he is going to do when he quits School. I am glad to hear you get along well with your Stepmother.

---

[6] Gideon Shultz, brother of Charlotte Shultz Clinard and Carrie Shultz Grier, uncle of Frank A. and Edward C. Clinard

[7] Edward Clifton Clinard, second son of L. N. and Charlotte Elisabeth Clinard, brother of Frank A. Clinard, nephew of Carrie Grier

Livingston I am glad you sent the money if it was little, came in good time. Money is scarce—hardly to be had at all. If the "Savings Swindle" can live with my hard earned money, I guess I can live without it.

Tell Auntie she must not wait for me to write, that I am always so glad to get her letters. Give my love to all the relations when you see them. Has your Father or Mother been to see you lately? Remember me to your Mother when you see her. Has Miss Addie Herman returned from Europe? I must close and write a few lines to John tonight he will want to hear how his pet baby is. You must write again whenever you can, write me a long letter and tell me all about the changes in Salem. I have never found out yet whether the Cars run to Salem or not. Mary sends a kiss to your baby. Accept much love, all of you.

From yours affectionately,

Carrie S. Grier

A. D. Clinard to Livingston N. Clinard

Newton House
Athens, Ga
Feb 16th 1872

Dear Bro.,

Your welcome letter of recent date containing photographs of yourself & wife came to hand a few days ago. We were all delighted to hear from you and especially to get the pictures. We all like the looks of your wife very much.

This has been the roughest winter I have ever seen in Ga. There hasn't been 3 good days in three weeks. I have had a very severe attack of neuralgia in my head for 10 days, confined to my room most of the time, I am up today.

Our court has been in session 2 weeks. We have had a good deal of company at the hotel which made my services more needful.

My wife's health is some better than it was. Blanche is well and is going to school. I am glad that Frank is such a fine clerk. I send to you two of our town papers from which you will gather some items of interest. I must close. Mollie & Blanche send much love to you & family. Present my regards to all.

As ever, A. D. Clinard

Write soon

A. D. Clinard to Livingston N. Clinard

Newton House
Athens, Ga
Aug 18th 1872

Dear Bro.,

Yours of the 15th inst came to hand today. I was greatly shocked to hear of the death of Sister Clarissa[8] as I had heard nothing of her being sick, I feel very odd indeed at her death. When I was at home over 15 years ago she was a little innocent child and slept with me. Since that she has become a grown woman and died without me having seen her since a child. I regret to learn that you have been sick but am glad to learn that you are getting well. Myself & family are in usual health. Business has been very light this summer. I still hope to visit you all sometime, nothing would afford me greater pleasure. I have nothing of interest to communicate therefore will close. Molly & Blanche join me in love to all. Write soon.

As ever,
A. D. Clinard

---

[8] Emily Clarissa Clinard, July 20, 1850-August 13, 1872

Salem Main Street circa 1890. Thomas Boner building on right, location of Livingston Clinard's first business operation. Private Collection; Photograph Courtesy of Old Salem Museums and Gardens

Personal Letters of L. N. Clinard 1873

A. D. Clinard to Livingston N. Clinard

Newton House
Athens, Ga
Feb 13th 1873

Dear Bro.,

Your welcome letter of recent date came safely to hand a few days ago. We were very glad to hear from you and to learn that all were well. Myself and Family are in usual health.

We are keeping the hotel again this year. Travel has been tolerably good this winter. Considering the very bad weather it would afford myself & family great pleasure to visit Carolina this spring, but I don't see much prospect of doing so. I have not received a letter from Mother for some time. Hope she has become better reconciled to the death of sister. I have no news of interest to write. Let us hear from you soon. Present our love to your wife & sons. As ever, A. D. Clinard

A. D. Clinard to Livingston N. Clinard

Newton House
Athens, Ga
June 29th 1873

Dear Bro.,

I have not rec'd a letter from you for a long time and drop a line to you hoping thereby to hear from you. I am running the hotel and have a fair prospect to do well. I have employed a clerk to assist me but he don't suit me. If Frank would like to come out here and you are willing, I would be glad to take him in with me as a clerk. I will give him $25 board & room per month. I only wish him in case it meets your approbation. Let me hear from you at once. Mrs. Wharton[9] is still very feeble. Mollie, Blanche and myself

---

[9] Ann F. Wharton, b. abt 1818-d. after June 29, 1873 (mother of Mary Adaline Wharton Clinard)

are well. I rec'd a letter from Mother a few weeks ago, all were well. I must close.

Write at once.

All send love. Yours, A. D. Clinard

F. A. Clinard to Livingston N. Clinard

Hickory, N.C.
Aug 9th 1873

Dear Father,

I received your letter this morning & was glad to hear from you & have been looking for one for several days. I am getting along right well. Every thing seems strange up here, the people are worse than the Spachs to trade with. We have winter up here, it is very cold for the time of year.

Tell Mother I have got a good boarding house. There are a good many strangers boarding at the same place I am. The Lady's name is Mrs. Black from Fayetteville, she keeps a good table. She says she knows Tom H's[10] folks.

Sunday Hill[11] & myself went to the White-Sulphur Springs. They are in a nice location & they have good houses there & a good many strangers.

Father, you wrote to me about Mary Fisher. You can rest easy with my word of honor that I have had nothing at all to do with Mary & you can tell people why I came up here. And as to Sal Hauser, I did make up with her, but she wrote me a note just before I started asking me to come up there & make it up & she saying I kissed her. When I told her good-bye, she drawed me to her & kissed me. You can rest easy about my writing to her. I never had such an intention & further more, I don't like her any better than I use to. I know a few things, she can't draw me in her wishes. I know too much for that. When I went up there, I did not stay five minutes.

Mrs. Hall has been sick ever since I have been here, she is getting better now. Mr. H.[12] & Mrs. H. board at the same place I do. There are some very nice people up here in Hickory, they all seem very kind & sociable. I have

---

[10] T. W. "Tom" Huske, apparently worked in retail store with L. N. Clinard in Salem, N. C

[11] Hill Carter, clerk at Hall Brothers store in Hickory, N.C.

[12] Joseph Gaither "J. G." Hall, operator of Hall Brothers store, also Hickory's first railroad depot agent, a flour mill operator, mayor, and president of Piedmont Wagon Company

not been to see any of the Ladies yet, but I think I will go tonight to see Miss Mag Lillington, she is up here on a visit.

I am so cold I can't hardly write, my hands feel right numb. Tell Mother to please fix up my winter coat & send it to me, for if it keeps this cold long we will have to move in our store. Some of the stores have fire now.

We buy a little of everything you can think of nearly, except roots. All kinds of vegetables & chickens worse than Hege Bro.'s. This country would just suit Zack Hege. Every body up here seems to think that you are trying to cheat them all the time. Tell Pfohl that Old Batch Spach is nothing at all to trade with in comparison to some of the people up here.

Tell Eddie he must write to me, also Tom. I would like the best in the world if I could see them both. Give my love to Aunt Eliza[13] & tell her I am getting along very well, & just not to believe half what Sal Hauser says. I regretted that I made up with her in less than no time after I did it.

Tell Mother that I ate my cakes when I got to Kernersville & was glad I had it, although it was some trouble. Mr. Hall & Hill send their best regards to you & Mr. Hall hopes you are getting along all right. Give my love to Aunty & Mother & tell Mother I am doing what I promised her. I must close as the customers begin to come in. Much love to you & Ed.
I remain your True Son,
F. A. Clinard

F. A. Clinard to Mr. and Mrs. Livingston N. Clinard

Hickory, N.C.
Sept 15th 1873

My Dear Father and Mother,

I got your letter & my coat this morning, my coat comes very good for we have had some very cool weather for the last week. I put my coat on right away as soon as Mr. P.[14] gave it to me & have been very comfortable in it all day.

Hill and myself went to Lenoir yesterday to hear Bishop Atkinson preach. He preached an excellent sermon, rather long, one hour and five minutes. Services lasted three hours. He confirmed seven. Three of the

---

[13] Elizabeth Butner, sister of Mary Butner Clinard (second wife of L. N. Clinard)

[14] R. L. Patterson, operated Patterson and Company in Salem, N. C., where L. N. Clinard was employed as a store-keeper, and a partner in Hall and Patterson, Hickory, N. C.

seven were Gertie Jones,[15] Sam Patterson & his wife. I seen all the Joneses & Pattersons. They all seemed glad to see me, also Mrs. Jas. C Harper. I walked up to her & spoke & she did not reckognize me till I told her who I was then she went on powerful & asked me over to see her & Mr. Harper. She said he would be glad to see me. I stopped at Mr. Cloyds & none of them knew me until I told them who I was. Mr. C. looks like always. His daughters have grown up to be young ladies & good looking ones at that. Wade looks like always. Mr. & Mrs. Cloyd said I should give their best respects to you and Mr. E. T. Ackerman's. Things have changed about Lenoir. There are a good many fine buildings gone up there since I was there last. Moore has got a fine block of buildings. I say buildings, I mean building.

George Harper has a fine house out this way from town opposite the Episcopal Church. Dr. Spainhower also has a fine house & office. I saw the Dr. today, he took dinner at our boarding house. Westman & Lark Gilbert look like always. They were both very kind to me & asked after you. Westman came to Hickory today, he still knows how to tell jokes. Fin Harper was here to day, he is looking old & seedy to what he use to. Mr. E. W. Jones asked after you & your health. I called on Mr. H. C. Hamilton & he is looking badly. He said he had been sick all the summer. Mrs. H. looks as well as ever, unfortunately Miss Emma had gone to Sunday School, so I did not get to see her at home, seen her at a distance. Mrs. Cilly was not at home, she was over at her Father's. I saw the Col. Mr. Cilly. I went on over to his Fathers today, she will not be back before next week.

Tell Tom I was sorry to hear that he has a sore foot. Hope it will soon be well so he can go to see Miss Lucy.

Mother, we get good eating chicken nearly every day for dinner, fried & dumplings. Mackeral for breakfast & waffels & battercakes for supper. I can't say as well for my washer woman at my boarding house. She done up my shirts awful bad last week, but she said she would try & do better.

I am getting better acquainted with the place now & like it better than at first. I nearly went up at first, but I did not let on any. The Boss asked me if I liked here as well as Salem & I told him I did not. He did not say much to that. Hill lied to him. He told him he liked it splendid & all the time, he is wishing himself away. I teased him right smart about it.

Tell Ed, I think he is a long time about writing to me & tell him nearly all the folks I have seen that I knew asked after him. They seem to be surprised

---

[15] Gertrude Estelle Jones, daughter of William Franklin Jones and Sarah Lenoir. Future wife of F. A. Clinard

to hear that he is as large as I am. Give my respects to all the clerks. Give my love to Aunt Eliza & tell her I heard from Mrs. M. & Rosa.

I saw Hort. Bowen yesterday, he says they are getting along very well. They have gone to Ark. now. Mr. Hall is making out his memorandum to go north. We talk about ugly calico down there, we don't know anything, if we haven't got the ugliest calico I ever saw. There ain't a respectable piece in the house. Goods are sold at a good profit up here, as shere as your born, from 1 to 3 hundred per cent. Berries are 15 cents here trade, 11 to 12 cash, just what we can get them at. I must close as it is late & my paper is full. Much love to you both.

I remain Your Affectionate Son,

F. A. Clinard

F. A. Clinard to Mr. and Mrs. Livingston N. Clinard

Hickory Tavern, N. C.
Sept. 23rd 1873

Dear Father & Mother,

I received your letter this morning & was glad to hear from you. You always put off answering my letters longer than I do yours.

Mr. Hall started north this morning. I got him to buy me a Sunday vest, & if he comes back by Salem please send me my boots. He said he would bring them for me. I am near bare-footed. It is getting too cool for my low quartered shoes.

Mr. R. L. P.[16] will be at Hickory this evening. Trade seems to be slacking up. We have not been so busy for the last few days. We occasionally buy a load of chickens & cabbage, bought one this morning. We got over 900 heads of cabbage. I was busy all day yesterday marking & shipping berries & fruit. We have got a Negro at our beck & call that does all the lifting. Mr. Hall keeps him here to help & do all the dirty work. He is the strongest Negro I ever saw. He carries a barrel of sugar from the depot by himself. I saw him carry a bale of yarn up stairs by himself.

I went to church twice Sunday to the Episcopal. We have five different churches here. The Episcopal, Presbyterian, German Reform, Baptist & Methodist. Also four Doctors. There is five Preachers live here. The Episcopal Liturgy is some thing like ours. I did not mention in my other letter

---

[16]R. L. Patterson

about the Altar & organ in the Episcopal Church in Lenoir. The Altar is the finest piece of work I ever saw, & the organ is splendid. The Rev. Mr. Oertel made them both. Miss Lena Oertel plays the organ, & she can play well, & Mr. Oertel has the best voice for singing I ever heard. He would make Mr. Grunert or Ebert ashamed of themselves. Hill is our Book Keeper now, he don't seem to like it very well. I call him Mr. Belo, he gets about as 'orabil some times when he gets bothered.

We have a good time sleeping. We sleep from nine to seven in the morning. We generally sweep out of an evening, & shut up at dark. I did not get to finish my letter in time to go off today, so I am finishing it tonight. It has set in to raining this evening, & Harrison Patterson is setting close to me eating sugar. He says tell Martha he will not be home in nineteen weeks. I felt right glad to see Harrison & the Boss. The Boss put me to counting interest & it like to got me. I missed it the first time 12 cents, but got it the second. I sold 819 heads cabbage this evening, it goes faster up here than it did for us down there last winter. Hill says if old man Lash is about to die, tell him not to forget his promise, that is will him his watch.

Give my love to Old Aunty, & tell her to write to me. Harrison keeps talking so much that I can't write for laughing so. I must close with my regards to all the clerks. Give my love to Aunt Eliza & Ed, & tell Ed to write to me soon. Give Hen my regards. Much love to you both.
I Remain Your Affectionate Son,
F. A. Clinard

F. A. Clinard to Mr. and Mrs. Livingston N. Clinard

Hickory, N. C.
Oct. 1st 1873

Dear Father & Mother,
Your letter reached me yesterday & I was glad to hear from you. We have got right cool weather now, hope it may continue, for I feel better & do better. I think I am improving. Gamo brought my boots to me this morning. I was glad to get them, for I want to save my other pair for Sunday. They do as well as any thing in this country. I paid him for bringing them.

The people here are making great preparations for the Fair. They are cleaning off the grounds & expect to have a big time. They have got a very nice place for Fair, but not very good houses. The best thing about the grounds is the race track, which is fine. It will be the 29, 30 & 31st of this month.

There are not many strangers here any more, General Mat Ransoms family & a few more are all that's left. Hickory still improves, there is a three story store going up next lot below this one. It is to be a large house, but I think the people here will over do the thing with stores. There is from 20 to 25 here now, & more going up. The place is larger that I thought it was when I first came. There is between seven & eight hundred inhabitants here. I was surprised when I asked the number, but they say there is that many. We have got some of our bills for our new stock & looking for goods every day. We begin to need them, as our shelves are looking right empty.

Mother, I talked to my washer woman, & she is doing up my shirts better than she did at first. Hill has been begging me to sell him some of my shirts. He says he can't get any body here to make a shirt fit to wear. I told him I could not spare any.

For the last few days business has been dull here. People are plowing in wheat. We still get in some berries. We have brought in about two hundred pounds today at 12 1/2 cents trade & long profits on the goods. A sheeting @ 15 cents, berries at 14 cents, common coffee 3 lbs to the $, & other goods according.

Are you going to the Raleigh Fair? You spoke of it before I left. Hope you will go & have a nice time. Mother, we still continue to get good eating at our house. We had hash & fish for breakfast, chicken & dumplings & vegetables of different kinds for dinner, and waffles & eggs poached for supper today. We have about that sum every day with some variations of beef steak & ham. Board $10 per month.

I was to hear Mr. Joiner preach Sunday. He is the Episcopal minister here, & he preaches well for a young preacher. Mrs. Black, the lady I board with, is an Episcopal. She asked me to get my Hymn book, if I could, for her to see. She says she has always had a desire to see the Moravian Liturgy. You can send it by Mr. Hall if you think of it, & can spare one. Send one that is not torn. She is a very nice Lady, always pleasant & got a good word for some one. She also has a very nice Daughter. Mrs. Black is from Fayetteville. She knows Tom Huske's mother, use to be neighbors.

Give my respects to all the clerks, & all inquiring friends, that is, if I have any that inquire. Give my love to Aunt Eliza & Ed. Hope he will write to me soon. Much love to you both.
Your Affectionate Son
F. A. C.

F. A. Clinard to Mr. and Mrs. Livingston N. Clinard

Hickory, N. C.
Oct. 8th 1873

Dear Father & Mother,

I received your letter yesterday & was glad to hear from you. I have been hard at work all day opening & pricing goods. You asked why I did not speak of Mr. Beard. I don't know what to say about him, except he looks like Eli Rominger & is like Mr. Barrow in pricing goods. He can't read the Bills. I had to read several & count up for him. I get along allright with him, he is a great talker. He is like Mr. B. in another respect. He pulls down goods & won't put up any. Hill & myself put them all up. We have got some nice calico this time. We opened drugs this morning, also stationary & have got a good many more to open, but have not got the bills. We look for Mr. Hall in the morning & I guess he will have the bills, & then we will have work. The goods are stacked up here now till we can hardly pass about in the store. We have had several cold days, put up the store yesterday, and it feels right good.

I heard some good music last night for the first time since I have been up here. Hill & myself stopped at our boarding house last evening, & had a very nice time. Miss Cowles from Lenoir, the widow Cowles Daughter, was there with three other Ladies & they made Mrs. Hall's piano sing. I forgot to mention, that Hickory has a brass band. They play right well for new beginners. Transau from Hauser Town was up here & taught them how to blow. They play several pieces that the Salem Band play, but can't play near as well.

Trade has slacked a little, people are plowing for wheat. Mountain wagons are bringing some very fine apples here now. They bring from $1.00 to $1. 30 per Bu. Butter 22 cents & Eggs 22 cents.

There has been a good many people passed here for the last three days, going to the Fair at Salisbury. Wes Clinard & a man by name of Pitts took two horses down yesterday. Pitts is going to run his horse for the race Premium. I hope they will hang the man that burnt Mr. Tise's barn. There was a man in the store today, with a hand of the finest Tobacco I ever saw. He is going to show it at the Fair here in Hickory. People up here raise a deal of cotton & Tobacco. I notice in the papers that M. V. Moore of Lenoir took the Premium at the Vienna Exposition on his manufactured Tobacco. We buy cotton & pay 15 per b. There is a good deal coming in now.

How is Jones getting along with his barber shop? Has he hurt Alex Gates any? Mother you ought to see me sew, mend my pockets & pants. Has H. W.

B. [17] sold Bally yet? He was talking of sending him off by Ron Cox when I left. Hill sends his respects to you both, also to all the clerks & Ed Ackerman. Give my love to Aunt Eliza & Aunty, also retain a greater share for yourselves.

Your Affectionate Son

Frank

F. A. Clinard to Mr. and Mrs. Livingston N. Clinard

Hickory, N. C.
Oct. 14th 1873

Dear Father & Mother

I received yours & Cousin Jennie's[18] letters this morning, & was glad to hear from you both. I was surprised to get a letter from Cousin J., glad you opened it. I supposed Ed got my letter today. I wrote him one Sunday night after I got back from the camp meeting. I had a very nice time, met a good many people I know. I saw some of the grandest mountain scenery I ever saw. The cars run up the Catawba River, close to the Linville Mountains. I saw Table Rock, Hawks Bill, & Short Off. We passed through some of the deepest cuts & over some of the highest fills that I ever saw. The fill there at Salem is comparatively a small one. I fared splendid. I met John Pearson, & he showed me round & introduced me to his sister, & several other Ladies. I had two invitations to dinner. I took dinner with John, & it was a good one I tell you. I heard Mr. Ivy of Lenoir preach. Also Mr. Roby of Lenoir. I recognized Mr. Ivy's voice before I saw him. You recollect what a peculiar voice he has, he begins to look right old. The camp ground is right on top of a small mountain, Mount Nebo, one of the nicest places, & the best stand & camp houses I ever saw any where. They are all new. There was the largest crowd there I ever saw, beat Friedburg.

Dr. Carter is here now, sitting here smoking & talking all he can. He looks like allways & he said I should give his very best respects to you & Mr. Henry Barrow. He came down to meet General Patterson. I saw Mr. Harper yesterday, & he was glad to see me. I thought he never would get through shaking hands with me. He was on his way to Raleigh Fair, so I did not get

---

[17] Henry W. Barrow

[18] Jennie E. Shultz, niece of Livingston N. and Charlotte Elisabeth Shultz Clinard, and cousin of Frank A. and Edward C. Clinard

to talk long with him. He said he would stop when he went back, & take a long talk with me. I also saw John Rainy, the painter. He asked after you & said I should give his best respects to you. Lark Gilbert is about his last, Dr. Carter says. Has got inflammation of the brain, had two convulsions yesterday.

I am some what tired this evening, have been pricing goods & packing cabbage & chestnuts all day. I am shipping clerk. I mark & see that all the goods get to the depot. We bought a load of cabbage & butter & chestnuts from Watauga today. Paid 22 1/2 for butter, $3.00 per bushel for chestnuts, & 2 cents a pound for cabbage, cash, part trade. I have not had the chance to ask Mr. Hall how long I was to stay up here. Mr. Hall is going to kill himself, he works hard & goes all the time as hard as he can rip. Sometimes I tell him some thing & he don't hear me. He is awful absent minded thinking about business. Mr. Hall just came in & gave me orders about cabbage. He said to tell you he was sorry that he did not get to see more of you when he was at Salem, & to give you his regards. Hill sends his regards to you & all the clerks. Also give mine to the clerks & brake Tom's head for not writing to me. We have got a new Depot agent, Mr. Fevee, John Fevee's Father. He is a very clever old gentleman.

Give my love to Aunt Eliza & Aunty. Also give much love to you.
Your Affectionate Son,
Frank

P. S. There was several Indians passed here on their way to the Raleigh Fair.

F. A. Clinard to E. C. Clinard

Hickory, N. C.
Oct. 21st 1873

Dear Brother,

I ought to have answered your letter sooner, but have been so busy that I did not have time. I just returned from Statesville this morning, went down on some business for H. & P.[19] Had a right nice time, considering it was so cold. I really suffered with cold last evening just as the sun was setting. I was on top of the Female College in Statesville. It was certainly one of the prettiest sights I ever saw. It was a little cloudy & you know how nice & red it

---

[19] Hall and Patterson

looks. The College in it self is a handsome building & the grounds round, are very fine. Statesville has more nice cottage houses in it than any town I ever saw. There is two very large Hotels there, & they were so full I liked not to get in. I happened to know several gentlemen stopping there & they got me in. Mr. Joseph Williams & several from Mocksville, & round there that I know were there, so I fared right well after all. I looked round for Charles Stockton, but did not see him & did not know where to find him.

Ed, I have been hard at work all day marking & shipping berries & fruits. I have not done any thing else all day & have suffered with cold, my hands would get right numb. I have weighed & marked about 60 barrels & bags today, besides getting up last night at 3 o'clock & coming 40 miles. Gaither gets lots of good work out of me, & is not hard on me at that, but keeps me moving round right sharp.

The Rev. Mr. Stroble lectures here tonight. Hill & myself concluded that we would not go. He would read, I would write to you, so here's at you. I saw Dolph & Will Nelson today, Faddy's boys. They look like always, got the same mules they had when we left, & look like they always did. I knew them as quick as I saw them. Dolph asked after you & Father, & how you were getting along. Ed, I saw Col. Harper. He was here last Saturday when I got your letter. I read to him what you said to tell him. He said he would like very much to see you & have a good talk with you. He invited me to come over & see him before I go back to Salem. I think I will have to go over on the river a day or two before long, if I can get off. I was disappointed this morning in not getting a letter from home. Hope I will get one in the morning. Tell John Brown, Mr. Gibbs said I should remember him & his family to him. Also tell him Miss Anna Gibbs was in the store this evening, & that she looks as rosy as a peach, but her red hair spoils her looks.

Ed, the Watauga wagons begin to roll in with apples, butter & cabbage. We have got some of the finest apples here now I have seen, & good ones too.

I suppose you have heard of Lark Gilbert's death, he died last week. Hill & myself send our best regards to the boys, & would like to send them to the gals, but we are afraid they would not appreciate them. (use your own judgement about that.) Give my love to Father & Mother, also to yourself. So good night.
Your True Bro
Frank

F. A. Clinard to Mr. and Mrs. Livingston N. Clinard

Hickory, N. C.
Oct. 23rd 1873

Dear Father & Mother

I got your letter Wednesday morning & was glad to hear from you. I have been hard at work all day on a bill of crockery, opened a crate & hogshead & sold goods too. H. & P. have got a splendid stock of goods for this country, one of the best that has ever been here. The goods are stacked all about every where, almost beat P. & Co., except we have not got as many fine goods. Mr. Hall sold a wholesale bill today & I sold one yesterday. We have got right smart Wautauga trade at this time. They are bringing in their chestnuts & apples, also lots of butter. Last Monday, I made a trade with a Watauga wagon & then went to Statesville & marked 55 lbs of berries & came back Tuesday. Statesville is a nice place & I think there is a good deal of business done there. I was in several stores, & they got good stocks. I saw the largest stock of goods there I ever saw any where in a few stores, it beat any thing I ever saw. I was surprised when I went in, the store is larger than E. A. V.'s[20] old store in S, & the goods were packed every where & in nice order. I was in H. X. Dwire's store. I knew him. He has traded at the store in S. lots of times. He reckolected me & traded with me last time he was in Salem. He told me he saw Mr. H. W. B. north and that they came back together. I went up to the Female College. It is a splendid building. I went up & knocked & one of the teachers came to the door, & I gave her one of my cards & told her I was from Salem, & she showed me round, & took me out on top, & I had a splendid view of the town, & all the mountains in the western part of the state. She asked me a good many questions about Salem, & the school, & asked me to call again. One of the Hickory Merchants was with me. I saw several gentlemen I knew. Mr. Jos. Williams was there, & a Mr. Baily of Davie & several others. They have got two very large Hotels in Statesville, & they were both crowded, so I liked not to get any place to stay. I thought I would get to see Charles Stockton, but I did not see or hear anything of him.

Next week is our Fair. We are going to have a big time, selling goods especially & not getting to see the Fair. They are going to have a pole, 30 feet high, greased, & a watch at the top for the man that climbs it. There is an

[20] Probably Ernst Augustus Vierling, uncle of Charlotte Elisabeth Shultz Clinard (first wife of L. N. Clinard)

18

old man, nearly eighty years old, is going to try it. He is a great hunter and climber. He is from McDowell. He says he will have that watch. Our Negro here says he is going for that watch.

Mr. Hall asked me yesterday when I wanted to go home. He said he would like to keep me all winter, that I suited him better than any body else he could get, but if I wanted to go back he would have to look round & get some one else. I told him, I would let him know. What shall I tell him?

Give mine & Hill's respects to Pfohl, & all the clerks. Also give my love to Aunty & Aunt Eliza. Why is it Aunt Eliza never sends me any word? I send you a paper, notice a piece of Poetry in it about the merchants. My best love to you both.

Your Son

Frank

F. A. Clinard to Mr. and Mrs. Livingston N. Clinard

Hickory, N. C.
Oct. 28th 1873

Dear Father & Mother,

Your letter came to hand this morning & I was glad to hear from you, & glad to hear Uncle Gid[21] is in Salem. Sorry I am not there to see him. You can tell him I am sorry I am not there, as I would like to see him the best kind. I guess Aunty rejoiced to see him.

We have got a bitter cold night, but the people are crowding in to the Fair. There is just lots of Ox wagons from Watauga here this evening, loaded with apples & cabbage, the Legal Tender of this country. I saw one of the funniest looking teams this evening I ever saw. I think the man had all the stock he had hitched to one wagon. He had an Ox, cow jinney, & a Bull. There is right smart of fine stock came in this evening.

I saw my old sweetheart today, & she looks better than ever. Miss Emma Hamilton. She was in the store & I talked a long time to her & about old times & she seemed to enjoy it as well as I did. I also saw W. D. Jones. He looks like Will Jones, yet only he is fleshier that he use to be. He was driving a mule wagon with a load of apples.

---

[21] Gideon Shultz, brother of Charlotte Shultz Clinard, uncle of Frank A. and Edward C. Clinard

We bought a load of cranberries today at $2.00 per Bu., the finest I ever saw. We sent half Bu. to the Fair grounds this evening. The man we bought them of says he has four hundred Bu. that was picked off one marsh, & they cost him 25 cents per Bu. for picking. He has sold two loads here @2.00.

Mr. Hall told me today that Black Brook's child is dead. I guess they take it very hard. I noticed old man Holland's death in the paper. You asked me where I saw Miss Lillington. She was here at her Aunts, Mrs. Tom Hardins, & at a mighty nice place too. I go round there frequently to see her & her Daughter. Most all the people here are people of means, & they live in good style.

You said I should answer frankly about coming home. I would like to be home by Christmas any how, if not before, but I leave that to you, as I am getting along alright up here & I think I am pleasing Mr. Hall from what he has said to me. I have not had a rough word from any one since I have been here. Mr. Beard treats me as kind as any man could, not to know me longer as he has, & Hill & myself are the same old seven & six, move along as smoothly as two old steers. Hill has gone to bed & I am going shortly.

Mother, if I had two of my shirts done up right nice, I would have entered them at the Fair. Mrs. Hall wanted me to, but I could not get them done up nice enough. I have one that was done up at home, but I had to have a pair to take the Premium. They say the Ladies have got Floral Hall fixed up in style & lots of nice things to show. I will write you after the Fair and tell you all. Gov Z. B. Vance is to deliver the address here Thursday. Give my love to all my friends & much to you.

I am Your True Son

Frank

F. A. Clinard to E. C. Clinard

Hickory, N. C.
Nov. 1st 1873

Tuesday morning, I did not get a letter from home this morning.

Dear Bro,

I ought to have answered your few lines sooner, but have not had time. I have been busy near all the time. Would not have time to write today, but it has been raining all day & I have been out in it & my coat is drying at the store, so I thought I would write to you.

I shipped 130 chickens & a crate of cabbage this morning & helped make coops & I got wet feet & back, so I put on dry socks & boots & so I feel better. Mr. Hall has gone to Palmyra this morning in the rain. I think he will have a bad time. He has gone after his wife & Miss Gertie,[22] will be home tomorrow. We have had some very cold weather up here. I have suffered some. I am more exposed up here than I am at home. I have to be out so much & we keep the doors open, so you know it is a hard matter to keep warm measuring apples & handling cabbage.

We are having right good trade from Watauga. I have traded with Billy Thomas twice, he had little Ed with him the first time, & he is a rough little fellow & can ask more questions than any fellow I ever saw. Watson, the drummer[23] from Baltimore, is in the store. He is talking to me so much that I can't half write.

Ed, it seems to me you ought to write me more than you do. It seems to me if I was there, I could find more to write about than you do, hope you will do better next time. Ed, I want you to whale Tom Huske for me. The little rascal has not answered my last letter, so I think rather hard of him for not writing to me. Ask him, "if he ever saw a whale". Tell him he don't know what work is, if he was up here to catch old nasty chickens in the rain & handle cabbage, he would get his sixty dollars back.

I would like to be home about this time, but I am getting along right well. I slept this morning till the train came in, so you know I get sleep enough. The train comes between 7 & 8 o'clock & we shut up at dark.

Last night I went to see a young Lady, an Episcopal Preachers Daughter. She is one of the prettiest & sweetest girls I ever met. I have fell about half way in love with her. You ought to hear her sing & play on the piano. She is the Rev. Mr. Hughes Daughter from Washington D. C. I call on her several times a week & have a nice time. I went to church yesterday & heard a good sermon. Give my love to all my friends, also to Father & Mother.
Your True Bro,
Frank
P. S. 4 o'clock p.m. I just now went in a man's store in town, & on the counter lay a watermelon. It looked out of season.

---

[22] Gertrude Estelle Jones
[23] A drummer was a commercial traveler or salesman sometimes using a drum to attract attention to his wares

F. A. Clinard to Mr. and Mrs. Livingston N. Clinard

Hickory, N. C.
Nov. 4th 1873

Dear Father & Mother,

I received your letter today, & was glad to hear from you. I guess the first thing on docket is the Fair. Well, I enjoyed myself very well, considering that I had to be in the Store all the time, except Thursday from 10 o'clock till 4. I went to the grounds & I bet you, I saw as much as the next fellow. You ought to have heard Gov. Z. B. V. He let himself out & you could see the old Mountain men going up & shaking hands with him & was as glad to see him, as if he had been one of their sons that had been gone & just returned. The Floral Hall was fixed up splendid. I thought, of course, I never saw one before, but people that was at Salisbury say that it beat Salisbury. The most fun was the foot race & the pole climbing, or rather, trying to climb the pole. No one could climb that. There was one fellow with a nice black suit on tried it & you can imagine how his clothes looked when he got through. The foot race was 1/2 mile for five dollars. There was about twenty started, & but one held out, & he started behind & came out winner. There was a very large crowd there Thursday, an extra train run from Salisbury & from the head of the road to Hickory & they were crowded.

I met a good many people I knew, & had a general good time, especially at our Ball. We had a fine time, no rows or disturbances of any kind. There was lots of nice & pretty Ladies there & I went for them all, & made myself as agreeable as possible. I met a Miss Erwin from above Morganton, a niece of Dr. McDowels, & had a mighty nice time. Also a Miss Walton & several more too numerous to mention. I danced nearly every set. You can imagine how I felt Friday night. I had only slept 3 hours Thursday night, & sold goods all day Friday & till after 10 o'clock Friday night & then went & helped Mr. Hall eat Oysters. You bet I would not refuse as it was my first, & I expect will be my last till I get back to Salem.

We have not been very busy this week selling goods, but I guess we have earned our board cleaning up. Hope I am through for awhile. Mr. Hall is at this time selling a large bill of goods to Mr. H. C. Hamilton. He is just going for them, been trading since about four o'clock & it is now after nine & he still holds on faithful.

I have seen some old acquaintances today, for instance, Jack Robbins & Wills Coffer. They brought down the staple that you know is apples & cabbage. Wills went on powerful about me & asked after you & Ed, & went on

& told all about old war times at the Factory, & how kind Father was to give him some thing to eat once when he was on guard duty there. Cute Jones, his wife, & Miss May came in town this evening after dark. They had a damp ride, for it has been raining all this evening & night.

I am suffering with a cold & cough tonight, so I can't half write. I keep coughing & sniffing so. I undertook a job, I am afraid I can't carry out, that is, to fill all sides of this paper with some thing that will interest you. I have improved a little since I am up here. I have gained 15 lbs & I think will gain more if my cold don't hurt me. I make apples & chestnuts git up & hop.

Mother, I was powerful glad you wrote to me. It helped me considerable, for I have been thinking about you a great deal since I have been here. I was looking at yours & Mother's pictures Sunday, & it came near making me home-sick. Don't you think it was the first time I have looked at them many, many nights, have took a good look at them before going to bed & thought of the good advice you both gave me. Tell Uncle Gid I am awful sorry that I am not there to see him & the photographs of my cousins. Tell him to leave them at home for me to see & keep. Give him one of my photographs to take home with him. You said in your letter that Grandmother is at home. Give her my love, & tell her I am sorry I am not there to see her. I tell you it has been right trying to me to be up here & hear of my kin being there & can't see them. Hope I may have the pleasure of seeing them at their homes in the future. Tell good old Aunty, I often think of her & would write to her, but I just have not had the time, give her my love. I would have liked to have seen her when she met Uncle Gid. I know she went on powerful, but nothing to compare with Aunt Cinthy. She talked & went on the best seven in eleven. I guess you are glad I am not at home for I would want to go home with Uncle Gid certain and see Cousin Misenhammar and git my pony. "O how" I would ride. Ed wrote me you asked about the old imposter. Hope he is in some penitentiary.

Cute Jones just came in the store. He looks like always. Give my love to all my friends and give my love to Aunt Eliza. Hill sends his regards to all his friends. It's getting late & I am tired, so I must close with my best love to you both.
I remain your Affectionate Son,
Francis Augustus Clinard

P. S. Mr. H. C. H. is just through & he said I should give his best respects to you. Mrs. Beard's Daughter was crowned Queen of Love & Beauty at the Coronation after the Tournament by a young man of Hickory. Jack Baker by name. Mr. J. G. H. says tell you he has just wound up selling between 3 &

4 hundred dollars worth of goods & to give you his best respects. I quit with my files carried out & it is after ten, so good night. I think I will sleep well.

F. A. C.

P. S. I will send you the paper you want.

F. A. Clinard to Mr. and Mrs. Livingston N. Clinard

Hickory, N. C.
Nov. 13th 1873

Dear Father & Mother,

I write you in a hurry this morning. We are having very cold weather, had a little snow yesterday. Trade is rather dull. Mr. Hall has gone to the Valley with his wife, went on Tuesday, we look for him back today. Mr. H said to tell you he wanted you to throw in Sugar to those Cranberries he sent down there if you could not sell them any other way. I traded for the cabbage we sent to Patterson & Co. I bought it from Mr. Morris. He tells me he was at Salem & saw you. He also say give you his regards. I bought another load from him yesterday. He hauls the finest cabbage I have seen. I traded with old man Penley, that lives up Buffalo. He asked after you. Tom Coffee was down on Monday, & H. V. P. sold him a bill of goods. He looks more like old man Caleb than like Tom use to, he looks old. Old man Charley Dickson & his two sisters were down & traded a good bill with us. I seen Joe Masten the other day & he told me he saw you last Monday a week & that you were well. I seen Ed Clemmons pass here Monday. I had a talk with him & he told me about his suit with O. A. K. I received Ed's letter yesterday, & will answer soon. Times are so dull, I can't hardly find enough to fill a page.

I guess Uncle Gid has gone. Sorry I did not get to see him. My hands are so cold I can hardly write. Please send me a copy of Blum's scrap book. I would like to see it.

How about my coming home. When do you think the boss will write for me? I think he is going to try and keep me here all the time. I am coming home Christmas if I have to come back.

Mother you ought to see me sewing on buttons and trying to mend torn places. They don't look like you had hold of them. When you see Aunt Eliza give her my love and tell her I would have written to her but I can't hardly find enough to fill a letter to you and she can see yours.

I have got nothing to write about since the Fair. I broke myself down writing that last letter to you, so you can't look for much this time. Here comes that fool Negro of ours with a bale of yarn on his back which weighs 250 lbs. Tell Tom Huske he is going back on me. He has not answered my last letter, give mine & Hill's regards to Pfohl & all the clerks. Give my love to Aunty. Hill says give his regards to old Dan, you can give him mine also & tell him I would like to hear him laugh once more. Much love to you both.
I Remain Your Son,
Francis.

P. S. Hill & myself wants to know how old man Jake & his old blind horse is getting along. Is he carrying the mail from the Depot?

S. B. Shultz[24] to Livingston N. Clinard

Clinton, MO
Nov. 16th 1873
L. N. Clinard Esq.
Salem N. C.

Dear Bro,
A short time after you wrote & with certificate enclosed, I wrote you a long letter, & as yet I have had no answer. I hope you will not have it as long as we have done heretofore, for I would be truly glad to hear from you all, have not had any answer from Aunty either. Our health is, and has been generally good. I hope this will find you all well. The weather this fall has been remarkable fine, no cold weather yet. The grass is still green in many places. The roads are fine. The crops have been good & every thing plenty, except potatoes & apples. Grain plenty, all kinds of stock plenty. It is no rare daily sight to see from 10 to 20 car loads of stock pass here. Business however, is rather dull & money causes flurry to the eastern panic, & value of most articles have come down.
Our town is still improving some. A joint stock Co. formed for mass farming impliments, are putting up a good brick building, 150 by 50 feet, 80 feet, 2 story high, balance 1 story, which when completed & set to running

---

[24] Sanford B. Shultz, brother of Charlotte Elisabeth Shultz Clinard, brother-in-law of L. N. Clinard, uncle of Frank A. and Edward. C. Clinard

will give a good many hands work & consequently add to the business of the place.

In my letter I asked you some questions about Lestie Carnes. Did you ever get my letter? Write me where a letter will find her.

The certificate you sent me enabled me to join here as an ancient O F since which time I have attended regularly and find it very interesting. Give my regards to Salem Lodge. No doubt there are some of the old members and many new ones. The members of 20 years ago I would be very glad to see. Our Lodge here is in poor working order. About 25 to 30 regular attendants.

It is now 20 years past since we left dear old Salem with its many friends and many the changes that have taken place. Most of us have had our joys and sorrows, often, yes often, when I get to thinking. I would wish myself back among my friends & relatives, but that may never come to pass. I sometimes think I will pay you all a visit. Did I say all? All would not find, as many dear relatives & friends have gone before, where we too soon will have to follow, & may God give us grace to be ready at all times to meet our dear ones where parting will be no more. Give our love to your family & to Aunty, & all of the other relatives & old neighbors & friends. I write soon. Yours as ever,

S. B. Shultz

F. A. Clinard to Mr. and Mrs. Livingston N. Clinard

Hickory, N. C.
Nov. 20th 1873

My Dear Father and Mother,

I received your letter Wednesday & was glad to hear from you. I began to think some thing had happened, as I did not get a letter Tuesday, but was glad to find I was mistaken.

We are having very cold weather, the mountains are covered with snow, so you know it is bound to be cold. I have suffered today, we keep the doors open & I have been measuring apples nearly all day & that you know is cold work. I did not get my dinner till nearly four o'clock. I am exposed & have suffered from cold so much that I bought myself some undershirts this evening, so I think I will keep warmer. I have got a cough & my breast was cold most of the time, so I asked Mr. Hall's advice about wearing undershirts, & he said he thought it would be better for me to wear them. I tell you, I don't get to set by the stove much, my hands are so cold, I can't hardly write. My coat is getting the worse for wear, the elbows are worn out. I had them mended yesterday, so I guess it will last me a while yet.

Mr. Hall & his wife, & Miss Gertie Jones arrived yesterday. Mr. Hall says General P. is right bad off. Mr. Hall is going housekeeping next week. I don't know, but I expect Hill & myself will board with him, he has not said any thing to us, but I heard that we were to board with him.

Trade is right lively just now, mostly barter, but very little cash. I had a right good cash trade today sold about 210 Dollars worth, but mostly apples, so I earned it measuring the things up. Mr. Hall told me the Boss wrote him that H. W. B. had over stocked you with goods. Has he grumbled much or not? Is he just blowing? Is Bismark in Salem now? If he is, I guess he blows about the panic considerable.

Hill has gone to bed, & I am cold, tired & sleepy, so I can't write a long letter this time, for I can't think of any thing to write about. Give my best love to Grandmother, Aunty & Aunt Eliza, also give my regards to all the clerks. How is Pole getting along? Does he go up town as he always says, so much as ever? How is Tom getting along selling goods? The boy owes me a letter & it seems he don't intend to answer it at all. You did not say what Dan said to our word we sent him. Good Night, with much love to you both.
Your Affectionate Son
Frank.

F. A. Clinard to Mr. and Mrs. Livingston N. Clinard

Hickory, N. C.
Nov. 25th 1873

Dear Father & Mother,

I received your letter this morning & was glad to hear from you & that you are all well. I had a talk with Mr. Hall about my staying here & he told me Mr. Patterson told him that I might stay with him till Spring. I told him I wanted to go home Christmas & he said he could let me off, but wanted me to come back. Shall I come home on a visit Christmas, or not? Just as you say, I am very willing to stay with Mr. Hall all the time. I have not got half dozen Bosses up here to order me round, & run in before me, when I am waiting on a customer. I am getting along selling goods as well as could be expected, as I am almost an entire stranger.

Since three o'clock yesterday, till nine this morning, our Negro & myself counted 18,000 shingles, & I have been busy buying cabbage & apples ever since till dark, & I traded with Tom Matney's son today. Tell Ed I thought of him, when I was trading with him. You know, I use to call Ed, Matney. Yesterday, I got another load from William Morris. David Farthing, his wife, & Jane Coffee were down last week. They look just like they use to. I had lots of questions to answer. Miss Margaret Coffee is dead, she died a few weeks ago. Col. Wat. Lenoir is living here now. He comes in the store nearly every day. Father, ask the Boss how Mr. Hall likes me. I would like to know if he is pleased with me. I think he is, if he was not he would not want me to stay with him.

We have got a cold, windy night. It is now after 9 o'clock. I just got back from calling on a young Lady. Preacher Gibbs Daughter. Spent a very pleasant evening. Heard some good music, instrumental & vocal.

You wrote me you would have me a coat made. I can buy a ready made coat at 10% on cost up here, or I could have one made. We have a Tailor in town. If I come home Christmas, I will want a pair of boots, as both pair of mine are about gone up. I am trying to make them last me, the best I can. I have had both pair mended twice, also patched. I look fancy with my dress suit, & patched boots, but I don't care much, as long as they will stay on my feet. I tell you, my undershirts feel good these days. I have hardly had time today to look at the store.

I hear our Negro loading shingles in a car this time of night. He is one of the faithfullest darkies I ever saw. He would brake his neck for five cents, or do a favor for Hill or myself.

Mr. Beard has gone to the Charlotte Fair, so the balance of this week we will have to dig to wait on all the customers.

Mother, I thought of your good mince pies today & wished for some. I hardly ever get my dinner till three or four o'clock, but when I do, I make it hop. We are kept so busy that there is no getting off. Hill is setting here by the stove, eating crackers, cheese & sugar, & just this minute got up & got some chestnuts. Miss Gertie went to Salisbury yesterday to meet the Boss, & came back this morning mad at him for fooling her. She went back with Mr. Beard today.

I must close this my hands are cold & it is getting bed time. Give my love to Aunty & Aunt Eliza, & all my friends. Hill sends his regards to you both & to all the clerks. Also give mine to the clerks, & brake Tom's head for not writing to me. So Good night, with much love to you both,
Your Affectionate Son,
Frank

F. A. Clinard to Mr. and Mrs. Livingston N. Clinard

Hickory, N. C.
Dec. 2nd 1873

Dear Father & Mother,

Your dear letter came to hand this morning, & I was glad to hear from you but sorry to hear of that young Lady's death. It seems that they are having bad luck in the Academy, measles & burns. I have been under the weather for the last four or five days, but am getting better.

We have been busy for the last week, buying trash of all kinds. Father, do you recolect Casper Cable, that very large man from Watauga? He was here today, & he asked my name & I told him Clinard, & he asked me if you was my Father, & then he told me a joke on you. While you was in Boon, about you buying crawley root. Do you recollect buying chick weed for crawley? The old man pitched in with me, & traded 35 dollars worth. He was talking about you most of the time. He gave me a very cordial invitation to come & see him, he said he would kill a chicken. I get lots of invitations to come to Watauga.

You say you think I am smitten with Miss Gibbs, you are mistaken. I think a great deal of her, for she is a pleasant agreeable Lady. I am smitten, but is with another Preacher's daughter from Washington D. C. Mother, you ought to see her, she is good looking, favors you except she has blue eyes. She left today so you know I feel rather blue. I have spent some very pleasant evenings in her company. Hill is smitten with her sister, she is good looking also. They both sing splendid & are smart as a fresh cut with camphor on it.

About my coat, it is nearly finished. Mr. Hall sold me the goods at cost & then added 75 cents to it, all cheaper than I could get one in Salem. The Tailor only charges three dollars for making, so you know that is cheap. I will have a nice coat. It is splendid goods & all wool. I am trying to sell my old coat to pay for making my new one. It looks very much like snow tonight. They have had lots of snow in Watauga this winter.

I forgot to tell you my sweethearts name. It is Miss Nannie Hughes, no kin to Henry of Salem. Lindsay is here tonight. He is on his way home, so I will send my letter by him. He has asked 10,000 questions, more or less. We had a Turkey dinner at our house Sunday, & one today. Mr. Hall is going to House Keeping tomorrow. He has been at work, scouring & fixing up yesterday & today. They are nearly ready to move in, will be tomorrow. I guess Hill & myself will board with him. I am about through, as I have not got

any thing else to write. Give my regards to all the clerks, & my love to Aunt Eliza & Aunty. Much love to you both. Good night.
Your Affectionate Son,
Frank

F. A. Clinard to Mr. and Mrs. Livingston N. Clinard

Hickory, N. C.
Dec. 9th 1873

Dear Father & Mother,

Your letter to hand today I read with pleasure. We have been busy all day, did not get to go to breakfast till half past 10 o'clock, & been as busy as we well could be. It has been a very warm day. I went in my shirt sleeves part of the day. We had another Turkey dinner today.

Hill & myself do not board at Mr. Halls, he has a house full. Gertie brought two of her cousins with her, so I think they have company enough. They came in on Mr. Hall when he was not expecting them. He had just got in his house, & was not fixed up for himself, let alone company. I am sausage hungry, have not had any yet, & no likely hood of any soon. I kinder feel as if I would like to come home. Mr. Hall works me outrageous hard, but I recon it is better for me than to be shut up in the store in Salem. I have not got a thing to write this time, so you will have to put up with a short letter this time. I don't get to see anything these days but Watauga Wagons with cabbage & apples. Yes, I did see a sight the other day. Judge Cloud went down on the train, he talked to me & asked me if I had quit whistling. I told him I had. He said if I would quit going with young Ladies, I would do, & cut off my moustache. Hill & myself are going to call on those young Ladies at Mr. Hall's tomorrow night. I was introduced to them this evening, they are going to Salem this week. I must go to bed, as I have a lot of cabbage & butter to ship in the morning, so I have to get up soon.

There is a good many buildings going up in Hickory, mostly dwelling houses. Some nice ones and some that ain't so nice. There has been several new familys moved here since I come up here.

Tell Aunt Eliza, I want to be at home Christmas to eat Turkey and chicken against her. I am in good practice & I think I can beat her now. I won't put the bones in my pocket, as she accused me of doing once. Also, give her my love, & best wishes, that is that she & Davy will make a match yet. I would like to see old Aunty, & have a talk with her. She would ask me more questions than Lindsay could, give her my love. Tell Ed to write to me & to write more than he usually does, he writes one page & quits. Give my best respects to old man H. W. B. & tell him I hope he will soon be married. Give my respects to Pfohl, Lev & Tom, also to my cat. Good night. Much love to you both.

Your Affectionate Son,

Francis

F. A. Clinard to Mr. and Mrs. Livingston N. Clinard

J. G. HALL,   R. L. PATTERSON,
of J. G. & P. C. HALL, Wilkesboro, N. C.   of PATTERSON & Co., Salem, N. C.,

OFFICE OF HALL & PATTERSON,
Dealers in General Merchandise,
AND BUYERS OF COUNTRY PRODUCE.
NORTH OF RAILROAD STATION
Hickory, N. C.,

December 17th 1873
10 o'clock P.M.

Dear Father & Mother,

I received your letter yesterday, & was glad to hear from you. I have just got through work. Mr. Hall is still selling goods, he has sold a bill of about $500.00 since sun down & is still selling. He is selling to one Davy Coffee, the man that swallowed the grubb worm for 40 cents, so you know he has a tough old time selling goods to him. We have had a busy time for the last two weeks, I have traded with a good many old acquaintances. William Morris, Tom Nelson, Doo hush Cloyd, Jason Martin, Ceaton Bradford & so on. Jason Martin can whine like always. Tom Norwood reached here today, he & Stephen Brown went on to Lenoir today.

You want to know when I am coming home. I will be home sometime between this & next Christmas. Mother, you will not want to see me, as I have got a little mending for you to do, & want my shirts done up decent once more.

We are going to have a big dinner at our house Friday. One of the boarders is going to get married tomorrow, & bring his wife home Friday. His name is Abel Shuford. Father, you recolect Abel, he is a clever good fellow.

We are having very warm weather, do without fire most of the time. The boys have commenced Christmas already, shooting off fire crackers & Roman candles. Hill & myself were going to see the Episcopal preacher & his wife tonight, but we had to stay & sell goods. We spent Sunday afternoon at Mr. Hall's & took supper with him, also Billy Morris. He spent Sunday with us. We went to church Sunday morning. I am tired & sleepy too, so I can't write a long letter this time, but will write you a long one next time.

Give my love to Aunty & Aunt Eliza & wish them a Merry Christmas for me, also to Ed. I have been looking for a letter from him for several days, but have been disappointed. Give my best regards to H. W. B., C. B. P.,[25] & T. W. Huske. Tell Dan he can't catch my Christmas gift this year. Mother, we have got some fine apples. I wish you had some of them. I often think of you when I get a fine large one, so I save them & give them to Mrs. Hall, but some times I give them to some body else. Mr. Hall is still selling & he has not had any supper. Much love to you both. Good night with a kiss for you both.

Your Affectionate Son,

Frank

P. S. I forgot to send Levin my regards, so please present them to him.

F. A. Clinard to Livingston N. Clinard

J. G. HALL,   R. L. PATTERSON,
of J. G. & P. C. HALL, Wilkesboro, N. C.   of PATTERSON & Co., Salem, N. C.,
OFFICE OF HALL & PATTERSON,
Dealers in General Merchandise,
AND BUYERS OF COUNTRY PRODUCE.
NORTH OF RAILROAD STATION
Hickory, N. C.,

December 18th 1873

Dear Father,

I cannot resist the temptation of writing you tonight, although I am tired. We have done the biggest days work ever done in Hickory. Since sun down last night, we have sold between 1500 & 2000 dollars worth of goods. We have bought out four, four horse wagons, & two, two horse, besides loading 4 teams. I sold in one hour $62.40. Besides we have measured 75 bushels apples & weighed 1000 lbs. cabbage & various other things, & waited on the local customers all we could. I got about five hours sleep last

---

[25] Charles Benjamin Pfohl

night, was up before day for one time & at work. What I mean by loading four teams is, we sold them apples & cabbage.

Our Negro calls this "the New York house." You ought to hear him talking to some of the darkies that work at the other stores. It would make a preacher laugh. I must close & go to a Temperance lecture. Mr. Hall & Hill have gone & left me writing, so good night with my love to you & Mother. Your Affectionate Son,

Frank

P. S. I am back from the lecture. I heard two very good lectures tonight, one by Mr. Andy Shuford & the other by our Depot Agent, Mr. Fevee. The Brass Band was in attendance & sent some of their sweetest notes forth to help the thing along. Mr. Hall said a few words in behalf of the Temperance cause. He is the Chief of Good Templars at this lodge.
Your Son,
Francis.

S. B. Shultz to Livingston N. Clinard

Clinton, MO
Dec. 25th 1873 Christmas

Dear Bro,

I will just add a few lines to the letter I wrote you in Nov., & failed to mail it. Hoping my scrawl will interest you some. Our health since writing has been generally good, hope this will find you all well. The winter thus far has been cold, but very little snow & no ice yet thick enough to save. Some rain last week & roads muddy now. On last Monday night we had a very destructive fire here, the particulars you will find in one of our city papers, which I mail to you today. Trade has been some better than last month.

We received a letter from our Son Henry. They are now living in Indianapolis, Indiana. They moved back last summer. They are well. Also received one from Joseph Shultz of Brownsville, MO. They are well. Joe passed here last night on his way to Oswego Kansas, where I think he has gone to marry a Miss Pigg, a former resident of Knob Noster. He wrote us he would stop on his return & give us a call.

How would you like to exchange papers for the year 1874? Write me, & give me the news & tell me how all the relatives & friends are & give them all our best Love. Now Christmas, but not Christmas like we were accus-

tomed to in our youth, & at such times & often wish myself back again at old Salem. Hoping you have a Merry Christmas & a Happy New Year. We Remain Yours As Ever,
S. B. Shultz

Personal Letters of L. N. Clinard 1874

F. A. Clinard to Mr. and Mrs. Livingston N. Clinard

Hickory, N. C.
Jan. 5th 1874

Dear Father & Mother,

I arrived here safely Saturday morning, & I am well at this time. Mr. R. L. Patterson got here this morning, & went right on to his Fathers. Hill went home today, so I am by myself. Trade seems to be duller than when I left. We have not had hardly any thing to do today. It has been raining all day & is very warm.

Mr. Hall's Sister & Cousin came today, so he has a house full again. I feel slighted. Mr. Hall gave Mr. Beard, Hill, & Henry a Christmas present & did not give me any thing. I think he treated me rather shabby. He gave them all five dollars a piece. Do you get more for my staying up here than at home? If you don't, I want to come back. He told Hill, that he would have give me some thing if I had been here, but as I had gone home, he did not expect to give me any thing. It's not the present that I care for, but the looks of the thing, & what he said because I went home, for I know that I tend to business & work as hard as any of them, if not more so. Hill was highly delighted this morning when he started. He took a gun & ammunition with him & expects to hunt most of the time.

Mother, my eating come good, I tell you. I gave Hill some of the sweet pickel & sausage, & you ought to have seen him go for it. He asked me if I got Turkey hash.

There is a show in town tonight & there has a large crowd gone to see it. Mr. Hall has gone. I thought I would not go, so I stayed here by myself, except my Negro. He is up in my room making up my bed. You ought to have seen him when I came back. He was as glad to see me as anybody. Major Tom Hardin just came to keep me company. He is a very clever gentleman, so I must stop writing, as I don't know of any thing else interesting to write you.

There has been two new families moved here since I went home. One of them has ten children.

Winter view of Union Square, Hickory, N. C.
Photo courtesy Catawba County Historical Association Archives

I went to hear a Lutheran Minister preach yesterday. Give my regards to Pfohl & H. W. B. Also give my love to Aunty, Aunt Eliza & Ed. Much love to you both. Good night.

Your Affectionate Son,

Frank

F. A. Clinard to Mr. and Mrs. Livingston N. Clinard

AL. MORGAN, Ag't.
FOR RUFUS MORGAN'S
Stereoscopic Views of Southern Scenery.
Hickory, N. C.,

Jan. 13th 1874

Dear Father & Mother,

Your letter came to hand this morning & I was glad to hear from home, for I have had the blues for several days We are having bad weather at present. It has snowed, whistled & rained today, but it seems that nothing will stop these mountain wagons from coming in with their trash. I helped unload three, four horse wagons, loaded with potatoes. I have not been in the store scarcely any today. I was tending to shipping things till twelve o'clock & then I had them wagons to see to. I have had on my over coat all day. Carter is not back yet, so I miss him these cold nights, all alone in the big store by myself, & the hardest bed you ever saw. Them new bedsteads in the store at Salem are nothing to compare with mine. I am sorry, I forgot my catsup. Would like to have it.

Has H. W. B. gone courting? If he has, tell him I hope him success, for if ever I did want to see a man married, he is one. I think if he does not succeed he will have to go to the insane asylum. I wrote to Ed last night, so I guess he will get my letter tomorrow evening, such a letter as it is. I have not got any thing to write about, so I can't write long letters. Things that transpire here would not interest you, as you don't know anyone here. By the way, Miss Emma Hamilton was at Mr. Halls one night last week, & I called on her & had a nice time. Talked of old times when we lived at the Factory, & how we use to love one another, & so on. I spent a very pleasant evening & heard some splendid music. Mr. Hamilton passed here yesterday on his way to Lincolnton. He looks like always.

We received a lot of new goods last week & sold about $200.00 worth before we got time to price them all & sold another bill since of $327.00.

We have got another clerk, Mr. Beard's Son. He is seventeen years old, & can ask more questions than Lindsay. I make out I don't hear him, so I think he will get tired of asking them soon.

I have let my fire go out & I am cold & tired, so I must close & go to my bed to keep from freezing. I pile on new blankets till it takes a good stout man to lift them.

Hickory is still improving more. New buildings going up, & there is three more churches going up before long, also marriages. There is a wedding in town tonight. One of the Hickory merchants is taking unto himself a wife. The commissioners are having more new streets cleaned out & you can see the street lamps about on the corners. Another Hotel is to open next week, it is about completed.

I wrote out my Sugar cake recipe tonight. I think I will get some this week, we have had once of my kind since I got back. Give my respects to all the clerks, & my love to Aunty & Aunt Eliza. I would like to know Aunt Carrie's[26] post office, & I will write to her. I heard from General Patterson yesterday, & he is no better. Much love to you both, with a good night.
Your Affectionate Son,
Frank

A. D. Clinard to Livingston N. Clinard

Newton House
Athens, GA
Jan. 18th 1874

Dear Brother,

It has been some time since I wrote you or received a letter from you, so I will drop you a line. Myself and family are in usual health. I am still keeping the Hotel. Business has been very light this winter, but I hope for better times in the spring. I hope to be able to make you a visit in May next. If business is anything like as good as it ought to be, I will be able to do so. I received a letter from Mother a few days ago and have replyed to it. The weather has been very mild here most of the winter, but we now have very cold weather. I have nothing of interest to write, therefore will close. All send love. Tell Frank to write. Let me hear from you soon.
As Ever, A. D. Clinard

---

[26] Carrie Shultz Grier

F. A. Clinard to Mr. and Mrs. Livingston N. Clinard

AL. MORGAN, Ag't.
FOR RUFUS MORGAN'S
Stereoscopic Views of Southern Scenery.
Hickory, N. C.,

February 8th 1874

Dear Father & Mother,

Yours & Cousin Jennie's letter to hand, & I was glad to hear from you both. Well, I am at the same business yet, marking & shipping produce. I was in the warehouse yesterday & today all day, & will be tomorrow. I have marked today about two car loads of peas. Yesterday was one of the roughest days we have had this winter. I hardly saw the fire all day & last night. I sat up with a wounded man till 1 o'clock this morning.

This young man fell from the comb of the new Hotel, & caught a plank that was nailed in the side of the house, & tore him open from one side to the other, plum to the hollow. The Doctors say they think he will get well.

I have been to our reading circle tonight, had a very pleasant time. Mother, I am nursing them beards very well. I won't want a blacking, for the things are black as a crow, more or less. Hill was right sick for a few days, but he is better, so he can go about. I have got a cold.

Tell Ed I will write to him if I owe him a letter. I had forgotten whether I had answered his last or not. Mr. Hall's Aunt came today to stay with him awhile. Mrs. Bell from Newton. I sent you a paper last week with an obituary notice of General Pattersons.

Our new clerk is the most disagreeable boy I ever had any thing to do with. He knows more than any body else, & is always sticking his gab where he has no business. There is hardly any body in town that likes him. He & his Father quarrel nearly every day. His Father tries to tell him but he thinks he knows it all & must take advice. Hill despises him, he took Hill's flute cleaner & cleaned lamp chimneys with it. You might know he was mad. He goes to our room & takes as much priviledge in our room, as if every thing belongs to him. I seldom ever speak to him, unless I am obliged to.

There was a drove of horses passed through here today. There is a good many horses pass through here.

I must close, as I am cold, tired, & sleepy, so give my regards to all my friends, & my love to Aunty, Aunt Eliza, & much love to you both. Good night. Your Affectionate Son, Frank. Feb. 4th - I am at the Depot shipping peas this morning. My cold is better. F. A. C.

F. A. Clinard to E. C. Clinard

Hickory, N. C.
Feb. 20th 1874

Dear Bro Ed,

I received your letter & was glad to hear from you, & to get the pens. I have been kept right busy shipping peas & all sort of trash lately. Some days, I don't sell $2.00 worth of goods. We have got over 1500 bushels of peas. I am going to ship about three hundred bags tomorrow.

Ed, you ought to see Hill & myself eat the good things Mother sent me. We have had supper several times here in the store & took breakfast here Sunday morning. I had saved my mince pie for Sunday so I could warm it & when I went to take it out, some grand rascal had got in my box & eat all the bottom crust & meal & left the top crust, & eat nearly all my sweet pickles & citron tarts. It was in my room & no one was in there but our Negro & our cub. Our Negro swears that it was not him & I don't think it was, for I have tried him to see if he would steal. I have got my own opinion about who it was but don't say anything. I know one thing certain, it was not Hill or myself, & the rats could not get in it. I have tried our Negro, left money & little things lay about in our room, & he never has taken any thing, unless he asked for it. Ed, I am going to the reading circle tomorrow night if the weather is good. We have had heavy wind all day today & it has been rather warm. We had a nice snow last week.

I am tired so I can't write you a long letter this time. I will write one of your kind, hoping to hear from you soon. Remember me to Catfish, Brown & Stockton, also Huske.

Carter sends his love to you all, & hopes he may have the pleasure of smiling on your sweet faces once more. He is sitting here reading his Saturday Evening Post. Give my love to Father & Mother.
Your True Brother,
Frank.
Good night.
Feb. 24th. It is cloudy this morning and looks like snow.

F. A. Clinard to Mr. and Mrs. Livingston N. Clinard

Hickory, N. C.,
Mar. 4th 1874

Dear Father & Mother,

I received your letter yesterday & was glad to hear from home. Well, the first thing I have got to tell you is, I have changed boarding house. I am boarding at the Phenix Hotel, & you bet they feed all right. It is a new house, & they have every thing in apple pie order & style. Mrs. Black has shut up her house, & a man by the name of Merrill is going to open a boarding house, so Hill & myself & four or five more have gone to boarding at the Phenix.

Next on the docket is Mr. Hall is a daddy. He has a son & is one of the proudest men you ever saw. He says he can almost tell the price of cabbage. Our firm has changed. It is Patterson, Hall & Son now. Dr. Carter was down come Monday & left today. He asked after you & said give his best regards to you. He is the same good, east sort of a Dr. yet. I had him to examine me & he advised me to get a India rubber truss. I am going to send by Mr. Hall when he goes north, & get one. Mrs. Hall is doing well, Mr. Hall says.

I got a very interesting letter from Aunt Carrie this week. She is well, & well satisfied, but says she would like to be back in old North Carolina. I also got one from Cousin Jennie. They are all well & she kinder owns up to me. She has a sweetheart, & says there is some likely hood of my getting a new cousin some of these times.

I saw Mr. E. S. Clemmons & George Morris pass by here today. George said he saw you yesterday Father, but he is such a lier. I did not know whether to believe him or not.

You asked if the family's that moved in here are men of means. Most of them are, & them that are not are Mechanics of different kinds. There are five painters here that are kept steady at work & one sign painter. There is a market house going up here, will be completed in a few days.

Mr. Hall just told me to say to you his wife was doing very well, that she suffered some with her breast. We have had a real spring day. I have had off my coat all the afternoon & we have no fire tonight. I shipped today 260 bags of peas & will ship more tomorrow. My foot has come to a head on the side & busted. I hope it will get well soon.

Remember me to all the clerks, & give my love to Aunty & Aunt Eliza. Much love to you.

Your Affectionate Son, Frank

F. A. Clinard to Mr. and Mrs. Livingston N. Clinard

Hickory, N. C.
March 18th 1874

Dear Father & Mother,

I would have answered your letter last night, but as usual I went to the reading circle. I had quite a nice time, there was quite a number of Gentlemen & Ladies turned out last night. I went with the expectation of reading, but I did not, will read next time. I took Miss Gertrude & by the by I saw Alex Hall for the first time last night - he is a right sharp looking baby. Mrs. Hall was setting up & seemed very cheerfull. She is looking right well.

I just got back from visiting. I have been to see Maj. Tom Hardin's daughter & spent a very pleasant evening.

Mr. Bynum brought my shoes, he told me he was on his way to see after his volcanoe, he says he is going to file an injunction & have it stopped. There is a great deal of talk about the roarings & quakeings of the mountains above Old Fort, lots of people are leaving. Some are preparing for the other world & they have got a general commotion up there among them selves.

I thought I was done with Peas for this year. But bless you, we bought 500 Bu. more today, so I will have to go to shipping again. I had a sweet job three days last week. I was boss, worked two hands & baled rags till I smell like an old rag bag. I shipped 34 bales. Mother, I wish you had some of our good apples, we bought a load yesterday at $1.50 cash per Bu. I had a good trade this afternoon, a struck a man from McDowell Co. I sold him $110.00 worth of goods for cash.

Ask Mr. Barrow what he ment by saying my sweetheart was married. Mr. Bynum said he sent me that word. I wish I had some of your shad, I could make them hop from a fur back. We had a very warm day, it was very foggy this morning.

Mother, I send you one of my Photographs with my beard. I have cut them & my moustache. My face is as smooth as a little babys. Col. Wat Lenoir came in the store today & very solemly asked me when the funeral would be preached & I did not know what he ment, & asked him "What funeral?" He said of my beard, every body that sees me has some thing to say about it.

I think Ed is mistaken, but I will write to him this week.

Remember me to all the clerks & tell Henry B. I hope he will succeed with his courtship. Give my love to Aunty & Aunt Eliza & receive a greater portion for yourselves. Good night.
Your Affectionate Son, Frank
P. S. Show my Photograph to Ackerman

A. D. Clinard to Livingston N. Clinard

Newton House
Athens, GA
March 21st 1874

Dear Brother,

It has been a considerable length of time since I received a letter from you. I do not now remember whether I replyed to your last or not. My business has been paying tolerably well this year, but is a little slack the past few days, oweing to extreme bad weather. Blanche is recovering from her spell of sickness. It has been more than 4 weeks since she was taken, and has not been out of the house yet. My health is good. My wife is also well, except rheumatism in one arm. Her Mother, who lives with me, is quite feble, but up.

Blanche & I hope to be with you by the middle of May, should nothing occur to prevent. My business will doubtless suffer during my absence, but it will be 17 years the 25th of this month, since I left N. C., and I feel that I must make any sacrifice to see my Parents, Brothers, & Sisters once more. I send my photograph, that you may see how I look at this time.

I sent five dollars to Mother in a letter over a month ago, and have not yet heard from her. Do you know whether she received it? I have written her twice since, and no reply yet to any of them. I directed to Abbotts Creek P.O., to as I had been doing for a long time. Dear Brother, I must close. Write soon. All join in much love to yourself and family.
As Ever,
A. D. Clinard

Andrew D. Clinard
Photo courtesy of North Carolina Department of Archives and History

A. D. Clinard to Livingston N. Clinard

Newton House
Athens, GA
April 22nd 1874

Dear Brother,

Your welcome letter of the 12th inst. came duly to hand. We were pleased to hear from you, and to learn all were well. My family are in usual health. We have had the wetest spring here. I have ever seen, which has done great injury to all branches of trade. It has injured my business considerably.

I expect to leave Athens for North Carolina about the 12th of May, if nothing occurs to prevent. I calculate being absent about 3 weeks. I will go to High Point by Rail and get Mr. Ward to take me to Fathers. Blanche will go with me. We anticipate much pleasure during our visit to the old North State. I would take my wife, but we can't both leave home. My business will suffer considerably any way, on account of my absence, but I am willing to make the sacrifice to see my Parents, Brothers & Sisters. It is now over 17 years, since I left Carolina. I must close. Mollie & Blanche send love to all.
As Ever,
A. D. Clinard
Write soon.

A. D. Clinard to Livingston N. Clinard

Athens, GA
May 8th 1874

Dear Brother,

I drop you a line, to let you know that Blanche and I expect to start for North Carolina on Wednesday morning the 13th inst. We will get to High Point the following day and stop at Brother Burns and go to Fathers the next day and remain a few days, and then go to Salem. Could you conveniently send a carriage, or some conveyance to Fathers for us, or come yourself? We expect to remain about three weeks from home. I wish to visit as many of my relatives as possible during that time. I hope your son Frank can come home whilst I am with you. I shall feel disappointed if I fail to see him. I wrote Mother a few days ago when she might expect me, also Burns.

We have had a very wet disagreeable Spring here. All kinds of business very dull, money very scarce. All join in love,
As ever
A. D. Clinard

F. A. Clinard to Mr. and Mrs. Livingston N. Clinard

J. G. HALL,   R. L. PATTERSON,
of J. G. & P. C. HALL, Wilkesboro, N. C.   of PATTERSON & Co., Salem, N. C.,
OFFICE OF HALL & PATTERSON,
Dealers in General Merchandise,
AND BUYERS OF COUNTRY PRODUCE.
NORTH OF RAILROAD STATION
Hickory, N. C.,

May 14th 1874

Dear Father & Mother,

I must put you off with a short letter tonight. I have been so busy today, & I am so tired that I can hardly write. The Grangers had a picnic in town today & I think every body in the western part of the state came here today. We have sold lots of goods today. I don't think I ever worked harder than I have this week. We have got a splendid stock of goods, some of the nicest styles of prints I ever saw. I would have written last night, but I was so tired, I went to bed right after supper.

I am boarding at the Western House now. There was about 100 people took dinner there today, & there is about twenty transient customers there tonight. Much love to you both. Good night.
Your Affectionate Son,
Frank

A. D. Clinard to Livingston N. Clinard

Newton House
Athens, GA,
June 5th 1874

Dear Bro,

We arrived home safe last evening and found all well. My business has been conducted in a very satisfactory manner during my absence. We came through Atlanta and had a very pleasant time there. The distance by Atlanta is 488, by Augusta 389, by the N. E. Road when completed, 307 miles to High Point. The weather was very dry here, but we are now having good rains. I feel very much gratified with my visit to N. C. All things having worked well. Our stay was very pleasant to us whilst at your house, and to your good wife, we shall ever feel greatful for her untiring efforts to make us comfortable. Blanche speaks in high terms of her Salem friends and sends love to Miss Ackerman especially. She says present her regards to Mr. Ackerman & Mr. Husk and bushels of love to your wife & Eddie. Also to the little girls, who so kindly visited her whilst at your house. Also Miss Butner, your wife's sister. All join in love to you and your family. Write soon. As ever, A. D. Clinard

F. A. Clinard to Mr. and Mrs. Livingston N. Clinard

J. G. HALL,   R. L. PATTERSON,
of J. G. & P. C. HALL, Wilkesboro, N. C.   of PATTERSON & Co., Salem, N. C.,
OFFICE OF HALL & PATTERSON,
Dealers in General Merchandise,
AND BUYERS OF COUNTRY PRODUCE.
NORTH OF RAILROAD STATION
Hickory, N. C.,

July 7th 1874

Dear Father & Mother,

I received your letter this morning, & was glad to hear from you, but sorry to hear you were both sick. You are mistaken when you say that I wanted to find falt with my pantaloons, for I did not. I was glad to hear that J. E. Mickey is not broken up.

I tell you, I have got a big job before me. I have to make out monthly statements for the past year, & about half of it, I have to take from the day book, make a journal of each day separate. I have made out about twenty today, besides entering & posting up my book. Mr. Hall is not at home, he has gone to Wilkesboro to see his wife. I look for him & the boss this evening. I just got back from dinner. I tell you I am living at the top of the pot.

You seem to be afraid that I don't know how to behave myself. I am a great deal better than if I was at home. I am trying to establish a good name for myself, which I think I will succeed in. I have a great many good friends up here, & especially Ladie friends. I go about five or six nights in a week to see the Ladies, so you know I am in no bad company. I am going tonight, so I thought I would write to you this afternoon. I have took John round to see some Ladies. Hill took him last night to see some Ladies. I went to see my old sweetheart that was up here last summer.

We are having very warm & dry weather up here, but we have cool nights. I sleep under cover every night. This place beats anything you ever heard of for fleas. I kill from 10 to 20 on me every day. I have to stop & go to work, as I have got a lot of it to do. John[27] & Hill send their regards to you & to all the clerks. Remember me to all, & my love to both Auntys. Much love to you both.
I am your Affectionate Son, Frank

A. D. Clinard to Livingston N. Clinard

Newton House
Athens, GA
July 15th 1874

Dear Brother,
Your welcome letter of the 14th inst. was received this morning. I was very glad to hear from you and to learn all were well. You say you have received but one letter from me since my return to Athens. I have written two. Regret you did not get the last. The mail agent on the Georgia R.R. is an ignorant Negro and whole packages of letters are frequently miss-sent and delayed for weeks. Blanche received a letter from Frank this morning. He was well and having a good time. My health has not been so good since I returned, as it was previous to my leaving. Mollie & Blanche are quite well. Blanche often speaks of you and your Dear wife, and the pleasant time she had at Salem. She sends much love to the kind friends whose acquaintance

---

[27] John T. Bohannon, clerk at Hall Brother's store in Hickory, N.C., later partnered with J. G. Hall in a tobacco manufacturing factory

she made whilst there. Good rains have recently fallen here and crops are looking well

My business has been very light this summer, but is beginning to improve. The commencement exercises of the State University will begin the 1st of Aug., at which time I will have my house full. I hope to clear 4 or 5 hundred dollars on that occasion, but I may fall short of my hopes. I will be very busy from this time, on fixing up for that occasion.

I must close, write soon. Present my love to your good wife, whose kindness I shall never forget. Give my love to Eddie, tell him to write me. Blanche sends kisses and love to you and Sister Mollie & Eddie. Also to Miss Ackerman and the little girl whose acquaintance she made. Also to your wife's sister. My kind regards to all.

As ever, A. D. Clinard

F. A. Clinard to Mr. and Mrs. Livingston N. Clinard

J. G. HALL,   R. L. PATTERSON,
of J. G. & P. C. HALL, Wilkesboro, N. C.   of PATTERSON & Co., Salem, N. C.,
OFFICE OF HALL & PATTERSON,
Dealers in General Merchandise,
AND BUYERS OF COUNTRY PRODUCE.
NORTH OF RAILROAD STATION
Hickory, N. C.,

July 17th 1874

Dear Father & Mother,

I would have answered your letter sooner, but I really have not had time. I am at work steady on my books from morning till night & when night comes I go to see some young Lady. John, Hill & myself have not missed a night in over two weeks. We have had two "Hops" in the last two weeks. I was one of the managers at both of them. We certainly had the nicest "Hop" the other night I ever was at in my life. Everything passed off quietly & the strangers said it was the nicest thing of the kind they had seen. Mother I am getting tomatoes & all kinds of vegetables, & we have had watermelon three days for desert. There are a good many strangers here at present. I hear my breakfast gong, so I will have to put you off with a short letter this time, as Mr. Hall expects me to get to work as soon as breakfast is over. It is nearly eight o'clock. I won't get my dinner till 2 o'clock. Much love to all.

Your Affectionate Son,

Fr. A. Clinard

F. A. Clinard to Mr. and Mrs. Livingston N. Clinard

J. G. HALL,   R. L. PATTERSON,
of J. G. & P. C. HALL, Wilkesboro, N. C.   of PATTERSON & Co., Salem, N. C.,

OFFICE OF HALL & PATTERSON,
Dealers in General Merchandise,
AND BUYERS OF COUNTRY PRODUCE.
NORTH OF RAILROAD STATION
Hickory, N. C.,

July 17th 1874

Dear Father & Mother,

I thought I would take time to write you more, as I have just got back from dinner & I want to rest a little so I will write you about the Governor.[28] There was four coaches passed by here with the remains of him. Most of the big officers of state was along. They all wore crepe & the train was festooned from one end to the other with white & black cloth & the engine had three crosses of boxwood on the cow catcher & had a wreath of crepe round the smoke stack. They still run the same engine on this road with its mourning on. It is to wave it for thirty days. There were about fifty Negros along all dressed up & had on mourning.

Hickory has a regular auction house. I think it is a good thing, at least we are getting rid of some hard stock. All the merchants are cleaning them selves of a great deal of old stock at good prices.

John Bohannan wants to know what you can have him a pair of pants made for, like mine. He says no body knows anything about pants up here. He also said to ask you to tell Henry Tiddall to write to him. I see in the paper that he has sold his house.

Tell Ed I will write to him some of these days when I get more time. I never was pushed up with work so much. The books are way behind & mistakes in the cash rest. & in Mdse. Acct, I have found six or seven. I am in hopes I will get up some of these days, so I can have a little rest. I like to keep books very well, & I think I will like it better when I get up once, if I get up. I bet you, I won't let them behind any more.

Mother, I am getting fleshy again, this is the only summer that I ever fattened. I lay under cover every night & then get cold in the morning. I have not suffered with heat any at all this summer & I am not sun burnt at all. My hands are as white as my arms are.

---

[28] Governor Tod Robinson Caldwell, 1871-1874, b. February 19, 1918 d. July 11, 1874. Buried at Forest Hill Cemetery, Morganton, Burke Co., NC

I understand Ed is going to Raleigh. I hope he will have a nice time. Next trip I make, I want to go to Georgia.

Remember me to all the clerks. John, Hill & Mr. Hall send their regards to you.

Your Affectionate Son,

Frank

F. A. Clinard to Mr. and Mrs. Livingston N. Clinard

J. G. HALL,   R. L. PATTERSON,
of J. G. & P. C. HALL, Wilkesboro, N. C.   of PATTERSON & Co., Salem, N. C.,

OFFICE OF HALL & PATTERSON,

Dealers in General Merchandise,

AND BUYERS OF COUNTRY PRODUCE.

NORTH OF RAILROAD STATION

Hickory, N. C.,

July 22nd 1874

Dear Father & Mother,

Your letter was received yesterday & I would have answered it last night, but I went to hear Col. Pool speak. He is a fine orator & handles his subject well, he will get all the votes in this part of the state & I hope will be elected. He is a fine old Gentleman, he spent Sunday here. There is quite a crowd at the Central at present, about sixty persons. That you know takes something to feed them all. I am always on hand when meal time comes, for if I was not there, I would run a slim chance.

Father, you wrote me about spending money. I am oblige to spend some money or quit going in society. I am placed in a different position here to what I am at home, you know that. I don't fool any money away, that I never did. I go with the very best society & I never run about any where. I go visiting every night & have not missed going a night in several weeks. I have met some of as nice Ladies here as I ever expect to meet any where. I said I had not missed a night - I did miss Monday night, as I had to write on my book. Last night I was with a Lady at the Hotel, the speaking was there. I am in the notion of going on the R. Road, or at least going for Pres. William Smith's Step Daughter. She is the nicest, & well every thing that is good & pretty. I spend some pleasant moments with her. She is one of the finest looking Ladies I ever saw. She was educated in Salem. Her name is Miss Loma Atkinson.

Trade is rather dull at present, a few berries are coming in. We pay 8 cents. Of course we don't get any cherries. John is going to practice Physics, or at least he thinks he is, as H. W. B. use to say to me. He is going for the Drug store up here, & Hill I think will go to Columbia S. C., so we have all got our occupations picked out. I am rather on the wild order, so I take the Rail Road.

Tell Ed I will write him about next Sunday. I am writing this before breakfast. I get breakfast at 8 o'clock, dinner at 2, & supper at 7 1/2 o'clock. I generally sleep till nearly breakfast. I don't do a thing but write on my books. Mr. Hall told me not to do any thing else.

I am sorry to hear that Aunty is so bad off. I fear I will never see her any more. Give her my love & also to Aunt Eliza.

Remember me to all the clerks. Much love to you both.
Your Affectionate Son,
Frank

Lawrence Winston to Livingston N. Clinard

Authorized Capital, $500,000.   Commercial Insurance Company,
Cash Paid Up, $100,000.   of Charleston, West Va.,
                    C. D. REYNOLDS, Pres't.
J. D. MOORE, Secretary   Raleigh, N.C. Agency,

July 23rd 1874

Dear Sir:
Yours of the 21st inst. is at hand for which accept our thanks. We will write to the Jones. No tickets of admission are required to visit the Asylums (Insane & D. D. & Blind).
Very truly yours,
Lawrence Winston
N. B.
Capt. L. is absent, or would himself have answered your letter. W.

F. A. Clinard to Mr. and Mrs. Livingston N. Clinard

J. G. HALL,   R. L. PATTERSON,
of J. G. & P. C. HALL, Wilkesboro, N. C.   of PATTERSON & Co., Salem, N. C.,
OFFICE OF HALL & PATTERSON,
Dealers in General Merchandise,
AND BUYERS OF COUNTRY PRODUCE.
NORTH OF RAILROAD STATION
Hickory, N. C.,

July 28th 1874

Dear Father & Mother,

As it is rainy & bad under foot tonight, I will write you. I was glad to hear from you. I suppose you are both very fleshy if you eat all the potatoes you raised but one bushel. I am sure you had a fine prospect when I was at home. I will find out as soon as I can what potatoes are worth up here. There are none coming in to market yet, the people up here have not dug their crop yet.

As to me running off the R. R. or having a smash up, there is no danger, as I have the Pat Steam Break attached to my engine & all my coaches & that you know will keep me strait. John says he is afraid of the Drug store, as some one tried to go with her the other night & got busted. I spent some time this evening listening to the blow of my whistle. It is a very sweet one, more so than any whistle I have heard. I spent a few moments in the Parlor after tea this evening & heard a few of the best songs of the day.

Mother, I would like some of your Tomatoes splendid. I have not had any stewed, but I have had them cut up in vinegar. I get one thing I am fond of, & that is beets, beans & cucumbers & we have every day. I get apple dumplings about every other day. I am improving in flesh to what I was when I was at home. Tell Aunt Eliza I often think of her when I am eating, as we have fried chicken every meal. I eat for supper, three gizzards & two thighs, one leg & a wing. I ought to improve under such eating as that, don't you think so? I would like to have some of Mrs. Charles' fine peaches about this time, all the peaches I have had were small ones & few of Pheby Dans pears would go alright about this time. I eat six today, the first I have seen.

I had a letter from Uncle Andy yesterday. They are all well & he is looking forward to a big time at the commencement in Athens. I am sorry to hear Aunty is failing so fast, give her my best love.

There are very few berries coming in yet, the people are holding them for better prices. We are still paying eight cents. Strangers still continue to come to spend the summer. The Hotels are about full & a good many privet boarding houses have as many as they can take. I never in my life saw the like of children there is at the Hotel. Every woman that comes has from one to six. One woman here has six.

Father, I want to ask a favor of you. It is this. Please drop the Tavern in backing letters to me, as we are all trying to stop it being called Hickory Tavern. Much love to all.
Your True Son,
Francis.

F. A. Clinard to Mr. and Mrs. Livingston N. Clinard

J. G. HALL,   R. L. PATTERSON,
of J. G. & P. C. HALL, Wilkesboro, N. C.   of PATTERSON & Co., Salem, N. C.,
OFFICE OF HALL & PATTERSON,
Dealers in General Merchandise,
AND BUYERS OF COUNTRY PRODUCE.
NORTH OF RAILROAD STATION
Hickory, N. C.,

August 7th 1874

Dear Father & Mother,

I would have written you sooner, but I have not had the time. I was at a "Hop" at Mr. Hardin's last night given in honor of his daughter. I had an excellent time.

The election passed off quietly & the election went all right. Pool got 302 votes, & K. K. K. Tommy got 15. Bully for Hickory, the radical vote fell short about 75 votes at this precinct.

8 o'clock p.m.,

I have heard from the county. It has gone over eleven hundred majority conservative, a gain of over two hundred over last election. Caldwell & Burke have gained right smart over last election. The Citizens of this place are going to have a bonfire tonight in honor of their county. Mr. Hall & Mr. Beard was electionering nearly all day. I give up my books & sold goods. We are having a good trade at present. We pay 7 & 8 cents per bushel for berries.

Mother, Carter is here by my side. He said tell you your mince pie was splendid last winter. Mother, tonight is the first time in a long time that I have missed going to see some young Lady & I would have gone tonight, but I stayed at home to write you. I don't get time to do any thing through the day. I am kept busy from morning till night on my books. Mr. Hall &

John have gone to Good Templars meeting tonight. They have a big festival tonight. Is Ed at home? He owes me a letter & I would like to hear from him. I was glad to hear you went to Raleigh & that you had a nice time. Mother, I am still fattening up & my whiskers are still growing, you ought to see my presbyterians.

Father, I will send you a copy of the Press Extra, it has the returns of the election as far as heard from. I voted my Negro, square out & out conservative & went with him to the polls & saw him put in the tickets.

We are having cool weather, I have on my winter clothing & sleep under three blankets.

Father, I wish you would tell Tom & Hen that they both owe me letters, & that I would like to hear from them once more. Remember me to all the clerks & my love to both Auntys. Much love to you both & Ed.
Your Devoted Son,
Frank
I have to write to Cousin Belle yet tonight.

F. A. Clinard to Mr. and Mrs. Livingston N. Clinard

Hickory, N. C.
Aug. 10th 1874

My Dear Parents,
I received both your letters & was glad to hear you had received my letter & that you are all well. You can rest assured if I was to get sick, I would write. I always write as soon as I have the time. I am kept busy from morning till night, so I don't get time to write in the day time, it is 1/2 past eleven now. I have been at work on my books tonight. I am trying to get them straight, so I can have a little rest. They are in the worst fix you ever saw any books in the world. Hill & John just came in. They have been to the Reading Circle. John is highly delighted with Hickory & more so with the young Ladies. He is fixing up his Photograph to give me in the morning. His sweetheart is going to leave, she is from Burke, Miss Faney.

Father, Uncle Henry Patterson was down here yesterday. He came in & Hill & myself both spoke to him at once & he stood & looked at us both & at last he asked which is Mr. Clinet. I told him I was the chap. He asked a great many questions about you & said give his best respects to you. He said he would give any thing to see you once more. He told me Old Kit died last week. He says he is going to quit farming. He was down here looking for a place to live, he wants to get to Hickory. He coughs like always.

We are having right good trade at present. Our sales for cash for the last week or so have run from 100 to 150 a day. That is big sales for cash. Lots of produce is coming in. I have not seen any potatoes yet. Much love to all. Good night.

Your Devoted Son,

Frank.

A. D. Clinard to Livingston N. Clinard

Newton House
Athens, GA
Aug. 17th 1874

Dear Brother,

I believe I am due you a letter, at any rate I will drop you a few lines. We are all well and getting on tolerably well. My house was full to overflowing at the College Commencement the 1st of the month. Travel is light at present, but will revive soon. I enclose a slip from an Augusta paper complimentary of my house, written by a visitor from Augusta. I enclose three photos of Blanche, one for you & family, one for Miss Ackerman, and one for Alice & Dora Butner.[29] Please hand them to the parties with Blanche's love & compliments. I enclose one of my wife for you & family.

I received a letter from Hiram a few days ago, informing me of the birth of Sister Sarah's Babe. We have a letter from Frank a few days ago. He was well and having a good time. Tell Eddie to write us. We would be pleased to receive a letter from him. I often think of you all and would be glad to spend a few weeks with you again if I could. Nothing could be more pleasant.

Corn & cotton crops are very fine through this section of country. Last week was the hottest of the season. Weather very pleasant now.

I must close. Write soon. Mollie & Blanche join in love. Blanche often speaks of the fun she had at Salem. She sends much love to the friends she made there.

Yours & c., A. D. Clinard

---

[29] Dora Ellen Butner and Alice Estelle Butner, nieces of Livingston N. and Mary Butner Clinard

F. A. Clinard to Mr. and Mrs. Livingston N. Clinard

Hickory, N. C.
Aug. 20th 1874

Dear Father & Mother,

I was sorry to hear the sad news of Auntys death. Mr. Patterson told me it was a very large funeral. I will write Aunt Carrie on Sunday. I am kept busy all the time. I will soon be up with my books, then I will have some rest.

We have very dry & hot weather now, it is hot in the day time & very cool at night. I have on my winter coat this morning & about twelve, I will put on a linen coat.

We are having a right fair trade at present, a good many berries coming in. Mr. P. went on up to the valley yesterday. He will be back tomorrow with his family.

If you see Ed Strupe, tell him I will write him in a few days & tell him about the Fair. Mr. Hall has bought a new desk for me to write at. It is a large high one. It suits me better than my old one.

The Hotels are crowded with strangers & still they come. The schedule on this road has changed them. Both trains take breakfast here at eight o'clock. I am glad of it. I get my breakfast sooner by the operation. It is nearly breakfast time, so I will have to stop or I will not get my letter in the mail. The mail is closed early.

Remember me to all my friends & give my love to Aunt Eliza & tell her I was glad to hear she had some chicken once. Ask her if Mary Spach delivered a message I wrote him to her. Much love to all.
Your Affectionate Son,
Frank

F. A. Clinard to Mr. and Mrs. Livingston N. Clinard

Hickory, N. C.
Aug. 27th 1874

Dear Father & Mother,

Your letter came to hand a day later than common. I was sorry to hear that Mother had had one of her bad headaches, hope she is well again.

Mother, you must not get home-sick to see me, I am not coming home till next March when I am 21.

I had a letter from Uncle Andrew. He sent me Blanche & Aunt Mollie's Photographs. I think Blanche is splendid. If I get time, I will have some taken in a few days, there are three Artists here.

You spoke of our having Balls & being a fast set of people. We are not so fast as you imagine, but we go in for having a little enjoyment once & awhile. We had a Masquerade Ball, which was a grand thing & passed off splendidly. I was dressed as fancy as you please. I had knee pants, blue with yellow stripes, red jacket & red sash with fringe. By the way, a Lady friend of mine let me have that, also a pink turban cap with a gold star in front & black & white plume. I was complimented very highly on my suit. I was the beaux of the evening. My suit & the expenses of the Ball cost me about $2.50. Most of it was borrowed property. John B. had him a calico dress made & you ought to have seen what a good looking woman he makes. His character was Mrs. Links & mine Capt. Links. Hill represented a old fashioned county Gentleman, he had a calico coat, spike tail, calico pants, old boots, & stove pipe hat. There was about 160 or 175 persons present, from all parts, & one can say, a great deal. There was no one miss behaved or was drunk, we danced till 2 1/2 o'clock.

Father, I will send you a premium list of the Hickory A. & W. Fair. I wish you would put it up in front of the store. John said tell Aunt Eliza he fooled every body worse than he did Uncle Davy when he tried to buy eggs. We had lots of fun, but didn't make any money. It is getting so dark, I can't keep the line so I will close & go to supper. Lee Masten is here spending a few days. Remember me to all my friends. Much love to you all.
Your Affectionate Son,
Frank
P. S. Taters are scarce.

F. A. Clinard to Mr. and Mrs. Livingston N. Clinard

Hickory, N. Carolina
September 2nd 1874

Dear Father & Mother,

I was glad as usual to get your letter, of course Mother I would enjoy your chicken, corn & tomatoes. If I do have them every day, they are things I never tire of. I have had the trial on chicken. I have not missed half dozen days since I have been up here having chicken. We have baked, stewed, & cut up tomatoes nearly every day, and vegetable soup, light rolls, waffels, fried chicken, boilt ham, honey & butter comprises our daily suppers. For breakfast, beef steak, hash, batter cakes, biscuits, fried & stewed chicken & to my joy, we have light bread I sop.

We are having busy times at present. I tell you what is the fact. I am working myself very hard. I stand up, I write the day long, as soon as I get my books posted, I have to draw off accounts & worst of all I have to collect.

Father, I expect you will scold me, but I could not resist the temptation of learning the fancy dances, so I am taking lessons. I will make some extra money & pay you back. Hill & all the other boys are learning. I am getting along splendid. I can dance five or six round dances. The young Ladies compliment me very highly on my dancing, so you know that makes me feel proud. I can assure you one thing, & that is none of the young men drink or miss behave that goes, they are all gentlemen, so I hope you will be as easy as you possibly can on me.

Mother, I would send you my sweetheart's Photograph to look at, but I am afraid you would keep it. In fact I could not do without it a week. Her beautiful hazel eyes would charm you so that Frank would not have the chance to look on them any more till he comes home, so I guess I had better keep it in my sight. Did you get the premium list I sent you? The fact of the business is by the by.

I saw Clingman Chandler yesterday. Old Cling looks cleaner about the mouth than he use to. He is driving a team for Gwyn, Harper & Co.

Why don't Ed write to me? He owes me a letter, so does Tom Huske. I wish you would get after them both & make them write to me. How is Miss Gertrude getting along? You will have to keep me posted as to her health. Mother, make Hen tell you my sweethearts name, he knows who it is. I am too bashful to tell you myself, so I will leave that to him.

Father, I wish you would send me one of your Photographs, send me the one with you & Mother if you have no others to spare. I will be powerful glad to get it. Give my best respects to Levin, Henry, Charley, Tom & all my friends, & my love to Aunt Eliza & tell her if she will get married at Christmas, I will come to the wedding, provided she asks me. Much love to you both.
Your Affectionate & Dutiful Son, Francis.

P.S. I thought of you Sunday, Father, it being your birthday. I hope you had a happy one. F.

F. A. Clinard to Mr. and Mrs. Livingston N. Clinard

Hickory, N. C.
Sept. 8th 1874,

My Dear Father and Mother,

Your letter to hand this morning & I was glad to hear from you, but sorry to know you think I care for nothing but the frivolities of this world. You are mistaken. I do take hold of solid matter a great deal more than you think I do. I am all the time endevoring to improve myself, more so than when I was at home. I am steadier & go in the best of society & never think of frequenting a place of ill fame. From what I can learn, I bear as good a name as any young man in the place & try & make every body like me. I attend church regularly, have not missed but one Sunday this summer. I was at church three times last Sunday. I don't intend to go to any thing any more if you are so opposed to it. I will make a perfect hermit of myself.

Father, you wanted to know my account. For the last year up to date, which is over a year, & I owe nothing any where else.

$139.48
$25.00 of it - my trip home Christmas
$10.00 in May
$16.67 Mr. Hall ch. last time going home
$12.00 for washing
$6.00 for postage
$16.00 for 2 coats
$2.50 for undershirts
$3.00 for collars
$3.00 for shoe mending
$3.00 for paper & envelopes
$95.67

My acct. on the book at present is 80.33 with 175.00 credit this month not included. I don't fool any money away foolishly, as to that dancing money, I will pay you back if I have to cut wood at night to do it. I will trade my watch & make somebody else do the paying for me, as I make it I will give you credit for it. I don't buy all sorts of nic nacs. It's true, I have spent some money for watermelons, but not as much as I did last year at home. I will not need any thing this winter, but a pair of undershirts & a pair of shoes.

I think Mr. Hall ought to give me as much as he does John Bohannan any way. I work harder & steadier now than I ever did in my life. I have got more to do than Levin has. I have to enter from two to four pages in the day book every day, & keep them posted up, besides a single entry set of books. I fill two to three pages in that day book every day. As soon as I am through them, I have to make out statements. I seldom ever leave my desk, only to meals & then go & come in a hurry. When I am my own man he will have to anty up some more or I will go south, where I can get pay for my work. Mr. Hall raised Mr. Beard's salary. He was getting 600.00 last year. I have not found out how much. Mr. Beard quit, but he hired him back. Much love to all. I hope you will be satisfied with my statement as it is correct.
Your Affectionate Son,
Frank

A. D. Clinard to Livingston N. Clinard

Newton House
Athens, GA
Sept 11th 1874

Dear Brother,

   I believe I am due you a letter and will drop a line. We are all tolerably well, and getting along about as usual. Times are beginning to get better here. I hope to have a good run of customers this fall. I have to attend the U. S. Court in Atlanta next week, as a witness in a case. It is very inconvenient for me to leave home, but there is no chance to get relieved from going. I don't remember whether I sent you one of my photographs last taken or not. I enclose 2 for you and Eddie. I sent one to Frank. Blanche is going to school now, and is very busy with her studies. She often speaks of her pleasant trip to Salem. She says she is going again some time. She sends much love to you & Sister Mary and Eddie and all her Salem friends. Mollie joins me in love to you and family. Write soon.
As ever,
A. D. Clinard

F. A. Clinard to Mr. and Mrs. Livingston N. Clinard

Hickory, N. C.
Sept. 17th 1874

Dear Father & Mother,

I was very glad to hear from home this morning. I was uneasy about you, especially this morning as I asked for a letter & Hill told me there was none for me. He had it in his pocket to fool me. He gave it to me in about an hour afterwards. I was sorry to hear you had been sick Father, hope you will get well soon.

Most of the summer visitors have left for down the country, but there is plenty of excitement here at present. The Fair will come off in about a month, & John Robinson's Circus will be here the 9th of October. The bill posters & contracters were here on Monday. They had a fence built about 100 yds long & 12 feet high & covered it with pictures of all kinds of animals. They have 40 cars of their own. H. & P. have the contract to furnish all their provisions & Forage.

We have had right heavy rains for a few days past. I had the pleasure of hearing Gov. Z. B. Vance make a speech last week, he had quite a crowd.

Mother, I have been having eating to suit me for the past week or so. Soup, good vegetable & coon soup, & apple dumplings for desert.

The cabbage & apple trade has begun & chickens to no end. We are having a coop built 40 x 20 to keep chickens in. I believe we deal in every thing that any body ever heard of in this country, grapes & all such things as that. We have on hand at present about 100 watermelons. I see Miss Maggie Lillington is in the store. Hill is paying her a good deal of attention. I think John is engaged to a Miss Fancy that lives above Morganton about 4 miles. He is going up there in a week or so, he has asked to get off. I have an invitation from the young Lady to come with John.

Mother, I had that Photo taken you wanted. It is not good, but as good as I could get up here. Tell Aunt Eliza I would like to have her up here to eat chicken. I think she would get her fill. Give her my love. Much love to you all & tell Ed to write to me. I had a letter from Uncle Andy & Aunt Carrie this week, they are all well & I got a photo of Uncle Andy & one of Aunt Carrie's little girl.
Your Affectionate Son,
F. A. Clinard

B. F. Rogers to Livingston N. Clinard

OFFICE OF **MERONEY & BRO.**
FOUNDRYMEN,
AND DEALERS IN
General Merchandise,

Sep. 23, 1874
Mr. L. N. Clinard

Dear Sir,
I send you today by Exp. a number of Posters of our Fair. Will you please employ a boy and have him to paste them up like Circus Bills in Salem & Winston (as they will not stay up any other way) and forward Bill to me. Mr. Patterson, who was in our Town a day or two since, gave me your name and directed me to send the Bills to you. Enclosed find ticket which please accept. Should you visit our Fair I will do every thing in my power to make your stay a pleasant one.
Very Resp'y
B. F. Rogers Sec.

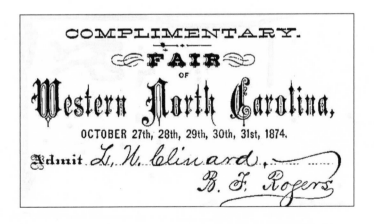

F. A. Clinard to Mr. and Mrs. Livingston N. Clinard

Hickory, N. C.
Sept. 30th 1874

Dear Father & Mother,

Your dear letter to hand this morning & I was sorry to hear that you had been sick Mother. I hope you are well by this time. I am enjoying splendid health at present. I was threatened with fever, but I would not write you that I was. I am in perfect health & weigh as much as I did last winter. We are having a splendid trade at present. They call on me to wait on customers. It is after supper now & there are several customers trading now. I have not had time to count out the money yet.

You wanted to know what I wanted in the way of clothing. Nothing at all but a pair of under shirts and I will get Mr. Hall to buy them for me when he goes north. I will make out on what I have and make my boots do. I will get a pair of gaiters that are warranted and hand made and Mr. Hall offers them at nearly cost to me. I will save you this winter what I have spent this summer. I am saving and economical as any young man can be. I have spent no money foolishly, except the money for dancing and I will try and pay you back that. I am working a scheme to make it now. I will not come home til in March at my birthday. I work hard and faithful and try to do and learn all I can. Give me half a chance and I will make my way through this veil of tears. I stick to my business close. My journals run to over $1,000 nearly every day. Sept 28th it run to 1,800, 29th to 1,400 and today nearly as much. It keeps me digging to keep up. I am ruining my handwriting. Can't write near as well as I used to. I write in a hurry all the time.

Everyone is all excitement about the Show. I hope I get to go to see the elephant if nothing else. I dread the day for we are going to have an awfull large crowd here & you know how they will bother us & buy nothing.

I promised some Ladies to help them sing tonight for a church concert, so I will have to count the money & fix to go & help the fair creatures. I have had two bouquets awarded me for singing this summer & a live geranium plant which I watch over with a great deal of care.

Give my love to Aunt Eliza & tell Ed to write to me. Much love to you both.
Your Affectionate Son,
Frank

F. A. Clinard to E. C. Clinard

ORDERS FOR COUNTRY PRODUCE, &c., SOLICITED

OFFICE OF HALL & PATTERSON,
Dealers in General Merchandise,
AND BUYERS OF COUNTRY PRODUCE.
NORTH OF RAILROAD STATION
Hickory, N. C.,

Oct. 6th 1874

Dear Bro,

At last you wrote to me. I was very glad to hear from you once more. I am sorry to hear Father is in such bad health, hope he will be better soon.

Ed, Hickory is all excitement about the Circus, every body is expecting a good time, except us poor souls. We will have to stay here & be worried to death with people asking questions.

Mr. Hall is Mayor, he is fixing up a Police Force, he has 25. John Bohannan is one! We teas him a good deal. We had Mayors court in my office this evening. Put one poor fellow in the lock-up for fighting.

We are going to have a musical concert next week for the benefit of the Episcopal Church. John, Hill & myself have to go to practice tonight. We have been several nights & have a nice time.

I was some what disappointed this morning at not getting a letter from home. I am afraid Father or Mother is sick. John, Hill & myself wish to be remembered to all the clerks & tell Tom Huske I am anxious to get a letter from him. Give my love to Father & Mother & to yourself. Write me soon.
Your True Brother,
Frank

F. A. Clinard to Mr. and Mrs. Livingston N. Clinard

ORDERS FOR COUNTRY PRODUCE, &c., SOLICITED

OFFICE OF HALL & PATTERSON,
Dealers in General Merchandise,
AND BUYERS OF COUNTRY PRODUCE.
NORTH OF RAILROAD STATION
Hickory, N. C.,

Oct. 8th 1874

Dear Father and Mother,

I was very glad to get your letter this morning as I was uneasy about you. I write hastily as we are very busy & I guess I will have to help sell goods. I think half of Watauga Co is here & they say the balance are on the road.

Father I am sorry to hear your health is so bad, hope it will improve soon. Henry just took a sack of chestnuts up stairs it made me think of you & wish you had some of them. They are very plenty this year. We shipped a lot today. I will have to work late tonight so I can help in the store tomorrow. Business is good but I never saw money so tight in my life. Mr. Hall keeps me working all the time to get money to pay for produce. Some days I don't return five dollars to the safe.

Mr. Hall and wife are going to the Raleigh fair. I wish I was going.

I had a letter from Ed at last. I answered it one day this week. Bill Fletcher just come in the store. I guess he brought old man Winkler's hog down to sell to Robinson. Much love to all.

Your Devoted Son,

Frank

F. A. Clinard to Mr. and Mrs. Livingston N. Clinard

Hickory, N. C.
Oct. 14th 1874

Dear Father and Mother,

Father, I am glad to hear of your improving in health. Hope you will continue to improve. Mother, you are about right when you say Hickory is a great place for boys to improve. I have improved fifteen pounds since I was at home & weigh as much now as I did last winter when I was at home.

Well Mother, we had our entertainment last night. We had a right good crowd considering that it came so soon after the circus.

Well, about the Circus, such a crowd never was heard of in Hickory before, all ages from the cradle to the grave & in all kind of conveyances, from an ox cart to a mountain slide. The crowd began to come in Thursday morning. Thursday night the town was encircled by one immence encampment, the crowd was estimated at about twelve thousand persons. Robinson said he had a larger crowd here than at Salisbury. He had a good circus & lots of animals. His procession was a grand thing. He had two splendid bands of music. The camels are queer looking things & one of the largest elephants in America. I saw a cow with five legs & two bags that she give milk from, one of them is on top of her back. I saw them milk her myself. The sea lions are queer looking things, the blackest, slickest looking things you ever saw.

He had two Australians, they are the funniest looking things to be humans that you ever saw. Their heads are about the size of your two fists & the blackest hair & eyes. His educated hog took my eye & they had white mice trained. I thought of Jim Reich when I saw the elephant. The zebra is a beautiful thing. They took the lion through the streets loose on top of a wagon & four Ladies seated by him. I had two complimentary tickets given me & Mr. Hall told me he would pay my way. The riding was splendid & they had as fine a lot of horses as I ever saw & Shetland ponies they had twenty, sixteen to one Carriage. Mr. & Mrs. Hall have gone to the Fair this week.

I just caught up with my books yesterday evening. I got behind during the show & waited on customers. Busy is no name for it. We just had more than we could do, sold five wholesale bills. I sold one.

We will have our Fair the 11, 12, & 13 of November. If it keeps on we will have cold weather for it is cold for certain now. We put up our stove today. John & Hill are setting close up to it now. I am afraid I will have a cold time this winter, for I suffered this morning. I am so far from the stove that it does me no good.

Remember me to Charlie, Levin & all the rest of my friends.

Your Affectionate Son,

Frank

F. A. Clinard to Mr. and Mrs. Livingston N. Clinard

Hickory, N. C.
Oct. 23rd 1874

Dear Father and Mother,

I was glad to hear from you & get the papers you sent me. I took it round to show to our Episcopal Minister, he always takes such an interest in our church, he read it. I said it seemed like this church. He is a splendid preacher. I like to hear him about as well as any preacher I ever heard. I go to see him often. I like to hear him talk, he is sociable & kind.

I guess you will think I am getting better after dancing & going to parties all summer, then to go to see preachers. I am staying close home now every night nearly & read & write till about 9 o'clock, then go to bed. We are having busy times in the barter business. I never seen money so scarce in my life & hard to collect. I have disarmed men in town so much I am ashamed to meet some of them. I counted the accounts on our books this evening, they are over eight-hundred. Of course they don't all owe us, we owe some of them. You know it keeps me busy to keep up. I stick close to it though, go to work as soon as I get up & work all day. I never get my breakfast till after eight o'clock.

We are having beautiful weather now. I have on my light coat & feel comfortable. Well, we are going to have our Fair at last on the 11th, 12, & 13 of Nov. Every wagon comes to town goes off with an advertisement pasted on them.

Hall & I have two articles for exhibition. Two hogs. We have one very fine fellow. Henry stuffs him. Mr. Hall told him he would give him half the premium if he could make his hogs fat enough to take it.

Father you ought to be here to eat chestnuts. We have got more chestnuts & ___ than any one else. I eat every day till I get tired. I believe that is what is fattening me so. I weigh 140 with my thin clothing on. I want to reach 150 or 160 this winter. We are getting John B. fat. We are going to show him at the Fair for the fat boy.

Mr. Hall bought a fine yoke of Oxen this evening, one weighed over 1300 & the other one over 1400.

We have some of our new calicos. Philo[30] is north buying goods & I will bet he buys things that won't suit us in this market. I will give you prices of

---

[30] P. C. (Philo) Hall, brother of J. G. Hall, operator of Hall Brothers store

this market for produce. Cabbage 2 cents. Butter 30 cents cash. Eggs 20. Chickens 16 2/3 to 20. Wheat 125 & 140. Chestnuts 2.00. Apples 60 to 65. Irish potatoes 60 & 65. Dried pumpkins 1.00 1/2 cents per lb.

Give my regards to all the clerks & love to Aunt Eliza. John just came up to my desk & asked me to remember him to you all & to Aunt Eliza. Hill went home today, will be back Monday. Tell Ed to write to me. I wrote to Granny Shultz last week.

Much love to all

Your Affectionate Son,

Frank

F. A. Clinard to Mr. and Mrs. Livingston N. Clinard

J. G. HALL,	R. L. PATTERSON,
of J. G. & P. C. HALL, Wilkesboro, N. C.	of PATTERSON & Co., Salem, N. C.,

HALL & PATTERSON,
DEALERS IN
General Merchandise,
NORTH OF RAILROAD STATION
Hickory, N. C.,

Oct. 28th 1874

My Dear Father and Mother,

We are having busy times now buying produce. Mr. Hall & Beard have gone to the Salisbury Fair, so I have to wait on customers. I sold a bill of $125.25 this morning to one man & this evening I sold another small bill of $16.00 & worked on my books besides. We are getting our new goods. We priced last night till after ten o'clock. We bought a load of stone ware last night after nine o'clock & unloaded it & paid the man for it.

You said you did not get my letter last week. I wrote you last Friday.

I saw Mrs. Clemmons was here today on her way to Salem. She told me her Mother was at the point of death. I had a cup of coffee sent her from the Hotel.

Mr. Hall sent his large oxen to Salisbury Fair & is going to send them to Charlotte Fair. We are having splendid weather. There is a special train runs from here to Salisbury every day. Fare there & return $1.50 during the Fair. I think we will have a right good Fair considering it is so late in the season.

Tell Ed to write to me, also Tom Huske. I am glad to hear Aunt Eliza has got some bacon to eat once more. I guess it comes from Davy's new gro-

cery, that is what made it so good, tell her this. Remember me to all my friends. What has become of my cat? Much love to all.
Your Affectionate Son, Frank

F. A. Clinard to Mr. and Mrs. Livingston N. Clinard

Hickory, N. C.
Nov. 4, 1874

Dear Father & Mother,

I received your letter this morning & was glad to hear from you. We are having busy times at present. You wanted to know Aunt Carrie's P. O., it is Prestonburg KY. I am glad to hear my cat is getting along alright. I saw Mrs. Clemmons as she passed here. She told me her Mother was very low.

Mother, I weigh 142 lbs. I can't button the top button on my shirts. I wear 14 1/2 collars. I have turned my beard out all over my face, it makes me look too heathenish. I will have to take it off.

You are kinder getting after me about the Preacher. I will send you Miss Fannie's Photo, but I want you to send it back next week as I know not the hour she might want it back.

You say last but not least, the Hickory Fair, you are right about it not being the least, as every one is trying to make it a success. I saw a Turnip last night that weighed eight pounds, it beats any thing I have seen. There has been a good many entries made. The Fair ground is in splendid condition. They are going to have a Tournament in gander pulling to amuse the crowd. We have had some cold weather for the past week, has turned some warmer & I fear we will have rain for our Fair. We have got nearly all our new goods in, some right nice styles this fall.

I never saw the like of chestnuts in my life, we can buy them for $1.25 per Bu., they started at $4.00.

I wrote to Grand Mother Shultz some time ago. I am sorry to hear she has had such a bad time.

Father, did you know Dolph[31] & Abel Shuford's Father? Last Saturday he took his cows to pasture & did not come back till dinner, so his family got uneasy about him & made the alarm round the neighborhood & searched for him till 9 o'clock Sunday morning, when they found him in the Creek

---

[31] Adolphus L. "Dolph" Shuford, Hickory businessman

drowned. He was subject to epelectic fits. They think that was what caused his death.

Much love to all & tell Ed to write.

Your Affectionate Son, Frank.

F. A. Clinard to Mr. and Mrs. Livingston N. Clinard

Hickory, N. C.
Nov. 12th 1874
11 o'clock p.m.

Dear Father & Mother,

I have just returned from the Deaf, Dumb & Blind concert. I don't think I ever spent a more pleasant evening in my life, they act splendidly.

I was at the Fair ground today about four hours. They have more on exhibition this year than last, but not so many people here, I mean Watauga & the surrounding counties. Judge Watts, or Greasy Sam as he is more generally known by the latter name, delivered the Address. Gen Leach could not come. There was some nice racing today, several blooded horses from a distance was here. Lady Rebel, Haden's mare, Dolly Vardin & several other names I have forgotten, they made half mile in 47 seconds. Trade is very poor this Fair, but like all public times we are bothered to death for nothing.

John has just come in, he has been with his sweetheart to the concert. He says he will send you the money for his taxes in a few days, as soon as his sweetheart leaves. She is the widow Faney's daughter of Burke, he is a heavy coon. He wants some of those John's River bottoms.

Mother, you want me to send you Gertrude's Photo. I will, also another one of my acquaintances, but you must send them back to me, as it is impossible for me to do without them long at a time, especially one of them. The other one, I don't care if I don't see it in a long time. I am sleepy, so I will close & write you more about the Fair next week. Much love to all.

Your Affectionate Son,

Frank

F. A. Clinard to Mr. and Mrs. Livingston N. Clinard

Hickory, N. C.
Nov. 19th 1874

Dear Father & Mother,

I rec'd your letter yesterday & would have answered it last night, but Mr. Hall kept me at work till 10 o'clock writing letters & makeing entries. I am kept busy all the time, I never get any rest, only at night.

Father, I am sorry you had such bad luck with your teeth, I know you look funny. How do you make out to kiss Mother?

Well, I will tell you about our Fair. We had rather bad weather, rained some two days. There was a right good crowd here, but not as many as last year. The display of stock was much better this year than last & the racing much better. Floral Hall was much better this year than last. Judge Sam Watts delivered the address, Gen. Leach could not come. We had an Entertainment given by the Deaf, Dumb & Blind from Raleigh, which was a success. I enjoyed myself very much. Mr. Nickols, the superintendent of the institution & Betties Father, was along. I showed him round & paid him right smart attention for Bettie's sake. He recognized me as soon as he got off the train.

You wrote for a paper with a write in it about Mr. Hall. I could not find one, or I would have sent it to you. It was more on us boys than on him. I will write you what I recolect. "While Mr. Hall is at the Fairs jockeying steers, his boys are having fine times. Henry is boss & Frank ditto, while Hill makes John and Horace git-oh. Henry is negro here that does our out work."

Billy Morris & Martin Dougherty was here today. We are having a heavy Produce trade from Watauga at present, money is awfull tight. I bet we buy more chickens & all kinds of fowls here than any other place in the state. We killed one of our Oxen, it averaged 185 to the quarter, it was fat I tell you. Mr. Hall got several premiums on things at our Fair, on his hog for instance.

We are having very disagreeable weather at present, cold & rainy. I have a cold & bad cough. I have a sore neck, also a mole on the side of my neck, just below my shirt band, got sore & it hurts all one side of my head & neck & my arm. Dr. Baker is working on it, it is better than it was. He says I ought to have it cut out, but I don't want to have it cut if it will get well without it.

Give my love to Aunt Eliza. John is rather of the same opinion you are about the Bottoms & shore so about the "gal," he sent you a P. O. Order for his tax.

Mother, do you want to know what that young Lady's name is right bad? If you do, I will tell you. She is worth $100,000.00 and likes the look of F. A. C., so she says, but I never said I liked her more than a friend. You know who ---. Much love to all,
Your Devoted Son,
Frank.

P. S. Don't be uneasy about my neck & cough. I will be alright in a few days.

F. A. Clinard to Mr. and Mrs. Livingston N. Clinard

Hickory, N. C.
Nov. 26th 1874

Dear Father & Mother,

We have been very busy today. Watauga with it's full force fell in on us today. We have bought an immense amount of produce in the last week. If any merchant in Salem had on hand half what we have, they would think themselves broken up.

We are having cold weather at present & looked like snow for several days past. My neck is nearly well, & my cold is much better, so I am getting along finely. Lots of work, no time for fooling.

You spoke of killing your hogs shortly. When you kill write me the weight & age. I want to show them to Dolph Shuford. He is a great man for hogs, & always bragging on his. He took premiums on his at our Fair. He killed today, he has not been round yet to tell the weights. You asked what pork is worth up here. It brings eight cents, but none of any consequence has come in yet. We have bought one pig. I would like to have some of our sausage & liver pudding. It would go well, as I am tired to death on chicken. I get good fare & plenty of it & cooked well. Mother, I get coffee that is nearly as good as yours. We have been having milk every day for dinner for the last month & apple dumplings every day.

Mr. Hall just come in from Good Templar meeting & I will have to go to work. I have been at work & it is late & I am tired, so give my love to Aunt Eliza & much love to you both.
Your Affectionate Son, F. A. C.

F. A. Clinard to Mr. and Mrs. Livingston N. Clinard

Hickory, N. C.
Dec. 3rd 1874

My Dear Father and Mother,

Your letter was duly received & I was glad to hear from you. You wanted to know about my shirts, what alteration I wanted made. I want wide pleats, especially the middle one & please make the bosam's out of fine linen. I think these shirts I have got have lasted very well. They are about gone. I have had some of them patched & one is gone.

Father, you wanted to know what we do with all our produce. We get orders every day for it from different places. Raleigh, Charlotte, Columbia, & all points along the Rail Road. We have shipped an immence amount of produce this fall & at high prices. Chicken 18 cents, Turkies 100 @ 125, Ducks 20 cents, Geese 50 cents, apples 1 .00 per bushel, Irish potatoes $1.00, cabbage 2 cents per lb., partridges 125 per doz., sweet potatoes 65 cents, buck wheat flour 3 1/2, flour 4 1/2, onions 1.00, mountain cheese 12 1/2, chestnuts 1.50 per bu., beef hams 8 to 10, butter 25 to 30 cents, corn 75 cents, wheat 125 to 140, peas 85, white beans 100 to 125 per bu., eggs 20 to 25 cents per doz., bees wax 28 and 30. We are having a big trade, but it is all is such stuff as I mentioned above. I know one thing, it keeps me moving to keep up with my books. I have worked several nights this week till after eleven o'clock. I am getting right good at book keeping, if I do say it myself. The part I dread is collecting. I have been trying all week to raise some money, but every body is hard up.

Charlie Hamilton just come in the store, he is a great big boy. He asked after Ed & you all. Mother, you say you wish I had some of your sausage & pudding. I wish so too, send me some by mail, can't you? Or will you save me some till I come home? Mr. Hall & John have gone to Good Templars meeting, so I don't have to work tonight, unless Mr. Hall comes in after the meeting is over. I owe about half doz. letters, so I will take tonight to answer them in.

Last Sunday morning old Mr. Link went out to feed his hogs & found a dead infant in a sack in his hog lot. The hogs had torn the sack & partly eaten the child. No clue to the murderess as I know of. They suspect a woman that cooks for Mr. Hall. Mr. H. lives next to the lot where the child was found. Give my love to Ed and Aunt Eliza & much love to you both. Your Affectionate Son,
F. A. C.

F. A. Clinard to Mr. and Mrs. Livingston N. Clinard

Hickory, N. C.
Dec. 9th 1874

Dear Father & Mother,

Your welcome letter to hand this morning. I was glad to hear from you & grand Father & Mother. I can allways tell when Grand Father comes to Salem. There is an Old Man, comes here to get his pension fixed up, we cash his check. Business is brisk, lots of produce coming in, but money is scarce. I have been out all the evening trying to collect, but made a poor out.

I saw Dr. Butner today. He inquired for me & Beard, told me there was a man at the train asking for me. I walked up to him & he asked me if my name was Clinard. I told him it was. He told me his name was Dr. Butner. He told me about Uncle Gideon & Lewis.[32] I had a long chat with him. The train stops here half hour for dinner, so I had a good chat with him.

Mother, I had my fill of sausage today. I eat a little too much. It had sage in it & made me about half sick, but I can go some of yours when I come home. I expect I will have a dull Christmas. I hear some talk of several parties, but I don't know whether there will be any or not. Harry Mast has come back to Watauga, he wants to get in here to clerk.

Hickory is still improving, good many houses going up. You said we got good prices for our goods. I will quote a few prices. Domestic 11 to 12 1/2, Ham 1. 40, Coffee 25 to 33 1/2, Calico 8 to 12 1/2, sugar 11 to 14, rice 12 1/2, Alamance Plaids 18. We some times stick them on small articles, oblige to do it or loose money. We sell leading articles as cheap as any where, but I admit we put it on some goods.

Remember me to all the clerks & tell Pfohl I said spank Josh for me. Much love to you all & Aunt Eliza.
Your Affectionate Son,
F. A. Clinard

---

[32] Lewis Shultz, brother of Charlotte Elisabeth Shultz Clinard (first wife of L. N. Clinard)

F. A. Clinard to Mr. and Mrs. Livingston N. Clinard

Hickory, N. C.
Dec. 23rd 1874

Dear Father & Mother,

You need not think I don't want to write to you because I have not written you long letters. I have been very busy every night writing on my books & just now quit writing on my books. I wish you all a very Merry Christmas. I don't expect to have any, Mr. Hall is going to give us all a big dinner. The Turkey is dead, & hanging out at our window. He weighed fifteen pounds dressed.

I got two of my fingers badly mashed today. We have got some dumb bells here for sale & I was using them this morning & mashed my thumb & one of my fingers real bad.

We are very busy now, more trash coming in than I ever saw. We are having very fine weather now.

Tell Ed I am very much oblige to him for the nice collar button he sent me. That is a nice way of answering letters. I wish some of my other correspondents would do the same way. I had a letter from Cousin Jennie Shultz this week. She is married. She married a Brown from Davidson, one of her second cousins.

You wanted to know what Mr. Hall is coming to Salem for. I think he is going to buy out Mr. Patterson's part in this store, say nothing about it.

I was writing late last night & the boys thought they would have some fun out of me, so they got some cockleburs & just all under my sheet & pillow. I heard them laughing up stairs, so I felt of my pillow before I went to bed, so I found it out. Hill had a skunk skin put in his pillow, so he thought he would pay me back with burs.

Last Sunday I was elected Librarian for our Sunday School. Nick Martin of Stokes Co. was up here last week looking round for a house & lot. He wants to manufacture Tobacco. This is a good point, lots of Tobacco comes here from Wilkes & Caldwell. We have one Tobacco Factory here now, also a news store. We can get any paper we want & there are several cabbage stores here. Tell Aunt Eliza I wish her a Merry Christmas, also Eddie. Much love to you all.

Your Affectionate Son,

F. A. Clinard

Personal Letters of L. N. Clinard 1875

F. A. Clinard to Mr. and Mrs. Livingston N. Clinard

Hickory, N. C.
Feb. 11th 1875

My Dear Father and Mother,

I was glad to hear from you & hear you are better. We have had quite a snowy time. It snowed all day Sunday & last night sleeted on top of it, so we have quite a snow.

Mr. R. L. P. has not arrived yet. I got the plot you sent, there has been a man here two days waiting on him to buy his land. He said that Mr. P. was to meet him here on the 10th, which was yesterday. John B. went to Morganton today on some business to buy up Eggs. I guess he is out about the widow Forney's by this time tonight. We are paying 20 cents cash for eggs.

Mr. H. sent you a check (or draft) for $169 52/100. I hope it reaches you safely. He rec'd the draft you sent in favor of P & Co.

About my lost time I was mistaken. He only chg'd me for the time I was at home last May & he said if you exacted it off him he would pay you that. He said tell you that he was compelled to have that rule about chg. lost time, as old man Beard looses right smart of time & charged him & all the rest with lost time, even half day, that is in my contract that I am to take notice of all the time that is lost by the clerks & ch. it up to them. I believe I wrote you that he gives me ten days & charges me with no lost time. I have been trying to learn John Neely to keep books so he could keep mine while I am at home. I tell you he is awful slow to learn.

The Boss & Levin kinder went for us in the statement we sent them of their Acct., but I guess we cleaned them up nicely, got them in two mistakes. One for five dols. & the other seven & some cents & have forgotten. I have been very lucky, but mind you I am not bragging about it. I have made but few mistakes & had the good luck to find mistakes in other people's Acct's. Don't say anything about what I said about finding mistakes in P. & Co's Acct. It might make them mad.

I think Mr. Hall is pleased with my bookkeeping. I know one thing, he puts a great deal of confidence in me. I carry the keys to every thing about the house, even his private papers & all the money. He often tells me things that he tells no one else & you can rest assured I will never betray my trust. I know what every man in the house gets. The clerks try to get out of me what the others are getting & what I am getting. How does Ed like Winston?

Capt. Avery had his in fare in Morganton, so I did not ask to get off as I want to come home & I did not care to loose any time going up there. I had a long talk with his wife. She kinder tried to tease me about how I flew round her in the summer, but she could not come that near me. I saw them today, they passed back down the road. Avery lives in Charlotte now. He is Political Editor of the Charlotte Observer.

Mother, I send you a strip off one of my cuffs. You can expect me on the 7th of March. I will leave here & stop at High Point & get Uncle Burns to take me to Salem, provided he is in a good humor. If he is Ashy, I will hire a horse & buggy of Barbel. Mother, you ought to see me going for Apple Dumplings, we have them every day, & beets. Them you know I love. I wish you had some of our nice apples. I often think of you when I am eating one. If we have any when I come home, I will bring you some, I can fill my trunk, as I have nothing else to put in it, so I can bring you some. I guess you will think I am in a good humor, as I am writing such a long letter. I just happen to have a little more time, as we have not been busy today & I got through entering sooner than common. Harry is here at my desk shaving. He has not forgotten how to fix it up. If he has been all over the world, he has been in every state & territory in the Union except New Mexico. Give my love to Aunt Eliza & tell her I am all right. Give my love to Ed & much to you both. Good night.

Your Affectionate Son,

Frank

F. A. Clinard to Mr. and Mrs. Livingston N. Clinard

Hickory, N. C.
Feb. 25, 1875

Dear Father & Mother,

I was truly glad to hear from you this morning. I thought you had forgotten to write to me this week. We have had heavy rains for the past week with thunder & lightning. The creeks & river are very high & there has been a big slide in the R. R. The train was six hours behind today. It has cleared up cold, so I guess we will have some nice weather again. My cold is better I am glad to say. There has been a good deal of sickness about here, but no deaths.

We are to have a big Temperance speaking Saturday night. Mr. Hall & John Neely are going to send forth their eloquence in behalf of the Temperance cause.

Father, I got after the Boss for charging me sixty cents for a box of pins when he promised to give them to me. He said you charged them up, they only cost 37 cents. You must recollect that I have not forgotten the old cost mark. Fifty cents would have been a big price for them. You never said a word about Hill in your letter. Is he with the new firm? We sold one man today $529.04 worth of goods. Tell Tom Huske I will answer his letter when I come home. Give my love to Ed & Aunt Eliza. Tell her she is getting so old by this time, I will have to call her Aunty. Much love to you both, & Mother I want some sugar cake.
Your Loving Son,
Frank

F. A. Clinard to Mr. and Mrs. Livingston N. Clinard

Hickory, N. C.
March 20th 1875

Dear Father & Mother,

I reached here this morning safely. I had a bad time getting here. I missed the train at Salisbury, I had to lay over there. I met Jimmy Menn & he took me to see some young Ladies, so I spent the time very pleasantly. I wish you could see my books. They are behind about two weeks. There has been nothing at all done to them since I left, so I will have to work hard to catch up. Mr. Hall says he has been very busy since I left.

Harry Mast has struck a streak of luck. He won $19,000.00 in the Lewisville Gift Concert. I must get to work, so I will write you again shortly. Much love to you.
Your Affectionate Son,
Frank

F. A. Clinard to Mr. and Mrs. Livingston N. Clinard

ORDERS FOR COUNTRY PRODUCE, &c., SOLICITED.
Office of HALL & PATTERSON,
DEALERS IN General Merchandise,
AND BUYERS OF COUNTRY PRODUCE
NORTH OF RAILROAD STATION.
Hickory, N. C.,

March 25 1875

Dear Father & Mother,

I received your letter this morning & it grieves me that some infamous scoundrel says I was drunk & carrying a bottle around Salem. I will swear before my Maker that I did not have a bottle of Whiskey while I was in Salem, & that I was not drunk. I was in your room each night. You ought to know that I was not drunk.
Your True Son,
Frank

P. S. I did not get off from High Point till three o'clock next morning. There was no train, so I missed connection at Salisbury. Mr. Hall starts for Salem today.
F. A. C. I am very busy or I would write more.

F. A. Clinard to Mr. and Mrs. Livingston N. Clinard

Hickory, N. C.
April 8th 1875

My Dear Father and Mother,

I received your letter this morning & was sorry to hear you were both sick, hope you will be better before long. We are having very fine weather & dull trade. We have been very busy this evening. We bought three loads produce, over 50 bu. apples. I wish you had some of them, they are fine.

We had a dance last night & had a nice time. I escorted Maj. Hardin's daughter, she is a very stylish Lady. My particular friend, Miss Perry, came back this morning from Richmond. She has been spending the winter in Virginia. She brought me a bouquet of flowers all the way from Richmond.

Miss Fannie Arthur gave me a beautiful bouquet last night, so I have a nice supply of flowers at present.

Mother, I have shaved clean since I got back, but I look so awfull funny that I will have to let my moustache grow again. I shaved off the day I got back & on Sunday night I went to see a young Lady & she nor her Mother, neither one new me when I first stepped in the parlor.

Mother, how is the best way to put away my winter clothing, pack it away in a box, or hang it up in a wardrobe with cloth doors? Father, have you any Prince Albert gaiters, or cloth gaiters, on the same style & what can you sell them at? These shoes I have are too heavy for summer wear.

You spoke of the Centennial. There is to be an excursion from this place to Charlotte to the Centennial.

I wondered why you had not sent me the Press, I thought you had forgotten it. I wrote to Ed a few days ago. Had a letter from Henry Lineback. He wrote me the cause of his delay in not sending my Photos.

Father, I had a sweet time getting our cash acct. straight. It was short eight dollars & I worked about one whole day on it & I found the mistakes. Mr. Beard had made them while I was at home. You wrote Mr. Robert Gray's property was advertised to be sold, so is Mr. E. W. Jones to be sold out for security money for I. Y. Bryce, his home place & the Devenport place. What do you recon Will Jones will do? I. Y. Bryce owns the house & lot that old man Elias use to live in, in this place. It is to be sold in May. I guess you know the firm of Hall & Patterson dissolve co-partnership the first of July. Mr. Hall says he has not decided what he is going to do yet, but he says he thinks he will continue the business. Give my love to Aunt Eliza & Eddie. Much love to you both from,
Your Loving Son,
Frank

F. A. Clinard to Mr. and Mrs. Livingston N. Clinard

Hickory, N. C.
April 15th 1875

Dear Father & Mother,

I received your letter this morning & also your paper. I was glad to receive both & I have trade a swap with Mr. Hall. I am to give him my paper, & he is to let me have the Piedmont Press, which I will send to you.

I received my photos on Monday, I am very well pleased with them. I sent H. Lineback a P. O. order for the amount. I wish you would ask him if he received it.

Mr. R. L. Patterson is here in the store now talking about the Jones case. The Bryce property was sold here in town today, it brought $2,000.00. It was the property that old man Elias use to live in. Mr. E. W. I. looks case worn and old. He left here this evening at 6 o'clock & said he was going all the way to the Valley tonight.

We are having very dull times at present, no mountain trade at all just now & all the Farmers are busy getting in their crops. The Boss is sitting here now bragging on Lambert Thomas as Corn Merchant.

Father, you did not answer my question about shoes.

There was a run off on this road one day this week. No one was hurt, but some of the cars were smashed up right smart.

Our Commissioners are improving the place right smart. They have worked the streets & side walks & trimmed the trees all over the square. The people here expect a large crowd of strangers here this summer, so I guess we will have a gay time.

Mother, I had a nice present given me the other day. It was a rose geranium. A young Lady sent it to me. That makes the second one I have received. Did I tell you about my flowers when I was at home? I have quite a selection. I have had quite a variety of Hiesinths. The young Lady that gave me the flowers is going to get married this summer & she says she wants me to be one of her waiters. I saw her this evening & helped her carry in her flowers so they would not freeze. We have right cold night. Mother, I will take your advise & pack my clothing away as soon as it gets warm enough.

We had the heaviest hail storm on Tuesday evening I ever saw. It beat the one we had while I was at home. It covered the ground like hail in the winter, only it was larger.

The Citizens of this place are going to build a Male College. They have most of the money made up, so I guess they will go to work on it soon.

I thought when I commenced to write, I could write enough to fill all sides of this paper, but I find I cannot. I could write you enough to fill it, but it would not interest you. John, Horace & Harry have all been out tonight. John just got in. He says give his kindest regards to Aunt Eliza & Uncle Davy. Give my love to Aunt Eliza & Ed, & tell Ed it takes him a long time to answer one letter. I write a letter nearly every night to some one. I think he might afford to write to me once a month. I think Ed treats me badly, to be the only brother he has. I have come to the conclusion that he don't care for me, at least he has a poor way of showing it if he does. I write to friends that answer my letters as punctual as any body can, & to think he is my only brother & won't write to me. It hurts my feelings, you have no idea how much. I am not void of feeling. If I do live out of the world he may live to see the time when he will wish he cared a little more for his brother than he does. He never even sends me any word in your letters. I have not heard a word with him since I am back. I must close with much love to you both & a happy good night.

Your Loving Son,

Francis

F. A. Clinard to Mr. and Mrs. Livingston N. Clinard

J. G. HALL,   R. L. PATTERSON

Office of HALL & PATTERSON,
DEALERS IN
General Merchandise,
NORTH OF RAILROAD DEPOT.
Hickory, N. C.,

April 22nd 1875

My Dear Father & Mother,

Your Post card received this morning & I was sorry to hear you were sick. I hope you are better by this time. John Brown arrived here this morning & I see he has bought a pair of P. & Co's no account shoes. I have often had poor shoes, but I don't think I ever had a pair as sorry as this pair I have now. They are worn out all over, even the soles & I have not done any walking of any consequence either. I think P. & Co. ought to give me another pair.

I was very sorry to hear of Tom Norwoods misfortune.

We have had some of the coldest weather we have had this winter. The ground & all the garden stuff is frozen & wheat is some what injured. We had a right heavy frost this morning.

Mr. Hall has another boy, so I guess after the first of July the firm will be Hall & Sons.

How about the Greensboro Lottery? Did you draw anything? Father, I feel proud. I have made out all my monthly statements to April 1st & proven them on my cash book & Ledger & they are correct. I found one mistake of 10 cents in my Mdse. Acct. & John had made that while I was at

home. Give my love to Aunt Eliza & Ed. I had a letter from Ed a few days ago & answered his letter yesterday. Much love to you both from
Your Loving Son,
Francis

F. A. Clinard to Mr. and Mrs. Livingston N. Clinard

Hickory, N. C.
May 14th 1875

Dear Father & Mother,

We are having right warm weather at present. I am in my shirt sleeves now, I am so warm. Everything up this way is backward. We have had only a few vegetables, lettuce, radishes, onions, & we have had young Irish potatoes once, & young was the right name for them.

We have had right smart of excitement this week. "The Hickory Dramatic Club" played two nights this week, & last night Miss Isabelle Armstrong, a English Lady, lectured here in the Temperance cause. She had a very large audience. I was certainly surprised to hear her lecture so well. She is the smartest lecturer I have heard, she was very interesting. But one thing I must say about her, she is the ugliest white woman I ever saw.

A great many people from this country are going to the Centennial. Mr. Hall & Harry are going down. I would like to go right well, but I will stay at home & go to the Philadelphia Centennial next year.

You asked me about my ringworms. I have killed them. I painted my face with tincture of iron & that cleaned them up.

Carrington's Circus is to be here on the 21st. From what I can hear of it, I hardly think I will go to see it. I understand it is a humbug of the first degree.

Father, I have got a nice job on my hands now. I am proving all my Personal Ledger entrys. I am getting along very well so far. I have proven all my other entrys to be correct. We are to have a Tobacco warehouse here, so Winston had better look sharp, or we will take some of their trade. The farmers up here are raising more Tobacco this year than they ever have before. Trade is very dull at present, no retail trade at all. We have sold several wholesale bills this week.

I wish you would say to Hill & Hen. that I am waiting very patiently for a letter from them. I sent you a paper last week & this weeks paper. Mrs. R. L. Patterson has been spending several days at Mr. Halls. She

gave me several very pressing invitations to visit them. I think I will go up there this summer & spend a few days. I have promised some body to take them up this summer. Remember me to Missus Barrow, Pfohl, Levin, & Thomas. Ask Tom if he has sold Hill a burial bust yet. Give my love to Aunt Eliza, Ed, & much to you both. Good night.
Your Loving son, Frank

P. S. I guess you will think I have written this letter very badly. I am in a hurry, I have to write some more tonight. F. A. C.

F. A. Clinard to Mr. and Mrs. Livingston N. Clinard

Hickory, N. C.
May 23rd 1875

My Dear Father and Mother,

I guess you was some what disappointed in not receiving a letter from me last week. I was kept busy so I did not get a chance to write. Mr. Hall, Harry, & Horace went to the Centennial, so I was kept busy.

The weather is very warm & dry. Our streets are very dusty. It is very disagreeable to go out any where, the dust is so bad. This place is so high that we have more dust here than any place to the size of it in the State.

Carrington's Show was here on Friday. They did not make expenses, a very small crowd went to see it. They did not show at all after night. They had their gambling man with them, but the Police watched them so close that they could not make any thing here. The Town Ordinance has a tax of $500.00 on all side shows & gambling & any thing of that kind.

Business is very dull, no trade coming in. Mr. A. C. Hege came up from Lexington yesterday. He is very much pleased with our town. He told me he saw you Father, on last Wednesday. I had a letter from Uncle Andy last week, they are all well. As usual, he writes the same old copy of his letters. As I write, a little to my surprise, we have a small shower of rain & the sun shining. I hope we will have more this evening.

Today, one year ago, I was at home with you. I wish I was there now. I was surprised to hear that Mr. R. L. P. was not at the Centennial. What was the matter? I thought he was one of the big men to be there. Mr. Hall & the boys are very much pleased with the Centennial. They say there was an immence crowd there. I took dinner at Mr. Halls last Sunday, & saw his baby for the first time. It is not as good looking as his other one. The last one favors him more.

Father, Wes Clinard is in a bad fix. He has consumption & I hardly think he will live to see another summer. He looks very badly.

John M. B. is still going for his John's River sweetheart. We have been running him heavy for some time. He had a dream that he acted in his sleep, & did not know any thing about it till I waked him. He threw his arms around my neck, & repeated three times these words "Miss Fannie God bless you, Now I do Love you" & wound up by kissing me. When he kissed me, I was so full of laugh that I waked him & the other boys & we lay for the hours teasing him.

Give my regards to all the clerks & my love to Ed & Aunt Eliza. Is Hen Ackerman dead, or married, or what has become of him? I would like to know. He has not written to me in over a month, neither has Hill. Tell Hill I said I would like to hear from him, give him my regards. Much love to you both. I must close as it is nearly Sunday school time & I must go.

Your Loving Son,

Frank

F. A. Clinard to Mr. and Mrs. Livingston N. Clinard

J. G. HALL,
of J. G. & P. C. HALL, Wilkesboro, N. C.

R. L. PATTERSON,
of PATTERSON & Co., Salem, N. C.,

OFFICE OF HALL & PATTERSON,
Dealers in General Merchandise,
AND BUYERS OF COUNTRY PRODUCE.
NORTH OF RAILROAD STATION
Hickory, N. C.,

June 24th 1875

Dear Father & Mother,

Yours just received & I am glad to hear Grand Mother is better, hope she will continue to improve. Mr. R. L. P. passed through here yesterday on his way to the Valley. He did not tell me about Tom getting his hand hurt. Is it shot much?

We are to have a mammouth pic-nic here on the first of July. All the Sunday School & different societys of the place have joined together & are going to have a big time. I am one of the committee. The Masons celebrate St. John's day this evening. We are to have a big supper at the Western Hotel

& a lecture delivered by the Rev. Wm. Hartsell, who is the Grand Master of this Lodge.

Trade is very dull, we have commenced taking inventory & I know I will be glad when we are through. I have to copy all of it, so you know it will be quite a job. Mr. Hall had a letter sociable at his house last night. I had a nice time you know. Mrs. Hall leaves for the Valley tomorrow, so Mr. Hall will be alone, except Miss Gertie. She is going to keep house for him.

You tell Hill I will write him in a few days, that I have been so busy lately, I have not had time to write to any one but you. It is very hot today & the flys are very bad. I never have seen the likes of fleas & flys. Mother, how are the pigs getting along this year? Hope they are nice. We had one here at the store that is fine. He will weigh over 200 lbs now. Visitors have begun to come in right smart. I hope we will have a large crowd here this summer. I must close. Give my regards to all my friends, especially Mr. H. D. Lott. Much love to all of you.
Your Loving Son,
Frank

T. W. Huske to L. N. Clinard

Hillsboro,
June 30th

My Dear Mr. Clinard,
    Your very kind letter was received last week & I do assure you, was very highly appreciated. In such a tedious time as I am having, it is surely pleasant & grateful to my feelings to know & hear there are kind hearts remembering me & think enough of me to write & say so.

This is the thirteenth day since my accident. All tell me I am getting along so well. The Drs. say far above any expectations they have had, but I'll declare - it is so bad to me. I am afraid I am an ungrateful boy. The sloughing has commenced & the shot & bone are making their way to the surface. I have twenty four shot from my wound.

It'll occur to me, it will be a long time before I enter the lists again. I am glad it so happens that I am not needed in the store, tho to be sure, I do wish the times were brisker. I hear of many clerks being dismissed on account of the dull times.

Give my kindest regards to your wife, thank her sincerely for her love & sympathy. My best respects to all of our friends at the store. I received Mr.

Pfohl's letter this morning. I am so much obliged & will answer it as soon as I can do so. Also send love to my chum, Hill. I received the clothing that he was kind enough to send me. I will reply to his letter. I hope he will not wait on my slow motions & write again. He ought to be aware of my anxiety on some subjects & keep me well informed to keep up my spirits.

  With very kindest regards & many thanks for your kindness, believe me.
Yours Most Truly,
T. W. Huskee
How many times a day can Mr. Barrow leave these times for home?

F. A. Clinard to Mr. and Mrs. Livingston N. Clinard

Hickory, N. C.
July 6th 1875

Dear Father & Mother,

  I have been so busy I have not had time to write. We have been very busy getting our inventory & Acct's. strait. I am about up with my work. We have got rid of three clerks, Mr. Beard, Horace, & Harry Mast. Harry started for Oregon on Monday. He said he was going by Salem to see Pat. John & myself & Ed Black are all that stay here now, except Henry.

  Last Thursday, July 1st, we had a "Pic-Nic." I did not go all day, I went just in time to get my dinner. All the Sunday Schools of the place joined together & had a nice time. Each school wore their badges. I will enclose my badge.

  Our place is getting a good many summer visitors & I understand there are about sixty at White Sulphur Springs. I have not been out there this season.

  Mother, I want you to do a favor for me, if you please. I want you to get Mrs. Davis, or send North, & have me a hair heart made. I will enclose some of my hair. I want it for a charm for my watch. Have it gold mounted & send me bill & I will send you the money. Please have it done as soon as you can for me.

  We are having good rains, but the weather is very warm. It looks like we would have a shower this evening.

  I had a letter from H. N. A.[33] this morning. He tells me there has been several deaths in Salem in the past week. He writes me his Aunt Delphia &

---

[33] Henry Nathaniel Ackerman

Charlie Fishers wife both died last week & that a man at Butners Hotel jumped out of a window & killed himself.

Wheat crops are splendid through this country, it will not bring over $1.00 per Bu. I have been rather unwell for the past day or two. I guess it comes from close application to business. Hope I will feel better in a day or two. I will not have to work so hard. You have no idea how strange it seems about the store, all the clerks gone. Tell Ed if he takes a trip any where this summer, to come up here. I will board him as long as he will stay. It would be a nice trip for him & he would enjoy it.

Hen writes me he has invested in a Horse & Buggy. Tell him I invest my money in something that won't die, or eat & grow larger. Tell Aunt Eliza I am looking for her at our dance. I sent her an invitation. Remember me to Henry, Charlie & Levin. Give my love to Hill & Ed. Tell Hill I will write him a long letter one of these days afore long. Much love to you both.
I Remain Your Loving Son,
Frank

F. A. Clinard to Mr. and Mrs. Livingston N. Clinard

J. G. HALL,   P. C. Hall
of J. G. & P. C. HALL, Wilkesboro, N. C.
Hall Bro's Successors to HALL & PATTERSON,
Dealers in General Merchandise,
AND BUYERS OF COUNTRY PRODUCE.
NORTH OF RAILROAD STATION
Hickory, N. C.,

July 15th 1875

Dear Father & Mother,

I received your letter this morning & was glad to hear from you. It has been nearly three weeks since I had a letter from you. I had a letter from Uncle Andy this morning, he is just like always.

We are having hot weather, but it rains nearly every day. Corn & vegetables are looking well. We have not had any corn or tomatoes yet, but I hope we will get some shortly. Summer visitors are coming in fast, so I hope our town will be more lively. We have several from Northern citys. Mr. E. J. Hale from N. Y. is here with his family, one young Lady from Philadelphia & one from Baltimore.

Mother I am much obliged to you for picking out my heart. Hope you got me a nice one. Mother, you ought to see my sweetheart. She is looking

better than I ever saw her & she is just as sweet as she can be. She made me quit using Tobacco. I haven't used any in a month. Father, Dr. Worth's son from Ashboro has been up here about a week. He is a splendid young fellow. I saw Tom Norwood the other day. He looks like always. He seems to be as lively as ever. I must close, as I have some work to do this evening. Give my regards to all the boys & my love to Ed & Aunt Eliza. Much love to you both.
Your Loving Son, Frank

F. A. Clinard to Mr. and Mrs. Livingston N. Clinard

J. G. HALL,   R. L. PATTERSON
Office of HALL & PATTERSON,
DEALERS IN
General Merchandise,
NORTH OF RAILROAD DEPOT.
Hickory, N. C.,

July 23rd 1875

Dear Father & Mother,

I received your letter this morning & was glad to hear from you. I began to think you had all burnt up down there. Last Saturday & Sunday was the hotest days I ever felt. I suffered very much with heat.

Last Saturday I took a horse & buggy & Miss Gertie & went to White Sulphur Springs, had a very nice time. Today & in fact for several days past, we have had very cool weather, considering how hot it was on Sunday. We have quite a gay crowd here now. I am enjoying myself very well. I go to see all the young Ladies & have a general good time. I have been at two dances this week.

I met a fellow here this week, that asked me if I had a brother in Winston. I told him I had. He said he had better look sharp or he would get in a difficulty writing & sending his photo to his sweetheart. Tell Ed I have treed him at last. If he has been shy about it, this fellow said he read his letter & saw his photo. I just now received the regular package containing the heart. I think it very pretty. Mother, I am very much obliged to you for getting it for me. You will find enclosed P. O. Order for three dollars. Much love to you all.
Your Loving Son, Frank

F. A. Clinard to Mr. and Mrs. Livingston N. Clinard

J. G. HALL,   R. L. PATTERSON

Office of HALL & PATTERSON,
DEALERS IN
General Merchandise,
NORTH OF RAILROAD DEPOT.
Hickory, N. C.,

July 30th 1875

Dear Father & Mother,

I have not heard from you this week, so as Lindsay is here, I thought I would write you a little hurriedly. I am not very well, been suffering with a very severe cold & cough. Hope it will get better soon. The weather is so very hot that I can not hardly stand it. We had our first corn & tomatoes this week. The Hotels are very much crowded. They had to turn off some yesterday. Trade is looking up, but I think berries are scarce this year, from what I can hear of the crop through this country. I wish I had some of your peaches & melons. We have had no peaches yet, but we have had some melons, but small.

We had a very sudden death here last week. A young man just my age was here at the Hotel & I had just finished talking to him, & he went up stairs to his room & in three minutes he was dead. He had a hemorrhage. He was from L. C. The proprierter of the Hotel had him fixed up in a $50.00 coffin & sent him to his parents. Much love to you all. The train is coming.

Your Loving Son,
Frank

F. A. Clinard to Mr. and Mrs. Livingston N. Clinard

Hickory, N. C.
Aug. 6th 1875

Dear Father & Mother,

I was disappointed today at not receiving a letter from you. I thought you probably did not get my letter last week, I gave one to Lindsay to take to you. Did you get my P. O. Order for $3.00? You did not say anything about it in your last letter.

We are having very pleasant weather, I was so cool the other evening, I put on my winter coat.

Our trade is increasing some, but the berry trade is small. We have bought right smart wheat in the past week, over 600 Bu., most of it at $1 .00 per Bu.

Father, I wish you would, if you please, have Jesse Riggs to front my boots that I left at home when I was there. He has my measure. Have him to make them as cheap as he will, have made out of good French calf skin & not to light soles. I want them to put on & near every day & Sunday too. I do not want too heavy soles, for I am not out much, only at my meals & Sunday.

Strangers still pour in, there are more here now than ever was before. Everybody seems to be very much pleased with the place & go away satisfied.

I will not say any thing about amusements this time, but I am not as big an expensive pack horse as you suppose I am. I try to keep in bounds with every thing. I do not go it as much as I did last summer, I am more quiet & reserved. Some of the young Ladies here got after me & wanted to know what had caused me to stay so close & be so quiet all this summer. I don't propose making a hermit of myself though, if I am engaged. I can show other Ladies marked respect & not love them either. I try & be polite to all. I have never lost any thing by showing Ladies attention. I know one thing, it has brought me out more than any thing else. If I had been in Salem, I would be like some other boys of my acquaintance. I feel quite confident I have made a good many friends from different parts of the country, both Gentlemen & Lady friends.

I am glad to know Ed Clinard pays Ladies attention. I heard from him & his Statesville sweetheart. I think Ed treats me very shabby by not writing to me. He never even sends me any word. I wish he could come up here about a week, he would enjoy himself I know. Give my love to Ed & Aunt Eliza. Much love to you both.

Your Loving Son,

Frank

P. S. Please be sure to send me this weeks paper. I am interested in "Eveni Page." I had a letter from Tom Huske yesterday, he is getting better. Father, you spoke about White Pine Shingles. You can see what they are. We shipped L. W. Fries a car load a week or so ago. We deliver them in Salem at 6.50 per, less freight. We pay freights that is by car load of 35. I think they are a splendid shingle & they make a beautiful roof. You probably could get Fogle Bro's to take the balance of a car load. We give 60 days time. Tell Pole & the balance of the clerks, I send my regards.

Your Son, Frank

F. A. Clinard to Mr. and Mrs. Livingston N. Clinard

Hickory, N. C.
Aug. 11th 1875

My Dear Father and Mother,

I was very glad to hear from you this morning. I thought you had made up your mind not to write to me any more. Father, you said I would not deign to say any thing about you selling your house. I did not think it necessary. I will tell you what I do think about it. You sold it very cheap, cheaper than I would have sold it. I think one thing you are missing it in & that is building a story & half house. I would build a two story always, & set it back from the street about 30 feet, room enough to have a nice yard in front. Have the L. build long enough for dining room & kitchen.

Father, you said if I ever had grown boys, I would think of your advice. I am thankful to you for all the advice you can give me. I am sure I meant nothing wrong the way I wrote you. It's true I have had to pay once or twice more than any one else, but the highest I paid was $2.00. I get ahead of them now, make them pay me at the door.

Mother, I am glad for you when you get in your new house. You will be better satisfied & I think will look more cheerfull.

Father, you got after me about not writing about the house & answering questions. I ask some thing in nearly every letter I write you that you pay no attention to at all. I asked after Ed in the last half dozen letters & you never say one word about him. Ed I think is above me. He thinks it would be lowering his dignity to write to such a fellow as I am, but I hope time will develop what we both are. I hope to be able to come up to his standard. It's true he had more advantages than I ever had, but never the less, I hope to be able to pass through this world alright.

I saw Judge Wilson & his son yesterday. They were here in the store. His daughter was here, but I did not get to see her. They went up to Lenoir.

You asked after the welfare of Hall Bro's. They are thriving very well. I have made a good many collections on old %, so you know that helps along things right well. I am going up the road in a few days to Morganton & Marion on business. I have been very unwell today, but hope to be well till tomorrow. Bishop Lymon preaches here tomorrow. Mr. Hall & John return regards to you both. Give my love to Aunt Eliza & Ed. Much love to you both.

Father, please hurry up Jesse with my boots. I want them so I can wear for Sunday this summer.
Your Loving Son, Frank

F. A. Clinard to Mrs. Livingston N. Clinard

Hickory, N. C.
Aug. 19th 1875

My Dear Mother,

I just received your letter today. I have been gone from home since last Friday. I went to Marion, I said, since last Friday. I returned home Sunday, & Monday morning soon I started for Wilkesboro. Reached Wilkesboro Monday night at 10 1/2 o'clock, went through the rain nearly all the way. The horse came near giving out. He traveled 56 miles. On Tuesday I rode 43 miles. All over the Northern part of Wilkes Co., I was buying Black berries. I got back home last night at 11 1/2 o'clock after driving 55 miles & getting lost to boot. I was in one of the hardest rains yesterday I ever saw fall. It fell so hard I could scarcely get my horse to go at all. I am awfull sore, got several blisters on my legs.

Last Friday, I went up the road with Miss Josie Wilson. Had a very pleasant time with her. The old Judge was along & he was talking politics with some men, so I sat by her & showed her the mountains.

Mother, I traveled about ten miles in the Brushy Mountains yesterday & did not see any living thing but flyes & not a track in the road & the first house I struck, I asked the way to Long's Store & they did not know any thing. I tried to get some thing to eat & feed my horse & could not. At last I got my dinner, had cold Rye bread without any grease on it, fried bacon & eggs & buttermilk. You bet I put it away. I was as hungry as a wolf. I saw Sam'l Horton & his wife & Amelia Church in Wilkesboro. I think Mrs. H. is breaking very fast. I called on her, she says she wants to go back to Salem.

Mother, I am very sorry you miss understood my letter. I assure you I meant nothing wrong in what I said & I am very sorry you miss construed it, for you know I would not say any thing to hurt your feelings for any thing in the world. You kinder go for me in your letter, you spoke as if I did not have any friends in Salem & had to leave there to find some. If such be the case, I am very sorry, but I guess I can live without them. You certainly are mistaken when you say I consider myself superior to Ed. I never thought of such a thing. You say I wish for something to him up to Ed's disadvantage. I am sure I never thought of such a thing. I would do any thing in my power to forward his progress in any thing I could. Ed is my only brother I love him & feel proud of him, but you will admit he has treated me rather shabby. As to my being superior to Ed in any thing, if I am I do not know it. He certainly has a better education than I have. It's true I have had more experience in business than he has, but I guess he could sell as many goods, if not more than I could.

There is a concert in town tonight. I hear them singing now. They are next door to us. The Orphans from Oxford are giving it. I thought I would stay at home & write to you. I have felt very badly about your letter all day. I am very sorry you think me such a man as you represent in your letter. Mother, I hope you will look at what I have written you in the right light. You know I love you & it hurts me to think you think me such a God forsaken demon as to try to wound your feelings or think of wishing my brother ill luck.

Tell Father to please send my boots by Express to Salisbury, care Capt. Whitley, W. N. C. R. R. Of course direct to Hickory & tell him Murrill feels alright over the election.

Give my love to Aunt Eliza & tell her I wish she could be here awhile. She could get her fill on chicken, for we have it twice a day regular. Give my love to Ed. I had a letter from Blanche a few days ago. She seems to be in fine spirits.

Mother, I want to tell you a remarkable surcumstance. I have not bought a neck tie this summer, wearing out my old ones.

Our town is crowded with visitors & they still come. I have not had but about three peaches this summer, but melons are very plenty.

Mother, please accept my apology, for it grieves me to think you think I try to wound your feelings in any way. Much love to you & Father. Good night. I am tired & sore, so I will go to bed & see if I can't get some rest.
Your Loving Son,
Frank

F. A. Clinard to Mr. and Mrs. Livingston N. Clinard

J. G. HALL,   P. C. Hall
of J. G. & P. C. HALL, Wilkesboro, N. C.
Hall Bro's Successors to HALL & PATTERSON,
Dealers in General Merchandise,
AND BUYERS OF COUNTRY PRODUCE.
NORTH OF RAILROAD STATION
Hickory, N. C.,

Aug. 31st 1875

Dear Father & Mother,

I have just returned from a trip up the road. I have been buying berries. I have really been so busy, I did not have time to write you sooner. Mr. Hall is gone nearly all the time & he has had me running all over the Western part of the state. We certainly have worked hard this summer. I am awfully behind with my books. Berries are active here, we lay all sorts of prices from 6 cents to 8 cents. I contracted yesterday for a lot at 6 1/2, another at 6 3/4, & another at 7 1/2 Btls. Included about 17,000.00 in all. I expect to start the last of this week on another hunt for berries. May go to Asheville.

I have heard since I reached home, of a case of suicide near town. I knew the fellow. The cause was on account of working the road. He was sort of a half witted fellow, and he said he never intended to work the road. So he was notified to work last Saturday & he left home & they did not see any thing of him any more till yesterday. He was found hanging to a limb, dead.

You will have to excuse me for not being prompt in answering your last letter. I have really not had the time. Much love to Aunt Eliza & Ed. I met Miss Alice Springs last night in Morganton. Much love to you both.
Your Loving Son,
Frank

F. A. Clinard to Mr. and Mrs. Livingston N. Clinard

J. G. HALL,
of J. G. & P. C. HALL, Wilkesboro, N. C.

R. L. PATTERSON,
of PATTERSON & Co., Salem, N. C.,

OFFICE OF HALL & PATTERSON,
Dealers in General Merchandise,
AND BUYERS OF COUNTRY PRODUCE.
NORTH OF RAILROAD STATION
Hickory, N. C.,

September 3rd 1875,

My Dear Father and Mother,

I received your letter today, also my boots. I tried on one of them, it went on very easy. I am very sorry Riggs made box toes, I dispise them. My reason for sending to him was principally on account of that, I thought he would not make box toes.

I wrote to you this week, I could not write last. I was kept so busy, I did not get to do any thing but work. I have worked harder this summer than last. I have been traveling round right smart & on forced trips in order to buy berries, before the excitement reached the Merchants through the country. I visited six different stores in one day through the country. We are having very warm weather at present & trade very brisk. We put up BB to 8 cents today. I hold my own right well, considering I have to stick so close & work hard & weigh berries.

Father, I am very much obliged to you for having my boots made. Don't I owe you some freight on them? Please let me know at once how much it all is & I will send you P. O. order for amount. I hope they will do me some service, for the last two pair of shoes I have had were no account at all.

Father, I notice in the Press, that you have begun your house. I hope you will have good luck & get it finished before cold weather sits in.

I examined my boots & I find one of them is ripped on one side of the sole. You can see half dozen stitches. I will have to have them sewed before I wear them. You get after Riggs about it.

R. K. Hege told me Ed had been to see his Bro at Lexington, I hope he had a nice time. Give my regards to all the boys & love to Aunt Eliza & Ed. Much love to you both.

Your Loving Son,

Frank

P. S. Mother, I am looking old again, I have chin beard. I trimmed them out by request of my sweetheart. I have not been to a dance, since Father wrote me about dancing. Your Loving Son, F.

F. A. Clinard to Mr. and Mrs. Livingston N. Clinard

J. G. HALL,
of J. G. & P. C. HALL, Wilkesboro, N. C.

R. L. PATTERSON,
of PATTERSON & Co., Salem, N. C.,

OFFICE OF HALL & PATTERSON,
Dealers in General Merchandise,
AND BUYERS OF COUNTRY PRODUCE.
NORTH OF RAILROAD STATION
Hickory, N. C.,

September 10th 1875

My Dear Father and Mother,

Father, I thought of you last Monday as it was your birthday. I wish you a very happy one if it is past. Mother, I know you baked him a nice cake, I wish I had a piece of it. I received your letter with tax receipt, am very much obliged to you for it. You did not say in your letter how much money to send you to pay for my boots. I will send you nine dollars & if it is not enough, I will send remainder. It is the worst fit I ever had in my life, there is leather enough in them for No 9's. I am sorry, but I will have to sell them if I can ever get any body with such a shaped foot as the boots are.

You spoke of being pushed up with work. I am so tired tonight, I can hardly write. It keeps me digging to keep up my books. We have had a very heavy trade for the past month or two, & we have bought so much fruit & berries that we have to work. We have bought every pound of F & B there is in town. We are paying only 8 cents in the store for berries, but we have bought large lots at a little down on 8 cents. If nothing happens to Mr. Hall he will make a glee smart money on Fr B this year. Our berries, on an average, has not cost over 7 cents. We had a heavy trade yesterday, sold five wholesale bills & two today. Our Mdse. Cr. yesterday was over $1,900.00, but it was not all goods sold yesterday. Our actual sales yesterday was near $1000.00. I sold two bills myself. We had a very nice shower of rain this evening, which will help things very much. The thermometer in the store stood at 90 degrees this evening at 5 o'clock. It has been a very hot day.

I am glad to hear you are getting along with your house. Hope you will get in it before cold weather. I had a letter from Uncle Andy this week. He said he had not heard from you in a long time. Tell Tom Huske, I am kept so busy that I can hardly get time to write to you, but will try in course of time to write him a few lines.

I attended my first Ball last night since you wrote me that letter, raking me about going to so many, but I have had a good excuse. I have been so busy. The Ladies got after me hot & heavy for not coming. I have a good many Lady friends. I went in a fancy costume last night. Mrs. Hall got it up for me. I represented a Spanish Cavalier. I had her silk velvet jacket, & by the way as handsome a thing of that kind as I ever saw, & a tall black hat with long black ostrich feather in it. Every body said I had the handsomest costume at the Ball. It fit me very tight, & showed my form off to advantage. Every body wanted to know where I got it. I told them you sent it to me Mother. Mrs. Hall & myself fixed that up before I went. I am boarding with Mr. Hall now, commenced last Monday. Give my love to Aunt E. & Ed. Much love to you both.

Your Loving Son,

Frank

Good night, I am very tired.

F. A. Clinard to Mr. and Mrs. Livingston N. Clinard

Hickory, N. C.
Sept. 19th 1875

My Dear Father and Mother,

I would have written to you sooner, but I have been kept so busy that I did not get time. Mr. Hall has been absent from home all the week, so I have been hard at work to keep up. Jinks Beard starts for Salem in the morning to clerk for P. & Co. He is a very clever young fellow & I expect will make a good clerk. Yesterday was a wet, cold day. I wore my over coat all day in the store, & was cold besides. I was going to the Valley yesterday if it had not rained, but the rain stopped me. We had very hard rains yesterday all day. We have got up the price of B Berries to 9 cents. We have bought the principal bulk of berries, bought in this country this year. We have a very fine lot of dried apples, but no peaches at all. I have not had but one good mess of peaches this year, & but one mess of cream & peaches.

I heard through someone, & I have forgotten who it was, that Cornelia Ackerman & Ciss Tise were to be married. Is there any thing of it?

Father, you just keep the remainder of that check after paying for my boots. I give you what ever it is for your trouble. I would like to come home Christmas & help you christen your new house, but I hardly think I can get off. I want to take a trip North next summer if I live, & nothing happens to me. I will stop by & see you. I want to go to the Centennial at Philadelphia next summer.

John Neely went up to Morganton to see his sweetheart yesterday. He has the advantage of me. He can go on the train, & I have to go in a buggy.

Father, Wesley Clinard died last Tuesday morning. I was there when he died, he died very easily. He was the most amasiated man I ever saw. He seemed very willing to die, talked to his family awhile before his death, also to Rev. Mr. Hartsell & told him he did not fear death.

Father, are you going to keep P. & Co.'s books all the time? I understand Levin has left you.

Mother, I understand from Old Man Hampton that you have picked out some nice evergreens for your yard. I am glad you are going to have a flower garden. I have a beautiful Rose Geranium. I wish you could see it. I will send you a leaf off it. I thought Tom Huske had gone back to Salem, till you wrote me he had not. I owe Tom a letter & must write to him the first chance I get. Remember me to Henry B. & Charlie P. I suppose Henry can't say what Bill Senly can, that he is Daddy. Give my love to Aunt Eliza & Ed. I'll bet Aunt E. is at our house this minute, 5 o'clock p.m., and Ed is looking after the Academy Girls. Much love to you both.

Your Loving Son,

Frank

P. S. I will send this by Jinks. It will reach you just as quick as by mail.

F. A. C.

F. A. Clinard to Mr. and Mrs. Livingston N. Clinard

J. G. HALL,
of J. G. & P. C. HALL, Wilkesboro, N. C.

R. L. PATTERSON,
of PATTERSON & Co., Salem, N. C.,

OFFICE OF HALL & PATTERSON,
Dealers in General Merchandise,
AND BUYERS OF COUNTRY PRODUCE.
NORTH OF RAILROAD STATION
Hickory, N. C.,

Oct. 8th 1875

My Dear Father and Mother,

I have not received a letter from you this week, but I suppose you are like myself, too busy to write to any one. I have just finished writing business letters, it is now about 1/2 past eleven. I have not worked every night I have been able for the past month. I am better, but not well yet. I have been right sick, but will be alright in a few days. We are having right cold weather at present, but have not put up our stove yet. I am chilly now as I can be. Watauga Wagons have commenced to run, so you know we are getting trash of all kinds. The Snitz trade has about played. [34]

Next week the state begins work on this W. Road, they are going to work convicts. They are to go up next week.

We are to have a Male College built here this fall for certain. The Lutherans are going to build it. They have the ground & the money all ready to go to work, are going to commence today a week. They are also going to build a church.

You are having weddings plenty in Salem at present. None of them here at present, but I think there will be this Fall & Winter.

Hope you are getting along alright with your house, would like to take my Christmas Dinner in it with you. Mother, I can imagine your good things, would take a slice of mince pie now if I had it. Or any thing else I could lay my hands on that you make, for it is all good.

Give my love to Ed and Aunt Eliza. Give my regards to Jinks, Tom, Charley, & all the balance. Tell Jinks I have not had time to answer his letter, will do so just as soon as I can, also Ed. Much love to you both. Good night.

Your Loving Son,

Frank

F. A. Clinard to Mr. and Mrs. Livingston N. Clinard

J. G. HALL,   R. L. PATTERSON,
of J. G. & P. C. HALL, Wilkesboro, N. C.   of PATTERSON & Co., Salem, N. C.,
OFFICE OF HALL & PATTERSON,
Dealers in General Merchandise,
AND BUYERS OF COUNTRY PRODUCE.
NORTH OF RAILROAD STATION
Hickory, N. C.,

Oct. 14th 1875

My Dear Father and Mother,

I received your letter & was glad to hear from you, but I think you might have thanked Gertie for the love she sent you, if nothing more. I feel hurt that you payed no attention to it at all. I am about well again, but worked very closely. It is now nearly 12 o'clock. I work every night. I have been

---

[34] dried apple slices

proving bills all night. Mr. H has bought a very large stock of goods, larger than we ever have had. He has not returned yet. I am anxious for him to come back, he will relieve me of some work. We are having right cool weather at present, we put up our stove yesterday.

I am glad to hear you are getting along so well with your house.

We are going to have our Fair on the 10, 11, 12 & 13 of November. We hope to have a good thing this year.

My particular friend, Miss Bettie Terry, is going to be married next Thursday & I think we will have a series of weddings here this fall & winter.

Tell Ed I will write him, as soon as I can. I am really pushed up for time, hardly get sleep enough to do me. I am always glad to see Sunday come, but I will tell you, for fear you may think other wise, I go to Church regular.

Give my love to Grand Mother & tell her I would like very much to see her. Wish I was at home about a month, it would do me good. I have worked very hard this summer. Mother, I will tell you after awhile what that wish is. Good night. Much love to you both.

Your Loving Son,

Frank

F. A. Clinard to Mr. and Mrs. Livingston N. Clinard

J. G. HALL,	R. L. PATTERSON,
of J. G. & P. C. HALL, Wilkesboro, N. C.	of PATTERSON & Co., Salem, N. C.,

OFFICE OF HALL & PATTERSON,
Dealers in General Merchandise,
AND BUYERS OF COUNTRY PRODUCE.
NORTH OF RAILROAD STATION
Hickory, N. C.,

October 27th 1875

My Dear Father and Mother,

I have anxiously awaited a letter from you, but I have not had one from you for three weeks. But Father, if you have been run half as close & hard as I have, I can excuse you for not writing. I have worked till two o'clock every night, except last night, for the past two weeks. We have been pushed with business. Mother, you might have written to me, but I guess you are like Father & myself, busy all the time.

We have got the largest stock of goods I ever saw any where. We run two rooms, wholesale & retail. Mr. Hall has hired two more clerks. He gave me orders yesterday evening, not to touch a thing but my books. I have been selling some goods since the first of July, till now. We run eight hands now & it keeps us all hard at work to keep up.

I got off one day last week to go to a wedding. I was first Groomsman, had a very nice time. We all went as far as Conover with the Bride & Groom. We have had four weddings here in the last week. Two were married at home, & two run away.

We have got two clerks, one named White, & one Black. We are looking forward to our Fair for a heavy trade, hope we will not be disappointed. You would open your eyes if you could see our stock of goods. I walk round & look at them with astonishment & accuse Mr. Hall of getting on a Bust when he was north, & buying more than he thought he did. He has made a good deal of money on fruit this year. I venture to say we have bought more fruit this year than any house in the Western part of the state.

Remember me to all the clerks & give my love to Aunt Eliza & Ed. Much love to you both. Good night. I am very tired & I take all the sleep I can get these nights. Please write to me soon. I am getting home-sick to hear from you.

Your Loving Son,
Francis

F. A. Clinard to Livingston N. Clinard

Hickory, N. C.
Nov. 2nd 1875

Dear Father,

I was some what surprised at the tenor of your last letter. I was not aware that I tried to hide, or cloak over any thing from you. You speak as if you are opposed to my marrying Miss G. If so, I am very sorry for it, for I think she will make me as good a wife as any body I could get. I never have written much about it, because I was not ready & don't intend getting married for a year or so yet. I intend letting you know in plenty time when I am going to get married & my future plans.

Father, it seems like you have some spite against me about some thing I know not what. I am trying to make a man of myself, & instead of you encouraging me, you try to dishearten me. You said I just picked you & Mother up to suit my own convenience & then dropped you when I pleased. Father, I am very sorry indeed to think you think me such a heartless Son. I love you & Mother dearly, & if you just knew how that remark hurt me, you would know that I do love you. I am steady & not half as wild as I was when I was at home. I work hard & try & do what is right. You spoke about me not consulting you before I engaged myself. If I had not loved her, I would never have engaged myself, & as to my ever marrying any one that I did not love, that I would not do if I never got married.

You asked me why I did not tell you that I was to be one of the groomsman in my letter. I did not know it myself when I wrote. The gentleman that married Miss Terry did not ask anyone till the day before he was married. He lived in Newberne and did not get here til the day before and he asked me to be his first waiter and I accepted. His wife now, used to be Miss Terry was one of my best friends in Hickory. Her father and mother are both very kind to me. When I was sick the Dr. waited on me and never charged me anything. I often go to see them and stay an hour or two. They are very kind to me.

Father, if you have any serious objections to me getting married to Miss G, I would like to know them. You said that I said nothing when I was at home about getting married. I expected you to say some thing to me as you wrote me a short while before I went home some thing about it & said you would talk to me when I come home, so I expected you to say some thing to me. I hope & trust you are not as much opposed to my getting married as your letter sounds like you are, for when I do get married, I want to bring my wife to see you & Mother, & I would feel perfectly miserable if you did not treat her kindly. I hope to hear from you soon again. Give my best love to Mother & much to yourself.
Your Loving Son,
Frank

F. A. Clinard to Mr. and Mrs. Livingston N. Clinard

J. G. HALL,
HALL BROTHERS, Hickory N. C.

P. C. HALL,
J. G. & P. C. HALL, Wilkesboro, N. C.

OFFICE OF
HALL BROTHERS,
(Successors to HALL & PATTERSON.)
Wholesale & Retail,
Dealers in General Merchandise,
And Buyers of Country Produce,
NORTH OF RAILROAD STATION
Hickory, N. C.,

Nov. 10th 1875

Dear Father & Mother,

I just returned yesterday evening from Lenoir. I have been up on some business. I am so sore, I can hardly work or do any thing. I am pushed up so close, I don't get to do any thing but work. We do lot of work here. You have no idea how much we do work, unless you could see us. I am certainly glad to see Sunday come. I get to rest & see my sweetheart.

We are going to have a bad time for our Fair. It is raining hard now & I am afraid it will not stop. Tell Aunt Eliza, I thought of her up at Lenoir the other night. I stopped at the Central Hotel, kept by Lucious Smith & it was after dark when I got there & he killed a chicken & fried it all for me & I was so hungry I eat it all & it nearly scared him to death.

If it hadn't rained we would have a nice time at the Fair. The Floral Hall is fixed up very nice & there has been a great many things entered for exhibition.

Tell Ed, I will write him just as soon as I can. I hope I will be able in course of a week or two to write to all my Relations and friends that I owe letters. Give my love to Aunt Eliza & much love to Ed. Much love to you both.

Your Loving Son,

Frank

P. S. I must go to breakfast now.

F. A. Clinard to Mr. and Mrs. Livingston N. Clinard

Hickory, N. C.
Nov. 10th 1875

My Dear Father and Mother,

I received your letter this morning & was glad to hear from you, & very glad to know I was mistaken in my idea of your letter, but it certainly reads like I wrote you, & I certainly am sorry I mistook your meaning. I ask your pardon, please forgive me.

I expect to try & do well & make a good husband. I have asked Mrs. Hall for her, & she says she is willing for me to marry her, if I live close to her, which I promised, provided I could make a living, which I think I can, provided I keep my health. I may get married in the Spring, about May, provided I can make arrangements to suit all round.

If it don't cost too much, I want to go to the Centennial. I am as saving & economical as I can be. I don't spend any money, but for what I am obliged to have.

I gave your message to Miss Gertie, & she said she was very much obliged to you, & said I should return her best respects to you both. She said I should say to you that she was very sorry that she sent you the message she did some weeks ago. She is afraid you will think her immodest in sending such a message to you, before we are married.

I am asked to a wedding tomorrow night. One of our clerks, Mr. White, is going to get married. We have a concert, dance & wedding in town tomorrow night. I think I will go to the wedding. You spoke of Mr. Faucett & Miss Mary Norwood getting married, it is Miss Lou & Mr. R.

I am compelled to work late at night to keep up my books. You have no idea how much work we do here. I will not be so busy from this on as I have been. I delivered your message to Mr. & Mrs. Hall & they both return their best regards to you, & Mr. Hall was talking about you tonight. It is now after 12 o'clock & I am very tired, so I will close.

I hope we will understand each other better here after. I am thankful for any advise you may give me. I think you might help me a good deal.

Mother, can't you give me some of your good advise? I wish I could see you awhile, I could talk to you. I think since I received your last letter, I understand you & myself both better than before. You don't know how much good it done me to get that letter. I have been like another man, ever since some body asked me what was the matter with me, that I looked changed from last week.

Give my love to Aunt Eliza & Ed. Much love to you both.
Your Loving Son,
F. A. Clinard

P. S. Callum from Greensboro is going to put up a Drug Store here. He has rented him a house. C.

A. D. Clinard to Livingston N. Clinard

Newton House
Athens, GA
Nov. 12th 1875

Dear Brother,

I believe I owe you a letter and should have written you ere this, but have procrastinated from time to time. I received a letter a few days ago from Mother, also one from Frank. They tell me you are having a very nice residence built. I am glad to hear you are getting along well. My business has been tolerably good the last six weeks. I hope it will continue improving. We are all well, except my Mother in law. She has been in bad health a long time. I have no news of interest. I write only to let you know that I have not forgotten you all. Mollie and Blanche join in love to all. Write Soon.
As ever,
A. D. Clinard

F. A. Clinard to Mr. and Mrs. Livingston N. Clinard

Hickory, N. C.
Nov. 22nd 1875

My Dear Father and Mother,

I have been expecting a letter from you for several days past & postponed my writing until I received a letter from you, but I have not had one yet so I will write.

We had a very nice time at our Fair. Floral Hall was decorated with some very handsome work of different kinds. Fine needlework of every description, hair work, paintings, & every kind of preserves & pickles & many other articles that you will find at such a place. I was out at the Fair ground one part of the day. Charles & Tom Griffith were both here, they said they enjoyed themselves very much.

We have a new Drug Store. Callum from Greensboro has opened one here, & old man Hines, the Tailor, is staying with him.

Jones Grier come to see me today. He looks like always, only he has grown to be a small man. He asked how "little Ed" was getting along, & I told him he wouldn't call him little if he could see him. By the by, Ed has his 18th birthday next Saturday. Tell him I wish him a happy one.

We had quite an exciting time in town this evening. A Negro & white boy had a fight, & the white fellow stabbed the Negro, so the Doctor says he will die before morning. The boy made his escape, but there are several following him.

I come very near going to Raleigh next week to the Grand Lodge of Masons. Our Worshipfull Master wanted me to go as a representative of our Lodge, but I could not get off very handy just now, so I declined. I felt highly complimented at being asked to represent & fill such a position. We are getting up a Concert for the benefit of the Oxford Orphan Asylum. It is to be given on the 27th of Dec. On the 27th, in the day time, we are to have a Masonic Lecture & March. Col. Cilly & Maj. Finger are going to deliver the Lectures.

Have you plenty of apples about Salem this winter? Mother, when you kill hogs please send me by Wootens Express some sausage & liver pudding. I will pay charges on it here. Mother, please buy for me at Blum's Book Store a nice book called "Keepsake of Friendship" for the year 1876, & send it by mail & write me price, & I will send you the money. I want it for a Christmas present for Miss Gertie. We are going to get married in June, if nothing prevents, more than we know of now, & expect to come to see you shortly afterwards. Give my love to Aunt Eliza & Ed & much to you both.
Your Loving Son,
Frank

Personal Letters of L. N. Clinard 1876

A. D. Clinard to Livingston N. Clinard

Newton House
Athens, GA
Jan. 7th 1876

Dear Brother,

Yours, not dated, came to hand today. We were very glad to hear from you and family and to learn you are getting on well. It is very gratifying to hear that you have succeeded in procuring a comfortable home. I have been striving for the same object, but thus far have not succeeded. My greatest desire now is to leave my family a comfortable home when I die.

The year just past was a very hard one with me. My business fell off one third compared with the previous year, oweing to the great scarcity of money and general prostration of business. I have again rented the Hotel, hoping this may be a more prosperous year.

I am very glad to hear so favorable an account of Frank & Eddie. I hope they will go to the Centennial. It will be of great advantage to them. Let them go, but caution them against the numerous swindling machines that will doubtless be set for unsuspecting ones. I wrote Frank a few days ago and hope to get a reply soon. I received a letter from Mother a few days ago, all were well. The weather here has been remarkably warm like May for the last three weeks. Blanche is getting on finely at school. She sends much love to you and Sister Mary and Eddie. Also to the little girls and Miss Ackerman. My wife joins me in love to all. Write soon.
A. D. Clinard

F. A. Clinard to Mr. and Mrs. Livingston N. Clinard

Hickory, N. C.
January 9th 1876

Dear Father & Mother,

I received your letter yesterday, & was glad to hear from you. You said you had written two letters to me inside of two weeks. The last letter I had from you was written on the 20th of December. I am glad to hear you are in your new house. Hope I will have the pleasure of staying in that nice room you have fixed up for me, before another Xmas comes. Mother, I am glad you thought of me when you were having the house painted.

I am sorry to hear old Bink is dead. Hope you will get another cow as good as she was.

Mother, I am glad you thought the cheese good I sent you. Hope you enjoyed the apples as well. We have more than 150 Bu. of apples on hand now, & more offered every day. I enjoyed my sausage & souse very much. I came very near letting one piece spoil in that warm weather, but I had it cooked & you bet I eat it. Mother, I have dreamed of being at home in your new house for two nights in the past week. Thought I had the biggest time there. Thought I met all my old friends & had a gay time generally.

Diptheria is raging here at an alarming extent. Miss May & Gertie both had it. Miss Gertie has not entirely recovered yet, but it getting better. There has been lots of grown folks had it. This town smells like a tar factory. Every body is burning tar, & every old log & chips, and all the wood piles in town have been burned up for the past few days. Every cellar & filthy place in town has been cleaned up. Even in church today they had a bucket of tar burning, nearly stifled me. I have been carrying a disinfective in my pocket till I smell like old Carbolic soap box in Patterson & Co.'s cellar. The grave yard looks bad, got new graves all over it. A good many familys have run from it. I myself am not afraid of it. Hope I will be fortunate enough to escape.

I had a letter from Uncle Andy this last week. He said he had not heard from you in a long time. Jinks got home last week, he likes Salem very much, but says he has not got much use for Pfohl & Charles Vogler. He has grown considerable since he has been down there.

Trade has been rather dull for the past week or two. It has been too nice weather for the Watauga Wagons to run. If it would snow & sleet they would roll in fast.

Give my love to Aunt Eliza & Ed, & remember me to Tom H., C. B. B., & H. W. B. I understand Ed got a goose in Winston Xmas. Bully for him. Would like to see him stepping high for that goose. Mr. Hall made me a New Years gift of six pair of half hose, something I needed. Much love to you both, & may you both live a long & happy life in your new home is the wish of
Your Loving Son,
Francis

F. A. Clinard to Mr. and Mrs. Livingston N. Clinard

J. G. HALL,	R. L. PATTERSON,
of J. G. & P. C. HALL, Wilkesboro, N. C.	of PATTERSON & Co., Salem, N. C.,

OFFICE OF HALL & PATTERSON,
Dealers in General Merchandise,
AND BUYERS OF COUNTRY PRODUCE.
NORTH OF RAILROAD STATION
Hickory, N. C.,

January 19th 1876

My Dear Father and Mother

I was truly glad to get your letter today, have been some what uneasy about you, have not heard in nearly two weeks. I have a cold, the first one I have had this winter, but I don't wonder at having it. We have the funniest weather for winter weather I ever saw, some days the thermometer is up to 70 degrees & next day down to 10 degrees, so every thing is continually changing. The Diptheria has abated to some extent, no bad cases in town now.

I am sorry to hear of Grand fathers ill health. I hope he will live till I can see him again. If you see him give him my love, also Grand Mother. Mother, I must fess up. I have been home-sick to see you all, dreamed about home two nights, would like to be there with you for awhile.

We had a stormy night last night & tonight is not much better. We had a storm this evening like summer time. Trade has been very good for the past two weeks. We are getting in lots of apples & other produce. We have orders to fill for all we get. We ship very little produce to Commission Merchants.

The people of Hickory are high up about getting another Rail Road to this place. The C. C. R. R. are going to extend their line from Lincolnton to this place & the L. & C. narrow gauge will pass by here. The greater part of the road is graded from the river to Lenoir.

When you moved did you get the old yellow wardrobe moved? I have thought of it several times & wondered if you could get it down & out of the house. It is getting late & I am tired, so I will close. Give my love to Ed & Tom Huske, also Aunt Eliza. Tell her I am sorry she has a sore finger. Tell her I would like to know when she & Davy are going to get married, if she don't mind. Davy will be old enough to die before they get married. Much love to you both. Good night. Your Loving Son,
Frank

P. S. Ask Tom Huske for me if he ever saw a whale

F. A. Clinard to Mr. and Mrs. Livingston N. Clinard

J. G. HALL,
of J. G. & P. C. HALL, Wilkesboro, N. C.

R. L. PATTERSON,
of PATTERSON & Co., Salem, N. C.,

OFFICE OF HALL & PATTERSON,
Dealers in General Merchandise,
AND BUYERS OF COUNTRY PRODUCE.
NORTH OF RAILROAD STATION
Hickory, N. C.,

January 27th 1876

Your letter received this morning & I was truly glad to hear you were both better. I have a little cold at present, the first this winter. We have had very fine weather for the past week, but looks like snow tonight.

Well! I & Mr. Hall have struck a Trade for another year. He is to pay me $500.00 & my board, which is $15.00 per month. I thought that would do, it is equal to $680.00 per year. He made me that offer & I thought I had better take it. I believe I could get more, but I thought I would be liberal with him. My business is strictly Book Keeping. I have nothing else to do, & in that contract, I am to have ten days vacation, for which I loose no time.

Mr. Hall told me he thought he would go to Salem this week & he would see you about my lost time. He thinks Patterson & Co. ought to lose it. He says he made the contract with P. & Co. for my time. I will see him in the morning & if he does not go, I will send you a check which will be about $170.00. I did not know.

Jennie Morefield had gone back to Salem. I go through the train nearly every day, & I never saw her pass down. Tell Ed to go it while he is young, for when he gets old he can't go it.

Mr. Hall promised me if he should burn out, or anything happen that I had to leave him he would help me get in a good place. I tell you the truth. I work like a Lurk, lots of work on these books. I tell you & I write a good many business letters & make out bills every day.

Tell Ed, Miss Emma Hamilton is here, going to spend a week or two. I have been to see her twice, & going again Friday night. She asked after him, she comes in the store every day. She brought me two sticks of nice candy she made herself. We have had lots of chats about our old times. She is splendid company. Harry said give you his best regards. I must close, as it is getting late & I have to write to my sweetheart yet tonight. I have had two letters from her since I wrote last. My love to all.

Your Affectionate Son,

F. A. C.

F. A. Clinard to Mr. and Mrs. Livingston N. Clinard

Hickory, N. C.
February 9th 1876

Dear Father & Mother,

I would have written to you sooner, but I have been so busily engaged that I did not have time. I have had the worst time with a cold & cough I think I ever had, it worries me at night. We have had bad disagreeable weather for the past two weeks, all kinds of weather you could think of. I am surprised that every body ain't suffering with colds. We had a right sharp snow & a heavy sleet.

I have been to three parties in the last week. Miss Gertie had one, had a candy stew & I was at a tea party at the Rev. Mr. Gibbs of this place, & at a candy stew at my particular friend Mrs. Whiting. Mother, she is an Artist. I wish you could see some of her paintings. They are perfectly beautiful. She makes her living by painting. She has some pictures worth $150.00, from that down to $5.00. She told Miss Gertie she was going to make some thing nice for her, a bridal present. She makes all sorts of nice work.

Father, we had an election in town last Saturday for Rail Road or no R. R., that is to pay tax on $25,000.00 worth of Bonds to build a R. R. from Lincolnton to this place. R. R. carried by 105 majority. Big excitement about it. The R. R. Commissioners are trying to make arrangements with the C. C. R. R. to extend their line to this place. I think they will succeed.

You wanted to know when we would be home, if nothing happens more than I know of, we will be there the last week in June, or the first in July. Think it will be June.

Father, please send me your Photograph or Pharo type. I have asked you so often for it, & you keep putting me off. You can step over to Henrys & have it taken in ten minutes.

Mother, I am going to trouble you again some of these days to do a little favor for me. I am very anxious to see your new home, & you too. It is nearly a year since I saw you, don't time fly? You spoke of Mrs. Hall being sick. She is better. She went to ride this evening & is going about the house some. Miss Gertie has been house keeper for several months & she feeds me alright. I am heavier now than I ever was. Miss Emma Hamilton has been spending several weeks at Mr. Halls. She asks a heap about Ed.

I told Jinks what you said Father. He said give his regards to you. He is painting a house inside for his mother to live in. Old man Beard is in Salisbury clerking for Smithdeal in the Hardware business. Our place keeps looking up. Several new familys have moved here lately & gone to Manufacturing, not gone to hawking dry goods & the rich like.

Give my love to Aunt Eliza & Ed. John Ward from Davie Co., one of my old customers, stayed all night with John & myself last Saturday night. He says he still goes to Salem every few weeks. Tell Pfohl I want to know how Josh is thriving, if he has to spank him any. Give my regards to all the boys. Much love to you both. Good night.

Your Loving Son,

Frank

F. A. Clinard to Mr. and Mrs. Livingston N. Clinard

Hickory, N. C.
February 21st 1876

Dear Father & Mother,

Yours rec'd & glad to hear the news of Henry being a happy Daddy. I guess he runs up home oftener than ever. I had a very pleasant time last week, was invited out to dinner twice & to a ball given at the Central Hotel. I was invited to a Circumcision of a new baby in this place. An old Rabbi came from Goldsboro. The Jew had quite a big time, & one of the nicest & best dinners you ever heard tell of. There were about 25 of the leading Citizens of the place present. They have services like the baptism of a child. We had a nice time at our dance, & the proprietors of the Hotel gave a big supper, which was splendid. We are having quite a rainy time at present, had a few beautiful days last week. Trade is very dull at present & money very scarce.

We are to have a Telegraph line up the W. N. C. R. R. They are at work on it now. They are at work on the R. R., have laid three miles of track lately & still going ahead as fast as they can.

I believe I forgot to write you that Hill had got home. He passed through here week before last. He says Nulli's not getting along very fast.

Mother, have you gotten use to your new home, & how do you like it? I would like mightly to be with you. It will soon be a year since I saw you. I think & talk about you often, when you better think your boy thinks of you. I hope, if nothing happens, next time I do see you, I can present my Bride to you. She often asks about you. Mother, you try & prevail on my brother to write to me. He found time enough to send me a comic Valentine. I think if he cares anything for me, he could find time to write. If he had half doz. Brothers to write to, I could look over it, but me his only brother & he treat me as he does is not humane. John Bohannon gets a letter from Frank every week, it does look like he might write to me once a month. I have had the pitifull of two letters from him in the last twelve months. Give my love to Aunt Eliza & Ed. Much love to you both.
Your Loving Son,
Frank

Southern Rail Road depot, Hickory, N. C.
Photo courtesy Catawba County Historical Association Archives

F. A. Clinard to Mr. and Mrs. Livingston N. Clinard

Hickory, N. C.
March 12th 1876

Dear Father & Mother,

I would have written to you sooner, but I have been to see Aunt Carrie & just got back Friday night, so I had to work to get up my books. Well, Aunt Carrie has come back to the Old North State, & she says she is going to remain. She is looking better than I ever saw her. She is nearly as fleshy as Mother was before she died. She looks younger & better than she use to. She has a very pretty & sweet little girl. Uncle John looks like he always did. Aunt Carrie asked after you both, & said she would like very much to see you and she was going to write to you. She asked me about every body & every thing about Salem. She cried when she saw me, she was so glad. She wants to see Ed very bad, she asked lots about him. When Ed comes to my wedding, he can go to see her. Aunt Carrie is just like always. She asked me a heap about you Father, & said she often thought of you & wished she could see you. She says she has not forgotten how kind you have been to her. She told me to write & tell you not to think hard of her for not writing to you oftener.

Mother, today one year ago you gave me my big dinner. I thought of it today & of you too. I would like to see you so much, I think of you often. I had a good dinner today, my sweetheart knows how to get up good dinners. She tries herself to see how much she can learn. She had baked chicken, rice, eggs, pickles, & ever so many other nice things for dinner. She says when we go home, she is going to get you to learn her how to make good things.

I was at a dining party in Lenoir on last Friday at Mr. Halles, Mr. Hamilton's Son-in-law. We had a Turkey dinner & everything that was nice. Col. E. W. Jones had a big dinner party the same day for Nath Gwyn & Lady. I was asked to that & the old Col. & Miss May just begged me to stay, but I wanted to get home.

I had a talk with Mr. R. L. P. when he was up here. He says he is perfectly willing for me to marry Miss Gertie. He says he is coming to our wedding.

Mother, I want to trouble you a little. I want you to buy me two scarf cravats. I want good ones, one pearl colored & you can pick the other one that you think will suit me. Give them to Mrs. Hall. She said she would bring them for me. Write me what they cost, & I will send you the money.

We had quite a thunderstorm this evening, but no damage done as I know of.

Mother, my shirts you gave me a year ago are about gone up the flue. They all wore out & left. The bosoms good. If I thought the bosoms would stand, I would have new shirts made for them. I have ordered myself a suit of clothing & will have to order some shirts soon.

Tell Cousin Chas. Hauser that Aunt Carrie asked after them, also Aunt Eliza & Mrs. Mickey. She talked like she might go to Salem about Easter. Did Aunty leave anything to her? I told her I thought she did. If she did, write me.

Father, I wish you would send me a Blums Alamanac for Aunt Carrie. She wants one & we have sold all of ours. I guess you will get the Piedmont Press regular now. I ordered the Press man to send you mine. I have not had a letter from you in over a week. Tell Ed I will write him this week, give him my love, also Aunt Eliza. Much love to you both.

Your Affectionate Son, Frank

F. A. Clinard to Mr. and Mrs. Livingston N. Clinard

Hickory, N. C.
March 20th 1876

Dear Father & Mother,

I was glad to receive your letter & especially your Photograph Father. I think it splendid, your spectacle case looks natural in your pocket.

We have had a bad day of it. It has been snowing all day & there is about seven inches of snow on the ground now. This evening it sleeted & there is a crust on the snow, but I think it is melting. I feel bad tonight, have been at the Dentist all evening. He has been plugging some teeth for me. He seems to be a very good workman, he did some nice work for me. I had rather wait till you can get some new neck ties. I supposed they had received their spring stocks in Salem.

You wanted to know why Aunt Carrie moved back to N. C. She says she came back where she could educate her child. She said there were no good schools in Kentucky. John has not decided where he will live, or what he will do yet.

Trade is very dull at present. I suppose farmers are at work when they can.

Mother, you say you are going to make me two shirts. I will be very much oblige to you, but I don't want you to think what I wrote you in my last letter was hinting to you to make me some shirts. Please make them lower in the neck & for spiral studs, as my old buttoned studs have given out.

I got some of Sully Welfare's wedding cake. Hege brought some with him & gave some to me. I understand Tom Huske is going to leave Salem. Where is he going? Tell Tom I owe him a letter & will try & write him shortly, also Ed. Hege says he went round to see your new house. He says it is a very pretty house, & likes it very much. Mrs. Hall wrote home, that she liked it very much & that it was a pretty house. Mother, I have dreamed of it more than once & am very anxious to see it. I often think of you & home. The man that composed the good old song "There's No Place Like Home" ought to have a monument erected to his memory, for I think it is one of the truest songs on earth.

How is H. W. B. & his daughter getting along? Can she talk about marrying yet? I suppose she will inherit her conversational powers from her Daddy, & of course, she will talk about that & nothing else. Give my love to Aunt Eliza & tell her I am glad to hear she takes such a deep interest in my welfare as to ask me about me, & how I am behaving myself. Give my love to Ed. Much love to you both.
Your Loving Son,
Francis

Carrie S. Grier to Livingston N. Clinard

Patterson, N. C.
March 26th 1876

Dear Brother,

I received a letter from Frank Thursday last in which he told me you were all well. You were no doubt surprised to hear we had come back to N. C. We have been here three weeks, but have not seen much pleasure. In the first place, Mary was so sick that I was very uneasy about her. She had such a severe pain in her side we could scarcely move her. She is now well again. Frank came up to see us, but I did not enjoy his visit, for I could not on account of Mary. I wanted to talk so much with him.

Frank told me how well you are getting along. I am glad to hear of it. Livingston, you have no doubt thought hard of me many times for my carelessness, but hope you will not think that I had forgotten you.

119

I can never forget your kindness to me. You were truly a brother to me and done more than one of my own brothers would, I have no doubt. If ever I see you to speak with you I can tell you many things that I think would surprise you. You and your children seem nearer to me than any of my relatives. I would so much like to see Eddie and all of you. Ed might send me his likeness.

Livingston, it seems rather strange to me that Willie Cooper never let me know that Auntie willed me anything. I thank Frank for telling me. I suppose they thought I would never come back to the country and I would be none the wiser for it. I can live without it, but if it were just one half dollar I want it because it was Auntie's will, and I would just as well have it as anyone else. I wish I could see you and talk to you. I am glad to hear Frank speak so highly of his stepmother. I would be so glad to see my dear old stepmother. If you have an opportunity let her know we have come back and tell her I would be so glad to see her once more. Write me and tell me if I ought to write to Will Cooper about that or what I had better do.

I do not know where we will live. John has had no chance to look around. The first week Mary's sickness hindered him and the past week the weather was so bad he could not get about.

We intend going to the Richlands to Margaret's tomorrow, and he will leave Mary and I there until he can look round and get us a place. I want us to get settled some place where we can live the remainder of our days. I have always wanted to live near enough so Mary could go to school in Salem. Neither one of us have ever been well satisfied since we left N. C. Frank is still full of mischief as ever. Don't you believe him that I weigh 225. Tis true I am a great deal fleshier than I was, but not quite as bad as that. Give my love to Cousin Charles and accept much for you and Mary. Write soon and I will try and do better hereafter.

John says he would be so glad to see you and sends his best respects. Tell Ed to write to me.

Livingston, if you don't mind to ask Will Cooper about that. I wish you would, for I do not want to write him about it.

Affectionately,

C. L. Grier

F. A. Clinard to Mr. and Mrs. Livingston N. Clinard

Hickory, N. C.
April 2nd 1876,

I was very glad indeed to hear from you yesterday. I thought you had given out writing to me. I had a letter from Aunt Carrie & she said she had written to you. She is going to house keeping in the Faithing house, this side of the Factory. We have had a gloomy day tonight it looks very much like snow.

Father, my shoes fit me very nicely, but I think the tariff rather heavy on them. Can't you do like the R. Road men, give me a rebate? Mother, they are kinder like that pair of boots Father wore once upon a time. I wore them to see my Sweetheart, & they hurt me so bad that I had to make an excuse to go to the Store, & when I went back she noticed I had changed & teased me about it. Father, I told Mr. Patterson when he was here to send me a pair of "Prince Albert" shoes. Please tell him I do not wish them now. He said he would send them when the spring stocks came in.

Father, I wrote to Ed about coming to my wedding. I hope you will let him come. We have given out going to the Centennial & will be married the 7th of June, if nothing prevents. We will go from here to Salem immediately, & spend our time with you instead of going North. We take inventory the last of June, so I will have to be here to get up my books.

Mr. Hall told me he called on you. He is very much pleased with your house, says it would suit him better that Mr. R. L. P.'s. Mrs. H has not returned yet, she has been visiting some of Mr. H.'s Kinfolks in Salisbury & Newton, will be home tomorrow. Mother, Easter is coming & it will be Sugar Cake & boiled sausage time then. I will think of it Easter morning.

The Hotels here are making preperations for the summer visitors. They are both building "Conditions," as John Petree would say. Where has Tom Huske gone to? I heard he was to leave Salem the first of April. Give my love to Aunt Eliza & Ed. Gertrude wishes to be remembered to you, with her kindest regards. Much love to you both.
Your Loving Son,
Frank
Good Night

F. A. Clinard to Mr. and Mrs. Livingston N. Clinard

J. G. HALL,
HALL BROTHERS, Hickory N. C.

P. C. HALL,
J. G. & P. C. HALL, Wilkesboro, N. C.

OFFICE OF
HALL BROTHERS,
(Successors to HALL & PATTERSON.)
Wholesale & Retail,
Dealers in General Merchandise,
And Buyers of Country Produce,
NORTH OF RAILROAD STATION
Hickory, N. C.,

April 21st 1876

Dear Father & Mother,

I have been sick all the week, was in bed yesterday, but feel better this morning, am at my work. I have not seen or heard of any shoes yet. Have you sent them? I have paid for them if you have not sent them. I expect it will be safer by Express, we have an office here. You did not answer me about Ed coming, would like to know. Much love to you both, from us both.

Your Son,
Frank

F. A. Clinard to Mr. and Mrs. Livingston N. Clinard

Hickory, N. C.
April 25th 1876

Dear Father & Mother,

I received your letter & my shoes. I like my shoes very much. I can account for them costing so much. They have such big heels that it took some thing near a side of leather to make them. I like them a great deal better than the Bush gaiters. I don't like them very much. When you send my jewelry, send it by registered letter as it is safer.

You did not say any thing about Ed's coming. I would like to know for certain.

Bishop Atkinson preached here last night. He had a very large congregation, confirmed one person.

122

I will enclose a list. If there are any persons left off that you want it will be alright to ask more, & if there are any on that you don't want, scratch them off. We are perfectly willing, except Gertie wants the Misses Sott for certain. You said you did not want any old folks, we put down Mr. & Mrs. R. L. P. Would like to have them, if you don't object. We hardly think Miss Carrie & Lettie will be there. They will be at our wedding & I think intend going to the Valley from here. You did not say how many you wanted, or I would know more about it, so if I have not got enough, you make out the list to suit your selves.

I was quite unwell last week, was threatened with pneumonia, but am better now, was in bed the best part of two days.

We are going to be married publicly in Church. Mr. Hall's house is so small that our friends can't get in it. I expect I will faint as I am so bashful, but will try & stand the storm. It is only six weeks from tomorrow. We are having right cool weather now, fire feels good. Give my love to Aunt Eliza & tell her I am straight as usual, also to Ed. As Uncle Andy would say, Gertie joins me in love to you both.

Your Affectionate Son,

Frank

F. A. Clinard to Mr. and Mrs. Livingston N. Clinard

J. G. HALL,   R. L. PATTERSON

Office of HALL & PATTERSON,

DEALERS IN

General Merchandise,

NORTH OF RAILROAD DEPOT.

Hickory, N. C.,

April 29th 1876

Your letter received this morning & I was truly glad to hear from you. I have felt anxious since last week because you said you were both sick.

So they have taken old man Boner to the Esylum at last. The death of Ike was a little unexpected to me, he always looked so stout. I thought he would be the last man to die with consumption.

You wanted to know how we are getting off our stock. We are getting along right well considering times are so dull. We took in over $100.00 today. I am trying to do right smart collecting. I think I will go to Marion on Saturday to collect some money due us up there.

I went to a concert last night given by a blind Lady by the name of Agnes Jones. She performed very well for a blind person.

You spoke of a circus. I saw the bill poster today. He says he thinks they will come here, they are going to Lenoir. I imagine it is a poor thing from the manner in which they travel.

I have got my book in apple pie order to close up the years transactions. Up to the first of April we had sold $47,000.00 worth. I made a general statement showing the Amt. Mr. Hall has offered me half of some % if I would collect them. I am going to try very hard. I will make some money if I succeed. He said if I would collect $1000.00 this week, he would pay me 1% on it. H said he would pay me any way, 1/12 of 1% on all that I collect this week, whether it is done or not. I am pushing up fellows round here all I can.

Harry received a present from a Lady today. He got a nice little box & thought he had something nice, but when he opened it he found a mole. He has put it in a box of dirt and put potatoes in it to feed it on. He is as proud of it as he can be.

Father, my shoes I got of P. & Co. are all busted round the sides. I never saw such bad shoes in my life. I must close as I am tired . I have been writing hard all day. Give my love to Aunt Eliza & Eddie. Much love to you both. Your Loving Son, Frank

V. R. Vogler to L. N. Clinard

ANDERSON, STARR & CO
Manufacturers and Jobbers of Clothing,
502 & 504 Broadway
(opposite St. Nicholas Hotel.)
P.O. BOX 1001.

Walter S. Starr
James A. Anderson
Andrew T. Anderson

New York,

May 1st 1876
Mr. L. N. Clinard
Salem N.C.

Your favour of the 25 to hand, we have shipped you as per bill enclosed one Blt cloth, for which I hope will please you. Also a suit for C. B. Pfohl, which I think is just what he wants. In referring to your measure, I see the words written under the measure, hold for orders, which is the reason I did not send it with Mr. Patterson't linens. My regards to your family.
Very Truly Yours,
Anderson Starr Co. Per V. R. Vogler

F. A. Clinard to E. C. Clinard

J. G. HALL,
HALL BROTHERS, Hickory N. C.

P. C. HALL,
J. G. & P. C. HALL, Wilkesboro, N. C.

OFFICE OF
HALL BROTHERS,
(Successors to HALL & PATTERSON.)
Wholesale & Retail,
Dealers in General Merchandise,
And Buyers of Country Produce,
NORTH OF RAILROAD STATION
Hickory, N. C.,

May 2nd 1876

Dear Bro,
I wrote you some time since to let me know whether you could come to my wedding. I want to know so I can make my arrangements according. Write me at once definitely, whether you can come or not. Gertie said to tell you she wanted you to be sure & come. If you don't come, I will have to ask

some one else, but had rather have you than any one else. I am to be married in Church in the morning, & leave on the train for home. You will only have to be gone four days. You will have a nice time. Give my love to Father & Mother & be sure to write me at once what you will do. I must know.
Your Loving Bro,
Frank

P. S. Tell Frank Bohannon that his Bro Tom is here with us tonight. He has been up on an excursion today that run up to the head of the road.
F. A. C.

F. A. Clinard to Mr. and Mrs. Livingston N. Clinard

J. G. HALL,
HALL BROTHERS, Hickory N. C.

P. C. HALL,
J. G. & P. C. HALL, Wilkesboro, N. C.

OFFICE OF
HALL BROTHERS,
(Successors to HALL & PATTERSON.)
Wholesale & Retail,
Dealers in General Merchandise,
And Buyers of Country Produce,
NORTH OF RAILROAD STATION
Hickory, N. C.,

May 4th 1876

Dear Father & Mother,

I received your letter, also neck ties. I think they are beautiful. You did not say what they cost. You can add the amount in with the bill for my jewelry & I will send you check for same.

I am very sorry indeed that Ed can't come. I am very much disappointed. You noticed that I offered to pay his R. R. fare back home, if he would come. You wrote me about my asking my cousins. I wish you would add as many as you like to have & who ever you want will suit us. The reason I did not put more on the list we sent, was I did not know how many you wanted. You can add Frank & Loula Fries & who ever you think suitable, the Miming girls & Emma De Schmeinitz for instance. There is John & Augusta Rich that are my cousins. I left them off because I did not think of them at the time. I don't believe I know who my cousins are. You can ask them for me. As to asking Mr. & Mrs. R. L. P., that is alright. Gertie did not want me to put them down when I did. They will not take any offense at it, I hope. Gertie is very much troubled about her dresses. She is afraid Mrs. Bill Hall

126

will not get them ready on time. She promised Mrs. H. when there to have them done by the 20th of this month & send them, & Mrs. H. had a letter from Mr. P. saying Mrs. Bill Hall said she did not know whether she could get them done, on account of the Academy girl's dresses. I think she ought to do what she said she would, or get some one else to finish them.

I don't want you to go & spend too much money for us. We are use to very common living & it will spoil us if you feed us up too high. Gertie is a very small eater any way. I have enjoyed a very nice place to board at, nice people & nice locality.

There have been two excursions up the road this week. Both crowded, & there will be one Sunday to Morganton to a big meeting. I stay at home myself, & do. Gertie said give her love to you both. Much love to you.
Your Loving Son,
Frank

Carrie S. Grier to Livingston N. Clinard

Blowing Rock
May 5th 1876

Dear Brother,

I wrote to you some time ago from Patterson, but have received no answer. We are all well, but do not like Watauga much. It is too cold up here for us. We have been disappointed in getting our plunder from Kentucky. John's brother Sam was to bring them for us. Received a letter from him last mail saying he had not yet started. There has been high waters to prevent him coming. John has become so disheartened about it that he has concluded to go back, and I feel perfectly willing to go. I would have been glad to have seen you and Eddie, if it had been so I could. I was so glad to see Frank, but Mary was so sick the day he came to see me that I could think of nothing I wanted to talk with him. If we go back we will leave in eight or ten days. We might hear that our things are coming and not go.

Frank wrote me that Will Cooper was going to pay you that money due me in a few days. I want him to do so. I hate to trouble you about it, but do not care about writing to him. Tell Eddie I would like very much to see how he looks, since he is a grown young man. He is very stingy with his Photos, has never sent me one. I have three of Franks. Write to me soon and tell me how you are getting along. I would like to see you and talk with you. Affectionately, Carrie S. Grier

127

F. A. Clinard to Mr. and Mrs. Livingston N. Clinard

J. G. HALL,
HALL BROTHERS, Hickory N. C.

P. C. HALL,
J. G. & P. C. HALL, Wilkesboro, N. C.

OFFICE OF
HALL BROTHERS,
(Successors to HALL & PATTERSON.)
Wholesale & Retail,
Dealers in General Merchandise,
And Buyers of Country Produce,
NORTH OF RAILROAD STATION
Hickory, N. C.,

May 15th 1876

Dear Father & Mother,

I received my package & am very much pleased with it. Enclosed, please find check for $18.00 to cover amount, and Mother, please accept my best thanks for your kindness in getting the set for me. I think it is beautiful. I am very busy & can not write at length. Much love to you both.
Your Loving Son,
Frank

Carrie S. Grier to Livingston N. Clinard

Blowing Rock
May 17th 1876

Dear Brother,

Your letters received all right. John went down to Patterson Monday - got back yesterday evening. He also went to Lenoir, received the money for the order sent. I signed the receipt - will enclose and return it to you. I am certainly much obliged to you for attending to it for me. I received $5.00 - one time while at Prestonsburg from you - suppose that was the only time you sent to that place. It seems to me that you said that would be the last I would get of my Savings Bank money.

Watauga is rather too cool a climate for me. We have to keep a big fire nearly all the time.

What I said in my former letter was in reference to my own brothers. Don't defer from what I said that I am dissatisfied, or unhappy with my lot - far from that. I do not wish any kinder or better treatment than I receive.

I was so glad to get Ed's Photograph - his eyes have the same expression they had when I last saw him. Frank and Eddie feel very near to me and I shall always feel interested in their welfare. Frank writes to me frequently. Hope he will have a happy future. He told me of his intended wedding - the time will soon be here. I would like to see Mother Shultz - have you seen her lately, or heard from her? Give my love to her when you do see her.

We do not know when we will start back - but think we will shortly. John thinks, and I do too, that we can do better there than we can here. It is time to send my letter to the office - must close with love to you all. Tell Ed, Frank told me about him going to the Judges - he might write to me I think.
Affectionately,
Carrie S. Grier

T. W. Huske to L. N. Clinard

Hillsboro, N. C.
May 22, 1876
Mr. L. N. Clinard

Dear Sir,

Will you please write or send record to E. Strupe & Son to send me two calf skins at their earliest convenience? And I will send the money as soon as I get the skins. Please give my kindest regards to all. I would write more, but haven't time. I will be very busy for a week or ten days yet and then will have not much to attend to. I may see you all sooner than you expect.
I am, as ever, very truly your friend,
T. W. Huske

F. A. Clinard to Mr. and Mrs. Livingston N. Clinard

J. G. HALL,
HALL BROTHERS, Hickory N. C.

P. C. HALL,
J. G. & P. C. HALL, Wilkesboro, N. C.

OFFICE OF
HALL BROTHERS,
(Successors to HALL & PATTERSON.)
Wholesale & Retail,
Dealers in General Merchandise,
And Buyers of Country Produce,
NORTH OF RAILROAD STATION
Hickory, N. C.,

May 24th 1876

Dear Father & Mother,

I guess you think I am never going to write to you any more. John B. has been gone two weeks, & I have been waiting on trade, so it took all my time to keep up my books. I have been under the weather for nearly three weeks. Nearly every body here is complaining. Flu is raging through the country to a great extent. I have fallen off 5 lbs. I am better now, & hope to improve.

If nothing happens, I will be married today, two weeks. Miss Annie Bitting will be here next week, she is to be one of Gertie's Brides Maids, & will go with us from here home & I suppose she will stop in Winston a day or two, so you can reserve an invitation for her to our party. She is one of Gertie's particular friends. They were class mates at St. Mary's. She is Joe B's. daughter. Mother, I & G. are perfectly delighted with the jewelry. I don't think I could have suited myself as well, if I had picked it myself. I will give you the names of my attendants; J. T. Bohannon, Hill Carter, Dink Graham & Jack Baker. Much love to you both.

Your Loving Son,
Frank

A. D. Clinard to Livingston N. Clinard

Athens, GA
June 23rd 1876

Dear Bro,

I have been expecting a letter from you the last 10 days, but have received none. Why have you not written me? I thought Frank would have written me after his marriage. Did he marry? What has become of him? We are all tolerably well. Times are very hard. I am doing nothing but hope business will improve soon. All join in love to all. Write soon.

As ever,

A. D. Clinard

Gertrude E. Clinard to Mr. and Mrs. Livingston N. Clinard

Hickory, N. C.
June 24, 1876

My Dear Parents,

We arrived safely last Thursday and would have written sooner, but we have been very busy moving our things to our boarding place. How are you both? I have thought of you very often, and of my pleasant visit to you. I can never forget your kindness to me. Every body seemed glad to see us when we came. Several came to the train to meet us, and Mr. Hendrix had several of our friends collected the same evening we arrived.

We are very pleasantly situated here - have a nice comfortable room and we like all the boarders. We gave them all some of the cake and they liked it very much indeed. We found brother Gaither all alone. Sister Annie & the children went to Wilkesboro on Wednesday. Frank took brother Gaither some of our cake, & he thought it so nice that he sent Sis Annie a small box of it by mail.

We went to a marriage the night we spent in Salisbury. It took place in the Lutheran Church. I do not know the names of either party.

I believe there is no news of interest in Hickory. Nearly all the children in the place have whooping cough. Business is dull, but Frank has been very hard at work ever since we got back. He is making up for lost time. He is with me tonight, but he is too tired to write. He has so much writing to do during the day. I feel tired too tonight and I am afraid I have written a very shabby letter. Please remember us kindly to all our relatives and friends and please let us hear from you soon & often. Frank joins me in much love to you both, & to brother Ed.

Your Loving Daughter,

Gertrude E. Clinard

F. A. Clinard to Mr. and Mrs. Livingston N. Clinard

Hickory, N. C.
July 5, 1876

Dear Father & Mother,

We were exceedingly glad to hear from you yesterday, but sorry to hear you have been so unwell, hope you are better by this time. We have been getting along splendidly. Gertrude has been at work on my old clothing & has got me wearing things I have not had on for two years.

We are having rain every day. While we were at home it rained every day up here, & the rivers got very high. The Catabaw bridge was damaged so that it could not be crossed for two weeks. Part of it on this side washed away. There were several mills up the river that washed entirely away.

I have been very busy since I got back, have worked hard & still at it. We are just winding up inventory.

Gertie & myself went to a Festival given by the Good Templars last night in our Town Hall. We had a very nice time, it was a free thing & of course it was crowded. They had ice cream, cake & lemonade in abundance. There is a dance in town tonight & we are invited, but we concluded not to go, & stay home & write to you.

Mother, I had your ring fixed, had a 1/16 of an inch put in, & it looks like a new ring. I hope you will be pleased with it & it will fit you. I will send it to you by Registered letter. I think it a nice job. Mother, please fix up my chest to send, also my chair. Father, please ship them as soon as you can as we need them, one to pack in & the other to rock in.

There are a good many visitors in Hickory now & more coming every day. Gertie says give you her love & tell you she will write to you before long. She has had a great many of her friends to call on her & she has been visiting some. Remember us to all our friends & give our love to Ed & Aunt Eliza & tell her I am smoking one of Uncle Dave's Cigars. Much love to you both.

Your Loving Son,
Frank

P. S. I wrote to Uncle Andy tonight.

F. A. Clinard to Mr. and Mrs. Livingston N. Clinard

Dear Father & Mother,

Gertrude has written to you, & I will enclose this note with hers. The ring was made 1/16 of an inch in circumfrence, that is what I understood you to say. It don't cost you any thing. am glad you are pleased with it, but sorry it is not large enough. Much love.

Your Loving Son,

Frank(In a hurry)

G. E. Clinard to Mr. and Mrs. Livingston N. Clinard

Hickory, N. C.

July 20th 1876

Dear Father & Mother,

We were glad to hear from you last week. You spoke of the warm weather in Salem. We can sympathize with you, for we have been having terribly hot weather here for some time. I believe it is the complaint every where. We enjoyed reading the papers you sent. You must have had a fine time in Salem on the 4th inst., wish we could have been there. We think Mr. Gray's speech very good. We had a letter from Uncle Andrew a short time ago. He said it had been a long time since he heard from you. He invited us to go to see him. Frank is still very busy, & it goes hard with him this warm weather. We are going to the Valley the last of this month if Frank can get off.

Mother, I am learning to crochet some pretty mats. Frank laughs at me for being so slow, but I tell him I will do better when I learn well.

Our house is full of boarders now. They all seem to like us, & we like them. There is to be a big Ball here on the 31st of the month. It is to be hoped that it will be cooler by that time. How are Ed & Bessie[35] getting on now? Please always remember us to all our friends, & let us hear from you soon. Frank joins me in much love to you both.

Your Affectionate Daughter,

G. E. Clinard

---

[35] Bessie Brown, future wife of Edward Clifton (E. C.) Clinard

F. A. and G. E. Clinard to Mr. and Mrs. L. N. Clinard

Hickory, N. C.
July 27th 1876

Dear Father & Mother,

We received your letter yesterday, & would have answered immediately, but wanted to receive the chest. It & the chair came today, & we are very much obliged for your trouble in sending them. I am also thankful to you for the articles contained in the chest. They will be useful to me, & I will prize them very much.

There has been a great change in the weather. It has been cooler here for several days past than it was Christmas day. It is very refreshing after such very warm weather. I hope it is cooler in Salem by this time. Father, Frank wants to know if you could bear a Linen coat during the hot weather. Frank is sitting back in our big chair reading. He gets cold beans every night for supper.

There are a great many visitors in Hickory now. We have at present a daily excursion train running from Wilmington to Henry's station. The whole crowd will stop over here next Monday night & we will have a grand "Excursion Ball" given by one of the young men of this place, who is also manager of the "Double Excursion." His name is Tomlinson. Frank says I must stop & let him finish the letter, so goodbye. Much love to you both & all my friends.
Your Fond Daughter,
Gertrude E. Clinard

Dear Father,

You asked me how I liked the nomination of Zeb. I like it very much & I hope & trust you will vote for him. We have a Tilden & Vance club here with over 200 members. The ladies are making a flag 12 x 24, which we will raise next Monday. We have the pole now, it is over 100 ft. high. There are but a few Rads in this town, what are have to be to hold their offices. We got up a club of between 40 & 50 at the store for a Dem. News Paper. I have subscribed for the NY Sun. I think it is the best paper I ever read, it has news of all kinds in it. I read the speaches that were made in Salem on the 4th. Good night. Much love to you & Mother.
Your Loving Son,
Frank
We have a bad pen to write with tonight.

Gertrude E. Clinard to Mr. and Mrs. Livingston N. Clinard

Hickory, N. C.
August 4th 1876

Dear Father & Mother,

Your letter came to hand yesterday, & we were glad to hear from you & hear that you were well. You asked why we had not been to the Valley. Frank has been so busy he could not get off. We think probably we can go some time this month, but can not tell certainty.

I hope that hot weather did not kill your nice garden Mother. We are having very pleasant weather here at present, except that it rains almost too much.

I believe I wrote you about the double excursion we had here last week & a part of this. The gayeties wound up last Monday night with a "Grand Excursion Ball" & the excursionests left Tuesday. We attended the Ball & had a very pleasant evening.

There was a very large "Tilden & Vance" Flag (made by the Ladies of Hickory) raised here last Monday. After the flag was raised they had speeches from several of our Citizens. There was a great deal of work on the flag. I assisted in making it.

There are a great many visitors in Hickory now. Frank is at the store this morning & does not know that I am writing. I will leave my letter open until I take it to him. He may have messages for you. Mother, please more write with Father when you have time. I will always be glad to hear from you both.

Your Loving daughter,

Gertrude

Love to all. I am very busy. Will write to you soon. Much love,

Frank

A. D. Clinard to Livingston N. Clinard

Newton House
Athens, GA
August 8th 1876

Dear Bro,

I received a letter from you some weeks back, but have neglected replying till now. My Mother in law has been very sick the last 10 days. My wife is now sick, but I hope it will not prove serious. I have been loosing money all this year, but had hoped the commencement of the University which took place last week, would set me up all right, but it proved a failure, there not being more than 4 the usual visitors here this year that have been here before. My receipts were about $200, where as here before, they have been from 700 to $1000. A new RR from here to connect with the Air Line will be completed by the first of Sept., which I think will double my business.

Frank wrote me some time ago and sent a likeness of himself & wife. They are a fine looking couple. I hope they do well and live long and happily together. I must close. Write soon. Present our love to your good wife. Tell her Blanche and I have not forgotten her kindness to us when at your house. We would be delighted to see her again, also you and Eddie. Love to all our friends there.

As Ever,
A. D. Clinard

I am anxious to hear from Father & Mother and Louisa. Tell me when you write.

F. A. Clinard to Mr. and Mrs. Livingston N. Clinard

Hickory, N. C.
Aug. 10th 1876

Dear Father & Mother,

I have just read your letter to Gertie. I was glad to hear from you. Gertie is now in the Valley, she went up last Friday to her Uncle's burial. I went up Saturday & came back Monday morning. She was coming home with me, but May begged her so hard to stay with her, that she stayed. I am going up Saturday to bring her home. We did not know Col. Jones was worse till we heard he was dead. We had just seen him at the Sulphur Springs two weeks ago & he said he was better. I am mighty lonesome with out Gertie, you have no idea how much I do miss her. It seems to me like she has been gone two months.

Vance & Settle speak in Statesville tomorrow. There is to be an extra train, run from the head of the road. I am going down to hear them. I want to hear old Gov. Zeb wear Settle out.

Trade is dull just at this time, berrys are very scarce & I think the Merchants are glad of it. There will be a good crop of dried fruit, but it will come in late & prices are low, as you know.

Our Hotels and boarding houses are crowded to their full extent & our place is right lively. They leave right smart money in our place through the summer season.

Father, you kinder go for me about not writing more. I told the truth when I said I was busy. I was just as busy as I could be that morning, had to get off some letters in the mail.

Mother, I had corn soup & stewed tomatoes for dinner. We have vegetables of every kind & generally a good table. We have a very pleasant time at our boarding house, every one is agreeable & do all they can to be pleasant to each other. When I was in the Valley, every body met me pleasantly & invited me to their homes & they all Coz'nd me. Sam P. said I should come to his house & make it head quarters & visit round among Gertie's relatives. Every body has treated us just as nice as they could, except R. L. P. Gertie thinks hard of him, the way he treated her. As to my part, I don't ask him any odds any way. He can go his way & I will mine. I am as independent as he is, if I haven't got as much money. Gertie will write you when she gets back home, which I hope will be soon. Much love to Ed, Aunt Eliza & to yourselves. Remember us to all our friends, especially "Cornelia Blick" (how funny). [36]

Your Loving Son

Frank

---

[36] Probably Cornelia Ackerman (sister of Ed Ackerman) who married Jacob Blickensderfer

F. A. and G. E. Clinard to Mr. and Mrs. L. N. Clinard

Hickory, N. C.
August 24th 1876

Dear Parents,

We were glad to hear from you yesterday, but very sorry indeed to hear you both had been sick, hope you are entirely well by this time. Frank brought me from Lenoir last Sunday. We had a pleasant visit to the Valley, though of course it was quiet. My dear Uncle's end was very peaceful & happy, which was a great comfort to all. While in the Valley I visited Dr. Carter, & Frank came to see me there. He & Hill enjoyed being together very much. The Doctor has not gone north yet, but will go next month I believe. Since he has been at home, he has had several right bad cases & been successful with them all. He had a case of brain fever when I was there. Cousin Sam was in Watauga nearly all the time I was in the Valley.

You seem to be having a good many marriages in Salem. There has not been one here lately, but the place is very gay with visitors. They dance every night now. Frank & myself with several of the other boarders from the house, went up to the Hotel last night to look on at the dancing, but we did not dance.

Are there any peaches about Salem this year? There are none here or in the Valley either. Mother, I was glad to hear you did not loose all your cabbage. Hope to hear from you both very soon. We were uneasy because you did not write sooner this time. Give much love to Brother Ed, Aunt Eliza, Miss Cornelia, & all our friends. Frank joins me in much love to you both.
Your Loving Daughter,
G. E. Clinard

Father, You will have to scold again for I am busy. I want to write you a long letter soon & ask you some questions about Settle & his party. I noticed what you wrote in the Press. Father, Vance is just as sure to be elected as this world stands till the 7th of Nov. This part of the State will go solid for him, I am glad to say.

Much love to you all. Hope you are better by this time. Mother, tell Cornelia, I am not in so big a jam calling her bluff.

There is to be an Excursion to the Centennial on the 20th of Sept. for $12.50 from here & return.
Your Loving Son, Frank

F. A. Clinard to Mr. and Mrs. Livingston N. Clinard

Hickory, N. C.
Sept. 5th 1876

Dear Father & Mother,

I would have answered your letter sooner, but last week we had preaching every night from Wednesday on till Sunday. The Presbyterians had Presbtery here, so there was a large crowd last Sunday. Mr. McKinnon preached & I think it was one of the best sermons I ever heard. Every body was delighted with it.

Father, tomorrow is your birth day. I wish you much joy & you may live to see many more.

There is a good deal of sickness generally through the country. Round about here fever & diptheria has again made its appearance. I know one family near here that has lost three children in the last week. There has been two deaths in town in the last week from fever.

And Aunt Sow is married. I guess she is satisfied. I have tried to think of the fellow she married, but I can't run him up.

Mother I am sorry to hear you are so thin, hope you will improve this fall. Sorry you & Father have both been sick. Gertie has been sick for several days & last night I was scared. She had a very high fever. She is better this evening. She says she wants to write some to you. I have the worst old scratchy pen you ever saw, you can tell that by my writing.

We have a good many summer visitors here yet. Our house is crowded to the garrett. Even the Kemmilies are full. There are over thirty persons in the house, all from Wilmington & just the nicest kind of people. Sam Hall's Sister in law is here in the house & I like her better than any body here. She is a middle aged widow & she is just like a Mother to us all. She looks after every body. Gertie thinks a great deal of her. She is a daughter of Mr. B. F. Mitchell of Wilmington.

Mother, I have just gotten through with the dentist. He filled eight teeth for me & he has just gotten through my pocket book to the amount of $23.00, but I have got a good set of teeth now & I am thankfull, he did some splendid work for me.

Father, trade is dull this fall. Money is very scarce & dried fruit is coming in very slowly. We haven't bought but 12 or 15 pounds yet. We have not been very anxious for it. I understand the chicken & cabbage crop is good in Watauga, so we will have a good winter trade.

Every thing in the West is for Vance & Tilden. Vance's election is run, so we look for better times.

Dolph Shuford has just finished the walls of a large brick store just above us.

There are a good many going from here to the Centennial this week. There is a through excursion for $15.00 set, ticket good for 30 days. Give my love to Aunt E. & Ed. Much love to you both.

Your Loving Son,

Frank

G. E. Clinard to Mr. and Mrs. Livingston N. Clinard

Hickory, N. C.
Sept. 5th 1876

My Dear Parents,

I was very glad to hear from you last week. Frank has written all the news, so there is nothing left for me to write. I have not been at all well for several days and still feel very weak & know account. Frank tells me that tomorrow is your birthday Father. I wish you a very pleasant day & many happy returns. I am sorry to hear you have been sick Mother. We are having very dry hot weather now. I hope you will excuse this note. I will write more when I feel better. I think brother Ed might write to us occasionally. Please give my love to all friends & accept much for yourselves.

Your Affectionate Daughter,

G. E. Clinard

F. A. Clinard Livingston N. Clinard

Hickory, N. C.
Sept. 6th 1876

Dear Father,

You asked me about Aunt Carrie & I forgot to write you last night. She is back from whence she came, Prestonsburg, KY. John treated her very kindly while I was there, & I asked her myself if John was kind & good to her, & she said he was always ready to get her any thing she wanted. She & her little girl were dressed very well & looked well. She told me he always stayed home with her on nights & Sundays. John had right smart money while he was here. I saw his package. He spent over $40.00 with me while he was here. Aunt Carrie seemed very well, contented, & said she was happy. I had a long private talk with her about several things & I asked her a good many questions concerning her life in KY. Gertie is better today, but she looks very badly, hope she will be better soon.

We have prospect of rain today, hope we may get it.

One of our clerks started for the Centennial today. His name is Craig Shuford, cousin of Dolph's. I must go get the mail, so I will close.

Your Loving son,

Frank Much love to Mother

E. C. Clinard to Mr. and Mrs. Livingston N. Clinard

September 13th 1876

Dear Father & Mother,

I thought you would be anxious about me so I will write to you. We are now sailing up the Potomac & expect to get to Washington tonight about 10 o'clock, but I don't think we will get there in that time. About 10 miles on this side of Greensboro, we passed where the cars had run off the track. It beat anything I ever saw in the way of a smash up, but it is a wonder to me how most of them escaped being killed, but none of them were hurt very much. Sam Patterson & Lady were on the train when it smashed up, but they escaped with a few scratches. Hill Carter was on the same train, he escaped also. All three of them are on the boat with us tonight. I have had a very pleasant time so far and I think I will continue to have a nice time. If you find any mistakes you must look over them for I wrote this letter in a big hurry, will write more to you from Baltimore.

Your Loving Son,

E. C. Clinard

P. S. We arrived in Washington all right

E. C. C.

F. A. Clinard to Mr. and Mrs. Livingston N. Clinard

J. G. HALL,
HALL BROTHERS, Hickory N. C.

P. C. HALL,
J. G. & P. C. HALL, Wilkesboro, N. C.

OFFICE OF

HALL BROTHERS,

(Successors to HALL & PATTERSON,)

Wholesale & Retail Dealers in General Merchandise,

Hickory, N. C.,

Sept. 14th 1876

Dear Father & Mother,

We are having very dull times just now. Fruit is very low & the people through the country are holding it for higher prices. The summer visitors are leaving now, so our town is rather dull. We have still got a house full at our boarding house.

I had a letter from Uncle Andy yesterday. He inquired after you, said he had not heard from you in a long time. I have been looking for a letter from you for several days, but have not received it yet.

Our town has a new enterprise, we have a "Daily Press." The editor said he was going to send you one.

Mother, I weigh 10 lbs more than I did when I was home & I have side whiskers, don't you know I look a sight. Gertrude is very well today. She had sick headache yesterday for the first time since we have been married. You ought to see me of nights, sitting back in my big chair, reading to Gertrude while she mends my clothing & darns my socks.

When does Ed speak of going to the Centennial? There is to be an excursion from here, on the 26th of this month. Fare $14.00 round trip, good for 30 days. There is an excursion on this road about three times a week. I can go from here to Charlotte & return for $1.00. There has been over 50 excursions this summer. One just passed here about half hour ago. Gertrude joins me in love to you both, Ed, & Aunt Eliza.

Your Affectionate Son,

Frank A. Clinard

P. S. Gertrude may write you some on this. She does not know I am writing..

F. A. C.

Sept 15th We are both quite well this morning. I am going to Lincolnton tomorrow to hear Vance and Settle. Gertrude says she will write next time.

Your son, F. A. C.

E. C. Clinard to Mr. and Mrs. Livingston N. Clinard

ST. CLOUD HOTEL
G. W. Mullin & Bro.
PROPRIETORS
Arch Street, Above Seventh,
Philadelphia

Sep. 17th 1876

Dear Father & Mother,

We arrived in Philadelphia yesterday evening. I tell you we had a nice time in Washington and Baltimore, we went to Smithsonian Institute which is a small Centennial its self. You can see most anything you want to in there, from the Institute we went to the Agricultural Buildings, Washington Monument, New State Building, Conklins Art Gallery, Post Office Department, Patent Office, Treasury, White House, Army Museum, Botanical Gardens, & The Capitol. The Capitol is the largest building I ever saw.

I went with Mr. Stockton to buy his goods in Baltimore. Mr. John Dannals gave me a fine knife & Mr. Jarboe a fine hat. I went to a Catholic Cathedral this morning, it is the finest church I ever saw, the Pope was dressed in purple velvet. I intend going to Wannimakers Sunday School this evening with Mr. Stockton. After we come from there, we are going to Mr. Jake Hesses for supper. We intend staying here till Thursday morning & then going to New York. From there we are coming home. I met Mr. Ebert & Bill Shultz this morning, also old man Wilson and his boys. You must write to me soon. Much love to you both. I remain your loving son,
E. C. Clinard

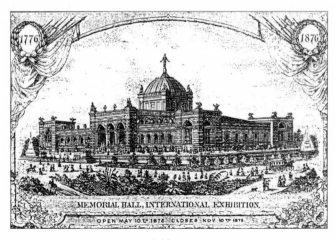

MEMORIAL HALL, INTERNATIONAL EXHIBITION.
OPEN MAY 10TH 1876 CLOSES NOV 10TH 1876

E. C. Clinard to Mr. and Mrs. Livingston N. Clinard

Old Rates, $3.00 Per Day
We did not raise our rates on account of the Centennial
St. Cloud Hotel,
Philadelphia
G. W. Mullin

Sep. 20th 1876

Dear Father & Mother,

I am having a splendid time. I just now came in from the Centennial grounds. It is the grandest thing I ever saw or intend to see again. You can see anything you want to from a pin to the big Corliss engine. I saw them manufacturing watches, pins, needles, and other things too numerous to mention. I went in the big glass works & saw them making different articles, they have a small engine made out of glass, it is shaped like the big Corliss engine.

The Odd Fellows had a big time today, they had their grand parade. There were more people in it than I ever saw before in one procession. The Centennial Grounds are a perfect jam, you can hardly get around in the different buildings. All of the hotels are crowded, the St. Cloud turned off over two hundred yesterday and about as many today. We were fortunate in securing a good room.

I saw the Sixty thousand dollar set of Diamonds yesterday. I tell you they are worth having. I went to see a fine painting that is not connected with the Centennial. It is called the Siege of Paris. It is 2 or 3 hundred feet long & about 1 hundred feet high. I haven't seen anything to equal it in the way of a painting since I left home. I have been to a theatre every night but Sunday night since we got here. We intend starting to New York in the morning, will leave there Friday night & get home Sunday morning.

Why don't you write to me? I have not heard from you since I left home. I must close my letter for Mr. Stockton wants to go to Supper. You must excuse my mistakes because I have to write in a hurry. Much love to you both.

I remain your loving son,

E. C. Clinard

G. E. Clinard to Mr. and Mrs. Livingston N. Clinard

Hickory, N. C.
Sept. 22nd 1876

My Dear Parents,

Your letter was, as usual, welcomely received, but we regretted very much to hear that neither of you were well, & hope you have both improved in health by this time.

Father, you & Mother must have changed your minds about going North. When we were in Salem you did not think you would go to the Centennial, but would wait until you are fifty & then take a long trip. However, if you desire to go to Philadelphia, I know it will be a pleasant trip for you both & I hope you will be well enough to go. I expect Brother Ed will enjoy his trip very much. Frank & I have given up all idea of going.

It has been raining almost steadily for several nights & days & still continues to do so. I hope we will not have another freshet. Cool weather is beginning to come at last, & I hope some of the boarders will leave now. This house is so very noisy. There are over a dozen small children boarding here & some of the children of a larger growth are as noisy as the little ones.

A few days ago there was a Negro killed by the cars running over him between this place & Morganton, I believe.

Last Labor Day Frank went to Lincolnton to hear Vance speak. He was very much pleased with his speech.

Father, I think it very good in you to write us such nice long letters every week, for we are both rather poor correspondents. I believe Frank does a little better than I do, but he has dropped all his correspondents but you & Mother, while I have a good many others, & it keeps me busy writing to keep up with them all. Give our love to Aunt Eliza & all our friends. Frank joins me in much love to you both.

As ever,
Your Affectionate Daughter,
G. E. Clinard

G. E. Clinard to Mr. and Mrs. Livingston N. Clinard

Hickory
Sept. 28th 1876

Dear Father & Mother,

We were glad to receive your letter yesterday, & hear that you both were better. We are having very pleasant weather now, & I hope it may not turn warm again. Frank is unusually busy because Mr. Bohannon has gone to Philadelphia, & brother Gaither has been in Charlotte several days.

We were glad to hear that Brother Ed enjoyed his trip so much. I hope you both may have a very pleasant trip. At what place do you expect to stop in Philadelphia?

Cousin Free Henry has been with Sis Annie for several days. She will leave town now. I rode out to the White Sulphur Springs with her this evening. I feel somewhat tired tonight from the ride.

John Robinson's Circus will be here the 28th of October. As I have never been to a circus, I have a great curiosity to attend this one. Frank already had two complimentary tickets to the Circus. We received an invitation to a Ball in Winston the other day. Mr. John Brown sent it. Is Bessie Brown at school in Salem now?

Frank says the country is just full of apples. The merchants here are buying the finest kind of apples for 25 cents per bushel. Frank says he would like mighty well to be on at the Centennial with you & so would I. Please let us hear from you again before you leave home. Frank joins me in love to all.
As ever,
Your Affectionate Daughter,
G. E. Clinard

Charles W. Vogler to Livingston N. Clinard

PATTERSON & Co.,
MAIN STREET.
DEALERS IN GENERAL MERCHANDISE, & BUYERS OF COUNTRY PRODUCE,.
Salem, N.C.,

Oct. 12th 1876
Mr. L. N. Clinard

Dear Friend,

According to promise I will now try to write you a few lines to let you know how things are going on at home. We are getting along very well and have had a splendid trade ever since you left home. Mr. Patterson said today that Trade has been better the last week than it has any week since 1868, so you may know we have been selling goods right along and only hope that it may continue. I truly hope that you and Mrs. C are well and are having a nice time at the Centennial Grounds. I told Mr. Patterson today that I wanted to leave about the 20th and he said all right, so you can take your time and please don't hurry home on my account, for the 20th will be soon enough for me to start. I heard the other day that Frank passed Greensboro on his way north. I am glad that he will meet you there.

We are getting along fine in the store. "Polly" is played out every night and "Matt" not much better, but your humble servant is all right. I got along first rate on pay day, better than I expected, if I did not have all the work to do myself. I had no trouble to make my balances and everything so far goes smoothly on. Mr. Patterson says that he is expecting to hear from you every day, has written you several letters in care of Wheeler & Pope. Kindest regards to all inquiring friends, hope you will excuse writing as it is getting late and I am very tired.
Very Respectfully,
Your friend
Charles W. Vogler

Julie Fries to Mrs. Livingston N. Clinard

Salem, NC
October 16

Misses Clinard,

I seat myself to drop you a few lines to let you know that I am well and doing well at this time and hope these few lines will find you the same. I am home-sick to see you all and hope you come home soon. Mother said she wants to see you mity hard and your hogs are getting along splendid. The cow is fat as ever. I made a mist stake and you must excuse me.

I will close my letter by saying good night.

Julie Fries

G. E. Clinard to Livingston N. Clinard

Hickory
Oct. 23rd 1876

My Dear Father,

I was very glad to receive your nice long letter this morning & hear so much Centennial news. Frank told me that he saw you & Mother in Philadelphia & I am so glad you both enjoyed the trip & that Mother stood it well. I would have liked to have gone with Frank & meet you both there. Frank got home last Friday & has been hard at work on his books since then. He seemed to enjoy his trip very much - has told me a great deal about it, but says he as not told half yet. Brother Gaither & Sis Annie went to the Centennial last Monday a week ago & I am keeping house & taking care of the children for them. They expect to be home the latter part of this week. Mary Jones has been with me ever since Frank left. She will go home next week.

Hickory is dull now, but Robinson's Circus will be here next Saturday (the 28th) & I expect it will be gay enough then. Yes, we hope to go to housekeeping in Jan. I think I will like it very much. I have not enough to occupy my time boarding. We have been having intensely warm weather for several days & it is very unpleasant for this time of year. Is it as warm in Salem? Give much love to all our friends. Frank joins me in love to you & Mother.

Your Affectionate Daughter, G. E. Clinard

F. A. Clinard to Mr. and Mrs. Livingston N. Clinard

Hickory, N. C.
Oct. 29th 1876

My Dear Father and Mother,

I should have written to you sooner, but have been very busy since my return home getting my books straight. On my return, I found Gertie well & keeping house for Sis Annie while she went to the Centennial. She just returned last Friday very much pleased with her trip.

Yesterday was a big day for Gertie, she has never seen any animals or Circus before, & Old John Robinson's Circus was here & she went to see it. Dr. Carter came down to the show & took Gertie with him. She was perfectly delighted, I wish she could have seen the Zoological Gardens in Philadelphia. As I came back, I had to lay over in Richmond a day, so I went to the Capitol Hollywood Cemetery & the Water Works, also to the Tredagar Iron Works. That was a show worth seeing. I like the Water Works in Richmond, better than Fairmount. I went out to Fairmount on Monday after you left & met several Ladies I knew from Newberne & walked round the Water Works with them. Monday night, I went to see "Paris By Night" or "Moonlight" & I think it the best thing I saw while I was in the City. Mr. Gormley, best of the A. F. & T. R. R., from Statesville to Charlotte, was with me. We came home together after we got through looking at that. We went to hear Clara Louise Kellogg sing & I was very much pleased. I saw Frank Fries, Frank Bohannon, old Red Hunt, & several other Salem people. As I came home the Train they were on ran off the track & we were delayed 6 hours. I thought for a while we would have to stay for the night.

There was a big crowd here yesterday from Watauga & Caldwell & they were all loaded with apples, cabbage & chestnuts. Apples sold here yesterday for 20 cents per bushel, & chestnuts at $1.00, cabbage 1 1/2 cents. We have sold cabbage this season as high as 5 cents per lb. It is very warm today. I am at an open window in my shirt sleeves. Gertie says give you her love & tell you she enjoyed the circus yesterday, ever so much. She just woke up a few minutes ago. She read herself to sleep after dinner. I have written to Aunt Carrie since dinner. Tell Ed to write to me. Gertie says give him her love. Much love to you both & Aunt Eliza.
Your Loving Son,
F. A. Clinard

P. S. Mrs. Newkirk said after you left Mother that she thought you loved me. I told her you did. She charged me 75 cents, like she did you.
F. A. C.

A. D. Clinard to Livingston N. Clinard

Newton House
Athens, GA
November 1st 1876

Dear Bro,
I received a letter from you some two weeks ago and would have replyed earlier, but as you were going to the Centennial in a few days, I have delayed till now supposing you have returned by now. I also received a letter from Frank stating he expected to start to the Centennial. I am glad you all went. I know it has been the greatest event of your lives. I hope to hear from you soon and shall expect a slight description of your visit. Myself and Family are well and getting along tolerably well. Business has improved in all branches. The weather is very warm and dry here. I have nothing of importance to write. Write soon. Mollie and Blanche join in love to all.
As ever,
A. D. Clinard

F. A. Clinard to Mr. and Mrs. Livingston N. Clinard

Hickory, N. C.
Nov. 12th 1876

My Dear Father and Mother,
I will have to ask forgiveness this time for not writing sooner, also for Gertie. I have been so busy & taken up with the election that I did not have time & Gertie has been busy making a dress for herself. She cut it out and made it all by herself. I am going to get her a machine. I can get a Wheeler & Wilson with all the attachments for $40.00. It is new, never been used any. Mother, do you know if they run easy? I was one of the clerks at the election. Our box cast 481 votes. 402 for Tilden & 79 for Hayes. Our county gave a majority of 1428. Father, do you recollect marking a local in the Peoples Press & writing aside of it "Not much"? What do you think of it now

the local was this; "Zeb B. Vance will be our next Governor"? Last Monday night Gov. Zeb. V. spoke here. We, about two hundred, went out to meet him on horse back. I was at the head of the procession, was Marshall of the crowd. At night we had a procession headed by a transparency three feet square with these mottos on it "Catawba Always True" "Victory Must Be Ours" "The People Win" "Hall Bro's Ad - Vance" I got it up and made it myself. It was as much as one man could carry. Next to it came our Tilden & Vance flag, then a torch light procession, which was very large.

We had a very good trade for the past week, except Election day, we all closed up. The Rads cut down our flag last Wednesday night & cut up the rope & tore it up right badly, but we had it mended & raised her again.

Father, I wish you would please look at Sandy Voglers & see what is the lowest you can buy me a set of good substantial furniture for & let me know. I did not buy in Philadelphia. Price his walnut sets, marble top bureau & wash stand.

Tell Ed I am glad he has not forgotten me, he sent me a Western Sentinel yesterday. I am much obliged to him for it. Gertie says give her love to you both & says she will write soon to you, also give her love to Bro Ed.

We had quite a snow here Friday. It covered the ground & the mountains all round here were white. It was real cold for several days, but today it has been very warm, so warm that we did not need any fire in church this morning. Mother, I wish you had some of our good apples. Gertie & myself are eating a large one now. Give my love to Ed, Aunt Eliza & much to you both. Your Loving Son,
Frank

G. E. Clinard to Mr. and Mrs. Livingston N. Clinard

Hickory
Nov. 21st 1876

Dear Father & Mother,

Frank & I have become uneasy about you, as it has been an unusual length of time since you have written. We sincerely hope that neither of you are sick. We are both quite well & hope soon to hear the same good news from you. The weather here is charming now. How is it with you?

Mr. Hendrix (the gentlemen we are boarding with) killed hogs this morning, so we are enjoying fresh pork now. I don't suppose you have killed your hogs yet. We hope to have some of our own to kill by this time next year.

We will go to housekeeping in January if we can get everything ready by that time & I hope we can, for I think we will both like it better than boarding. I have lately learned to sew on the machine & I like it very much, so Frank says he will get one for me. I tell him I will be smart then & sew a great deal.

There is still a good deal of excitement here about the election. The gentlemen were very much disappointed at not hearing any news today.

Frank is kept quite busy now. The mountain trade is heavy & he has to write a good deal at night. He joins me in much love to all. Tell Brother Ed I have not received the letter he promised to write & I suppose the mail must have gone wrong. Hoping to hear soon.

I am your loving daughter,

G. E. Clinard

F. A. Clinard to Mr. and Mrs. Livingston N. Clinard

J. G. HALL,
HALL BROTHERS, Hickory N. C.

P. C. HALL,
J. G. & P. C. HALL, Wilkesboro, N. C.

OFFICE OF

HALL BROTHERS,

(Successors to HALL & PATTERSON,)

Wholesale & Retail Dealers in General Merchandise,

Hickory, N. C.,

Nov. 23rd 1876

Dear Father & Mother,

I was very glad to get your letter today & glad to hear you are both well. We are getting along splendid & are anxious to go to Keeping House. You wanted me to explain what I wanted in the way of furniture. Bedstead, Bureau, Towel Rack, Closed Wash Stand, & Set Chairs. I am not particular about walnut, I just wanted you to price them for me.

Our Landlord killed hogs Monday & we are having sausage & liver pooding, pon hors & all kinds of pork. I am anxious to hear what your hogs weigh. If I live & nothing happens, more that I know of now, I am going to have some good hogs next year this time.

There is a Stock company building a Tobacco Warehouse back of our store, a company from Henderson, N. C. They are working hard to get up a trade & I think will succeed as there is a good deal of Tobacco raised here in this county. In McDowell County there is a good deal raised, also in the lower part of Caldwell. Mr. Hall is doing the building & we are going to do the paying off, the sales at the Warehouse. I think I will get to keep their books extra, which will be some help to me.

We are having quite a good trade at present, lots of Watauga Wagons coming in with all sorts of produce. Apples, cabbage & chestnuts plenty. We buy lots of chickens, turkeys & ducks low down.

We had a big time here last Tuesday night. Torch light procession, fire works, & speaking & general rejoicing over Z. B. V. election. I was appointed chief Marshall by the Citizens of Hickory & surrounding country for the occasion with several assistants. I rode horseback & had a heavy sash across my shoulders.

Gertie wrote you this week. She keeps busy sewing & mending. You did not write me what you thought of the Wheeler & Wilson Machine. I would like to have your opinion about it. Gertie sends love to you both & Ed. Much love to you & Ed.

Your Loving Son,
Frank

P. S.
I wish you would see Lineback & get him to print a large photo of mine & send it to me this week. I want it for Gertie's Christmas present. Send it so I will get it this week, if you please. If he can't do it this week, I do not want it. Let me know.

Your son,
Frank

G. E. Clinard to Mr. and Mrs. Livingston N. Clinard

Hickory
Dec. 7th 1876

Dear Father & Mother,

We were as usual glad to hear from you a few days ago. When you wrote Father, you were complaining of cold & headache. I hope you have entirely recovered. We have been having very cold weather for some time. Last Friday, Frank went over to the Valley on business & did not get back until 10 o'clock Saturday night. He was almost frozen. I expect you have killed your hogs by this time.

Frank got a Wheeler & Wilson machine for me a few days ago. It is very light running & I think I will like it.

Mr. Jim Beard is here clerking for Mr. Flaum. I reckon he has a very hard time to get along. His son Horace is at home in a very low state of health. He has consumption.

I have just finished working a large tidy for a chair. The pattern I worked it by is a beautiful one. The design is two birds sitting in a rose bush.

Several of our Sunday Schools are going to have Christmas trees for the children. The Episcopal School will have a tree & I have promised to do some work for it. Will you have a gay Christmas in Salem?

Frank is very busy writing tonight. He has not come from the store yet. He said I should give his love to everybody. Is Grandmother still with you? If so, give her much love for us. Cousin Will & Cousin __ Jones both have a little daughter. I don't know of any news about Hickory to write you. You ask what cabbage heads are worth here. I do not know, but will ask Frank when he comes. Give much love to all our friends & accept a great deal for yourselves.

Your Affectionate Daughter,
G. E. Clinard
Cabbage sells at 2 1/2 cents per #. Apples 75-80 cents per Bu. Cranberries $2.00 per Bu.

Gertie did not know who you meant by Jim B. Jinks is working where ever he can get work to do. We are kept very busy in the store now. I just finished my work 10 o'clock but I hardly ever work later than 7 o'clock. I am anxious to hear about furniture. Much love to mother and yourself.
Your son,
Frank

Jennie E. Schultz to Uncle, Grandma and Cousins

Dec. 7th 1876
Brownsville, Missouri

Dear Uncle, Grandma and Cousins,

We received your ever welcome letter sometime ago and I feel bad that I haven't answered sooner, but I have never had an opportunity till now. Uncle Sanford and Cousin Henry and family were here a long time this fall and Aunt Carrie was here a while, so I couldn't find time to write.

We miss our dear Pa a great deal since he is gone. We know not how dear our friends are to us till they are gone. Our Pa is one that is missed by all. He was always smiling, and seemed to love everyone and was loved by all. He had many friends and is greatly missed. It seems hard for us to live without him, but we must try and do as best we can, for we haven't long to stay, and we should try and live contented while here.

We have had the most changeable weather this fall that I ever saw. It is warm now, and very muddy. Yesterday it was snowing and cold.

Aunt Carrie is living in Brownsville. They are living with a man by the name of Dr. Hawkins. Joseph was there a day or two ago. They were all very well. They seem well pleased with the country. Cousin Henry Shultz' are living in Clinton, Henry county, about fifty miles from here, but I don't think Uncle Sanford will ever move to this state.

Grandma, I am going to send you my pictures before long. I have one that I had taken while Uncle Sanford was out here, but Ma says "it is not good enough to send you." I am a "great big" girl now, taller than Ma, but don't think I will ever grow much more. Eddie is small and Mary also, but Joe is very tall and looks like Uncle Lewis. We are looking for him out this winter (Uncle Lewis). Cornelia Ann is married to a Mr. Roninger. She was married sometime this fall.

Pa had his life insured last fall (perhaps he wrote to you about it) for two thousand dollars. We got the money yesterday and Ma had hers insured for the same amount that Pa did.

Tell Aunty to write to me. I wrote to her last summer, but have never received an answer, I remember her very well. How I wish I could see you all once more. Ma often tells us about all of you back there. I wish you would come out and live with us. Aunt Carrie will write soon if she hasn't written, it is only two miles to their house. How is cousin Henry Cooper? I hope he will get better, but am afraid he will not . Ask Cousin Willie if he has some photographs at Knob Noster for me. If he did, I have never got them. I must bring my poor letter to close, for it is getting late and I have nothing more to write. Tell Frankie to write to me. We would be glad to get letters from any of our relatives back there. Ma says, tell Grandma that "Mary looks like Uncle Gid's family very much." We will send one of Pa's pictures as soon as we can have some taken from ones we have.
Overlook all mistakes and believe me, as ever your affectionate niece.
Jennie E. Schultz
P. S. Write soon and often J. E. S.

A. D. Clinard to Livingston N. Clinard

Newton House
Athens, GA
Dec. 16th 1876

Dear Bro,

Your welcome and interesting letter of recent date was duly received and should have been replyed to at an earlier day. I was glad to learn that you went to the Centennial with your wife and got back safely. You did not say whether Frank and his wife went or not, he has not written me since his return, if he went. I have written him but received no reply.

My wife has been sick for 2 weeks, has had a severe attack of neuralgia. She is able to be out of her room today. Blanche is well. I have a very severe cold but keep going.

I have lost all this year that I had made the 2 previous years, but I have done as well as those in other branches of business or I would quit and try something else. I expect to keep the Hotel next year, hoping to do better. If the political trouble were definitely settled, my business would soon increase.

We have been having very cold weather the last 2 weeks, but it is now pleasant. I received a letter from Mother not long since. I will write her soon. I must close. Give my love to your dear wife, also to Eddie. Mollie and Blanche send much love to all. Blanche often speaks of her Aunt Mollie and says she is going to see you all again sometime. Write soon.
Yours as ever,
A. D. Clinard

F. A. Clinard to Mr. and Mrs. Livingston N. Clinard

Hickory, N. C.
Dec. 17th 1876

My Dear Father and Mother,

We received your letter last week & was glad to hear from you & wish we did have some of your sausage & sauce, although we have been very liberally supplied with them both. Our landlord killed six hogs, so we have had plenty of fresh pork.

Father, Mr. H said he saw you in Greensboro & he thought you were looking well.

About our furniture, you misunderstood me. We only want one set, if you can get me the one set for $67.00, less 5% delivered in Hickory, I will take it & would like to have it by Jan. 1st. We want bedstead like yours, bureau, washstand, table & chairs also, towel rack if it is included. We have enough to furnish one room now.

Your hogs were fine. I told Mr. Dolph Shuford what you said. He said he would run against you for amount of corn was fed. He has Essix & Berkshire that he got from Pennsylvania.

We have had fearfull cold weather here this winter & it still continues cold. The Blue Ridge has been blockaded with snow & wagons could not pass, but they have gotten through at last & are running us heavy with trade. Last Friday was one of the busiest days I ever saw. All the ice houses in town are filled with splendid ice.

We both wish you both a very Happy Christmas & send you a box for our Xmas present to you, containing apples & chestnuts, & Mother, Gertie put some cranberries in for you (but does not send the sugar). It will go forward tomorrow. I wanted to send you some nice cabbage heads, but could not get any nice ones. Cabbage is very scarce. We are invited to Maj. Whitings on Christmas night to a Christmas tree & on Wednesday night the Episcopalians have a tree. You know how the English people do up here about Xmas trees, they put presents on the tree for all the people that are invited.

Gertie & myself are both in good health. I weigh 150 lbs. Gertie is in better health than she ever has been. She is anxious to get to house keeping & she says tell you she is going to try to make all her clothing & mine also.

Father, you said you had just received my letter when you wrote me last. I don't understand the mails. Look at the date & you will see that I wrote it two weeks ago, for I read your letter & hurried round to my desk & answered it immediately. I am kept busy at the store now, making bills for goods sold & produce shipped & keeping up my books. Gertie is reading her "Home Guest" & says give her love to you both & Bro Ed, and accept lots from your loving son.

Frank

F. A. Clinard to Mr. and Mrs. Livingston N. Clinard

Hickory, N. C.
Dec. 27th 1876

Dear Father & Mother,

We have had quite a white Christmas. Snow fell here to the depth of 12 inches & then sleeted on top of that. With all the snow & bad weather we have had a very pleasant time. Xmas night we went to a Christmas Tree party & we both got several nice presents. Among the rest, I got a large jar of nice home made pickles. Christmas day we took dinner at Mr. Hall's & had a nice time. I received in all, 7 presents, Gertie the same. Mr. Hall gave me a sack of flour, which suited me very well. We are fixing to commence house keeping next Monday. Gertie is making curtains, towels & sheets & I am trying to get together our kitchen furniture. My understanding is that Vogler is to deliver my furniture in Hickory at price mentioned. Am I right?

There is a big Ball in town tonight & we are asked, but prefer staying home as our Ball time is over.

I have got a nice pile of wood & am having our house fixed up some at the expense of the Ladie I rented from. It is a cottage with 4 rooms & stands next to the Methodist Church. Got front & back yard fenced off from each other & a nice garden. Mother, I want you to please send me some garden seeds in the spring & tell me how to plant them.

Tomorrow night we are invited to another Christmas Tree party given by the Episcopalian Church. We had a Masonic lecturer here today & he installed the officers for the ensuing year. I was installed as Senior Deacon of our lodge & I feel honored, as it is a very important position in the lodge.

We bought out 4, four horse wagons today, loaded with apples, butter & cabbage. If you want any cabbage you had better write me to send you some, as they are scarce in our market this year.

The measles are raging in our town, but in a very light form, so say the Doctors.

I must tell you what Gertie gave me for a Xmas present. She had a charm made out of her hair for my chain. It was a square & compass, a Masonic badge, just like Mr. Yates has. She saw that when she was at home & had one made like it in Hickory. Gertie sends love to you both & Bro Ed & Aunt Eliza. Give my love to Ed & Aunt Eliza & yourselves.

Your Affectionate Son,

Frank

Dec. 28th -It is snowing this morning.

Personal Letters of L. N. Clinard 1877

F. A. Clinard to Mr. and Mrs. Livingston N. Clinard

Hickory, N. C.
Jan. 7th 1877

My Dear Father and Mother,

We just received your letter yesterday. We have not had a train on our road till yesterday, except an engine that run over the road to break the snow. I went down to Salisbury on it last Thursday morning & did not get back till yesterday. I went to telegraph Mr. H about his oldest boy. He has been very sick with measles & cold in his bowels. The Dr. thought he would die. He is some better now.

We have had the largest snow I ever saw, or ever want to see. Last Monday it commenced snowing at 2 o'clock a.m. & snowed till night. It fell to the depth of 20 inches on top of the first snow, which had not melted any. On the level it was over 30 in. deep. As bad a day as Monday was, we moved & I tell you, we had a rough time of it, for since then it has been fearful weather. The thermometer has been as low as 6 degrees below zero. Chickens & birds have frozen to a great extent. The snow is much deeper here than at Salisbury. Business is flat, owing to the roads being impassible.

We are getting along finely house keeping. Gertie likes it very much. She is going to churn tomorrow. We have got us a cow that looks very much like the one you had, when we were at home. We are fixed up right well, considering the bad weather & our furniture not here yet. You did not answer my question relative to the freight on the furniture.

If I get the office I referred to, which I think I will, I will keep it here at Hickory & the pay will be about $1500.00. It has been here to fore $2000.00 but will be cut down. Mr. Hall is doing all he can for me. We had a right heavy sleet yesterday, but today has been warm & the snow has melted considerably.

Gertie says tell you Mother, that she is glad you enjoyed the cranberries. The apples were not frozen when they left here, for we had them in the cellar covered with blankets & I examined them. The wood haulers here have gone up on wood from $1.00 to $1.50 a cord since the snow & we can't buy hay at any price. I bought some bale hay in Salisbury. Gertie says tell you she is satisfied keeping house & is going to try & learn to be a nice house

keeper. We have got a rough time just now getting something to eat, as we have not got any vegetables & can't get any. I bought a nice home made carpet for our room, paid 30 cents per yd. for it, so we look as cosey & happy as you please, which we are. We are sorry to hear you have been sick Father, hope you are well by this time. Good night from us both & much love.
Your Affectionate Son,
Frank

Gertrude Clinard to Mr. and Mrs. Livingston N. Clinard

Hickory, N. C.
Jan. 15th 1877

Dear Father & Mother,

We were glad to hear from you last Saturday & hear that you were well again. What sort of weather are you having now? We have had a very great change in the weather in the last few days. It has been quite warm for several days & today is raining - snow melting very fast.

I am much pleased with house keeping, like it a great deal better than boarding. We are getting on right nicely, but find it very hard to get anything to eat at present. There are few vegetables & no one seems disposed to kill fresh meat. We can't get pork or beef, so we have had to go on old hams from the store for some time & there is no prospect now of doing any better.

I have been somewhat discouraged about the cook we have. She is a colored woman who is not much account. She does not suit me at all & if I knew enough about cooking to undertake it all by myself, I should not keep her another day. Frank is going to try to get another cook soon. It is hard work to get good servants here.

We have a good gentle cow. She gives very rich milk & we have been making our own butter.

Last Friday night we had a very pretty tree for the Sunday School children. We had intended to have it Christmas, but the weather was so bad it was impossible to make the necessary preparations for it.

Sis Annie's little boys have been right sick with measles & one of them is still quite unwell, though both are better. I hear that you have chickenpox & whooping cough in Salem. Give love to Ed & Aunt Eliza for us, also accept much for yourselves from us both. Your loving daughter, Gertrude Clinard

A. D. Clinard to Livingston N. Clinard

Newton House
Athens, GA
Jan. 22nd 1877

Dear Bro,

Yours of recent date came duly to hand. We were glad to hear from you and to learn all were well. Blanche took violent cold 10 days ago and has not been to school since. She came near having pneumonia. She is up now. Myself & wife are well. We have had the roughest winter thus far I have ever seen in any country. Lots of snow & ice and not a whole clear day yet this year. All business is suspended. No travel scarcely. I have not received a letter from Frank since he went to the Centennial. I received a letter not long since from Mother. I am glad to learn they were in as comfortable circumstances as she writes. I must close. Write soon. Mollie & Blanche join in love to all.

As ever,
A. D. Clinard

F. A. Clinard to Mr. and Mrs. Livingston N. Clinard

Hickory, N. C.
Jan. 25th 1877

My Dear Father and Mother,

We received your welcome letter yesterday & with it the very welcome box, which we are very much delighted with. The sausage is splendid & we enjoy it very much with buckwheat cakes. We are more than much oblige to you for it & the seeds. The seeds are the very thing we wanted. We have a nice large garden & I think a right good one.

I am sorry to have to write you that Gertie has been very sick, but is better now. She over worked herself the other day when we got our furniture. She had scouring done & she washed off the furniture & got her feet wet & she had a hemorrhage of the womb & the Doctor said it was a merical that something more serious did not happen. He thought she would have a miscarriage. He says she is out of danger now, but will have to be very quiet & stay in bed five or six days. It is the first time she has been sick since we have been married & just the day before she was taken sick, she was talking about how strong & good she felt & what work she was going to do. Sis Annie has been staying with her for the past three days.

We have had right good trade for the past week. The mountain wagons has again made their appearance, so we have potatoes, cabbage & apples.

We like house keeping so much better than boarding that we are sorry we did not go to house keeping as soon as we were married. We are getting fixed up comfortably, would have had every thing alright if Gertie had kept well. Our furniture is very nice, some of it got rubbed right badly & the bed stead head board got cracked. We did not get a towel rack with it, did Vogler order it?

I have made arrangements to stay with Mr. H another year, provided I do not get the office I am seeking. Mr. H is doing all he can for me to get it & says he will get up my bond. I feel very hopeful at the present state of things. He is going to Raleigh tomorrow. If I am so fortunate as to get it, it will help me along very much & I will have an easier time than I have now.

The Tobacco trade promises to be a good one in Hickory. There is a good deal through this country & the farmers are fixing to put out large crops next year There has been several families from Granville county moved in here lately & they are stirring up our farmers to raise Tobacco.

Gertie says give a heap of love to you & tell you Mother, she is very thankful to you, not only for the sausage, but the garden seeds. I am writing at home tonight, by my own cheerful fire. Much love to you & Aunt E. & tell Ed he ought to write too.

Your Loving Son,
Frank

Gertrude E. Clinard to Mr. and Mrs. Livingston N. Clinard

Hickory, N. C.
Feb. 6th 1877

Dear Father & Mother,

We were glad to hear from you a few days ago. I am thankful to write you that I am well enough to be up & at work again, although I am not very strong yet. I have been making pillows, cases &c., for our spare bed room, have nearly finished everything. We are better pleased with house keeping than ever now because we have got a very nice white girl to cook & wash for us. She lives about two & one half miles from this place, but she has lived with several families in town before & they recommend her very highly. She cooked her first meal this morning, but she seems ready and willing to do any thing & I think we will like her. She will sleep here so she will be company for me when Frank is away. Frank is very busy, thinks he will have to go over to Caldwell this evening & if so he will be gone two nights.

Mother, I would not have known how to cook the sausage, but I was sick in bed when we had the first cooked & Frank remembered how you cooked it, so it was all right. You sent us so many nice garden seeds. I hope we may have a good garden.

Mr. Hamilton came down from Lenoir last week & took dinner with us on Sunday. He inquired after you Father. He said he thought we were very nicely fixed up for new beginners in house keeping. We have some chickens & ducks. The hens are beginning to lay. Please give much love to Aunt Eliza, Ed, & all our friends. Accept much for yourselves from us both!
Your Affectionate daughter,
Gertie

F. A. Clinard to Mr. and Mrs. Livingston N. Clinard

Hickory, N. C.
Feb. 18th 1877

My Dear Father and Mother,
We have been disappointed this last week at not receiving a letter from you. We are afraid one of you are sick. I was away from home nearly all week. Week before last was after some lame ducks, got some of them.

For the past few days we have had very cold weather again. The mountains are covered with snow, so we get the benefit of the cold. We had our garden worked up this last week, & planted onions, peas, radishes, beets & lettuce.

We are getting along very well, have got one of the nicest cooks in this country. She knows how to make good light bread. We had our Belona sausage boiled yesterday, will try some of it today for dinner. We have got most all of our sausage yet.

We had the first Tobacco sales in our new warehouse on last Thursday. Every body was well pleased with the sales. The highest brought 31 cents per #. There were several men here from a distance buying. The trade I think will be a good one here. There is right smart Tobacco in the country & a good many men are preparing to raise crops this year.

Gertie is again well as ever & is delighted & takes great pride in keeping house. She is raising ducks. A Lady friend of hers in town made her a present of a pair of ducks.

Philo Hall is going to move to Hickory the 1st of June. He is winding up their business at Wilkesboro now.

Our trade has been very good for the past month, but will slack now on acct. of farmers going to work.

I guess you have heard before this time of the misfortune that befell Lenoir, the burning of Davenport Female College. It is entirely destroyed, except the brick walls. All the furniture was saved & a good many of the sash. Charley Hamilton stayed with us last Wednesday night. He was at the fire Wednesday morning & told us all about it. It was supposed to have caught from a spark on the roof, was noticed burning about half past nine in the morning.

I heard yesterday that Ed Strupe had taken unto himself a wife. Is it a fact? Tell Ed Ackerman next is his time. Gertie says tell you she has been looking for a letter from you for over a week. She wrote you nearly two weeks ago & has not had an answer yet. She says give her love to you & Bro Ed. We heard Aunt Eliza was to be married this spring to Uncle Davy. Is it so? Give her our love & tell her we would be pleased to have her make her bridal tour to see us. Tell her Davy could make it pay, selling cigars up here. Much love from your Affectionate Son,
Frank

F. A. Clinard to Mr. and Mrs. Livingston N. Clinard

Hickory, N. C.
Mar. 14th 1877

Dear Father & Mother,

Yours received this morning & I am ashamed of myself for not writing you sooner. As Gertie said in her letter, that I was absent minded. Just been so, for the past week been working for my office & I feel right hopeful. Dr. Powell has promised he will do all he can for me in the matter & I think he will be president of the road, so he will be right smart help to me. I have got some friends at work for me who have written to some of the directors.

I am sorry to hear Grandfather is so feeble, hope he will rally. If I get my office, I will be home some time this summer to see you.

I think in the Cold Spring ofc that Mr. P. packed on board & interest very heavy, he has on Gertie's a/c several places amts run up as Sundries. I would like for you to write me if you know whether he has charged her for her watch. He told her it was a present from him individually. Don't say anything about it, but let me know, if you please about if you know.

We have Tobacco sales twice a week in our warehouse, right smart coming in for the cold bad weather.

We have a case of robbery in our town, but we have caught the thief. Burns store was broken open & we had a pair of pants stolen by the same Negro. He is in jail, caught him at Statesville. I am a witness in the case.

I am going to sell Gertie's part of Cold Spring, if I can get what I think it is worth.

Mother, I have had noodle soup twice last week. Gertie recollected how you showed her to make it & I tell you it was good. I didn't eat any thing else for dinner. She has been having hypocrite pies. I come nearer having Salem eating now than I ever have had since I left there. We have nice light bread & sugar cake. I must close, as it is nearly Train time. Much love to you all. Your Loving Son,
Frank

G. E. Clinard to Mr. and Mrs. Livingston N. Clinard

Hickory
March 18th 1877

Dear Father & Mother,

Frank told me this morning at breakfast that he had never mailed a letter which he wrote you last week, but still had it in his pocket, so I write again for fear you have become uneasy about us. Don't you think Frank is getting very absent minded?

I hope you have both been well since we heard from you last. I was sick nearly all last week, & was in bed Sunday, but I am well enough to be up & attending to duties again, & Frank is about as well as usual. We had a bad day yesterday, but it is delightful this morning, so bright & warm. I don't think we shall have much more cold weather. Our garden is coming on nicely. Everything we have planted has come up & looks flourishing.

One of our hens is setting now, another one is laying but her nest is inside the house & it is hard work to get any of her eggs on account of stray dogs around here. Frank has tried to poison several dogs, but it seems that they are too hard to kill.

I am sorry that our cow seems to be going dry. We are anxious to get another one this spring.

Last Friday evening there was a complimentary supper given by the proprietor of the Western Hotel to the Mayor & Commissioner of this town. We both received an invitation which Frank accepted & enjoyed very much.

Cousin Reube has given up the charge of the Cold Spring place at last & I am glad of it. I am very anxious for Frank to sell my half of the farm if possible, for I am not willing for him to pay my debt out of his own earnings. It would not be just to him.

Frank had three lines on a Postal from Brother Ed last week. Tell him I thought he could do better than that & I want to know if that is the way he writes to his sweetheart.

Give much love to all our friends, & accept a great deal for yourselves from us both.

Your loving daughter, G. E. Clinard

F. A. Clinard to Mr. and Mrs. Livingston N. Clinard

J. G. HALL,   P. C. HALL,
HALL BROTHERS, Hickory N. C.   J. G. & P. C. HALL, Wilkesboro, N. C.

OFFICE OF

HALL BROTHERS,

(Successors to HALL & PATTERSON,)

Wholesale & Retail Dealers in General Merchandise,

Hickory, N. C.,

March 27th 1877

My Dear Father and Mother,

We received your letter last week & was glad to hear from you. We are both well & getting along well. We will take your advice about selling Cold Spring. I am going to try & pay for it, or rather pay Gertie's debt.

We are having very dull times just now, farmers are preparing to plant corn. I will know in a few days what my doom will be concerning the Secretary office. The meeting of the directors will be held in Morganton on Thursday. I am going to the meeting, so is Mr. H. He is doing all he can for me.

Mr. Nickelson reached here today on his way to the Valley.

166

Mother, we have got a hen hatching, so if nothing happens we will have spring chickens.

Last night was one of the worst windiest nights I ever saw. It blowed all night.

I have been in the dog business for the past two weeks, have killed 14, most of them from the country. They have worried me no little, they run over my garden & have broken up my hens nests.

Father, you hardly ever send me the Press any more. The last one I received was three weeks ago. We had a Minister at our house Sunday for dinner. He is one of the best Preachers I ever heard preach. His name is Clapp, he lives in Newton & preaches here once a month. He is a German Reform Minister. Gertie sends love to Aunt Eliza, Ed & you both. Much love to you both.

Your Affectionate Son,

Frank

A. D. Clinard to Livingston N. Clinard

April 3rd 1877

Dear Brother,

Yours of recent date came duly to hand. We were glad to hear from you all, but regret to hear that Father was in such a precarious condition. He is now very old and in course of nature can not be expected to live long. I feel very sad to think that I shall never see him again. My circumstances are such that it is impossible for me to go to see him. Times continue very hard here, all branches of business are nearly at a stand still. We are all in usual health.

Blanche is going to school. She will graduate in June. She says tell Eddie he musn't get too deep in love or he can't get out.

I saw a Gentleman a few days ago who saw Frank recently. He spoke very highly of Frank. He said Frank expected to get the position of treasurer on some R. R., which would pay him very well. I am glad to know that

Frank and Eddie are such smart good business boys. I trust they may both do well.

Tell your good wife I often think of her how hard she labored when Blanche & I were there to make our stay pleasant and how well she succeeded. Blanche often speaks of the delightful time she had at Salem. Should my business ever improve, so as to enable me to do so, we will again visit you all. All join in love to all. Write when you can.

As ever,

A. D. Clinard

F. A. Clinard to Mr. and Mrs. Livingston N. Clinard

J. G. HALL,
HALL BROTHERS, Hickory N. C.

P. C. HALL,
J. G. & P. C. HALL, Wilkesboro, N. C.

OFFICE OF

HALL BROTHERS,

(Successors to HALL & PATTERSON,)

Wholesale & Retail Dealers in General Merchandise,

Hickory, N. C.,

April 5th 1877

My Dear Father and Mother,

I have been expecting a letter from you all week. You have heard before this of my defeat in the R. R. Col. F. E. Shobie said I stood next highest to the man that was elected, but for Maj. Fingers resigning in favor of Phifer Erwin. Col. Shobie did his best for me.

We have been very busy today, had a big Tobacco sale & consequently sold a good many goods. There was about $5000.00 of Tobacco sold here today. The best brought $40 per hundred & the cheapest $2.00. We have plenty of peaches here on the ridge, but none in the bottoms & but few apples have bloomed.

Mother, we have one hen with eleven chickens & another hen setting on 13 eggs. Gertie is very well, has been busy covering a lounge, has got it finished & is very nice. I have been having trouble with our cow. She has been sucking herself. I am going to get me another one, a young cow with a calf. I planted corn & beans last Saturday. My potatoes are coming up & my garden looks very well. My peas are large enough to stick. Mother, we had a Salem breakfast on Monday morning. We had sugar cake, sausage, light bread, boiled eggs & pickles. Gertie sends love to you both & Ed. My love to you..

Your Affectionate Son,

Frank

G. E. Clinard to Mr. and Mrs. Livingston N. Clinard

Hickory, N. C.
April 12th 1877

Dear Father & Mother,

Your letter was received yesterday & we were very sorry to hear that you were not so well. Hope you will both soon be well again. We are all well.

Frank had to go to Newton to court last Monday and Tuesday, but they let him off after that. He was witness against a Negro for stealing goods from the store. The latter was convicted & sentenced to three years in the Pen.

We had dreadful weather last week & the first of this, but yesterday & today have been delightful. Our garden is coming on right nicely, cabbage plants not quite large enough to set out yet. We have given up the cow we had & Frank is going to try to buy a cow with a young calf.

I think Frank has about cleaned out all the dogs, for we have not been troubled with them for several weeks. He heard of eleven that he killed (15 instead of eleven. F. A. C.)

Tell brother Ed I am glad he is getting a little better, but I don't believe he would have written to Frank if he hadn't been anxious to find out something the former told concerning himself and Miss Bessie. Tell him he must write to me next time.

My cook helps me a great deal with my sewing. She is piecing a quilt for me now, and it is nearly finished.

We lost two of our little chickens during the bad weather, the others getting on very nicely.

We were sorry to hear that Grandfather and Aunt Eliza were not well. Give much love to them and all other relatives, and accept much for yourself from us both.

Your affectionate daughter,

G. E. Clinard

F. A. Clinard to Mrs. Livingston N. Clinard

J. G. HALL,

P. C. HALL,

OFFICE OF
HALL BROTHERS,
Successors to HALL & PATTERSON,
Wholesale and Retail
Dealers in General Merchandise,
Hickory, N. C.,

May 8th 1877

My Dear Mother,

You can imagine my surprise at seeing Father with us. We were very glad indeed to see him, wish you had been with him. He was just in time to see his grand-son William Livingston.[37] Gertie & our boy are doing finely. Gertie has a great deal of milk, more than the boy can use. She has to have her breast drawn three times a day.

Father & Mr. Hall left yesterday for Charlotte. I sent you, by Father, some Maple sugar & a bottle of headache medicine, like I gave you at the Centennial. Hope it will do you good. I am much oblige to you for sending me Tomato plants, they are growing alright. Gertie & Livy send love to you. Much love to you & Uncle Ed.

Your Loving Son, Frank

F. A. Clinard to Mr. and Mrs. Livingston N. Clinard

J. G. HALL,

P. C. HALL,

OFFICE OF
HALL BROTHERS,
Successors to HALL & PATTERSON,
Wholesale and Retail
Dealers in General Merchandise,
Hickory, N. C.,

May 16th 1877

Dear Father & Mother,

We received your letter & was sorry to hear of Mothers being so ill, hope she is better by this time. Gertie is doing very well. She gets up awhile every

---

[37] William "Willie" Livingston Clinard, first son of Frank A. and Gertrude E. Clinard

day. She has a great deal more milk than the baby can use, has to draw her breast 3 times a day. Our boy is getting just as fat as he can. I measured him Monday, he is just 2 feet long & is a good cryer, but up on the whole he is very good so far. Gertie has a ravenous appetite, but she is careful what she eats on acct. of Willie. She ate some strawberries yesterday & gave him the Colic. Gertie & Willie send love to you both & kiss Mother for our boy. Give our love to Uncle Ed & Aunt Eliza.

Your Affectionate Son,

Frank

P. S. What sort of a man is a Mr. Harris that has been working for J. E. Mickey. He is here. F.

F. A. Clinard to Livingston N. Clinard

J. G. HALL,   P. C. HALL,

OFFICE OF

HALL BROTHERS,

Successors to HALL & PATTERSON,

Wholesale and Retail

Dealers in General Merchandise,

Hickory, N. C.,

June 4th 1877

Dear Father,

    Gertie is some better this morning, but is very sick yet. She has inflammation of the bowels. Willie is doing alright so far. Dr. Baker is very attentive to Gertie & does all he can for her. Gertie sends love to Mother & you. My love to you both.

Your Affectionate Son,

Frank

F. A. Clinard to Mr. and Mrs. Livingston N. Clinard

Hickory, N. C.
June 13th 1877,

My Dear Father and Mother,

We received your letter today & was very sorry to hear of Mother being sick again, hope she has recovered by this time. I am glad to write you that Gertie is improving rapidly & as to Willie, he is as fat as a pig. He has been a very good boy so far. He has eyes exactly like you Father.

Philo Hall has moved here, got here last week.

You wrote you had potatoes, beans & beets. My potatoes are fine & I have been eating them for the past two weeks. My beet crop is short, but I have had some fine beans. My garden is doing very well indeed, the tomato plants Mother sent me are the finest in town, have small tomatoes on them. We have had rain for the past week, so things are growing rapidly. I set out 44 more tomato plants this evening. My cucumbers are doing finely, so are the balance of my vines.

I have been real sick since Sunday, have had a bad case of dysentery. I am better now, nearly every body in town has got it. Mr. Jones & Mr. J. G. Hall are both past work now with it. The Doctors attribute it to the hot days & cold night. We had a slight frost last week.

Trade is exceedingly dull, the Farmers are harvesting.

Mother, I wish you could see little Willie. He is just as bright & playful as he can be, will lay on the bed & laugh & throw his hands about for an hour or two. He knows me, I put him to sleep nearly every night. I play with him & talk baby talk & he laughs & cooes the nicest you ever saw. Gertie thinks she will be well enough to write to you soon, she sends love to you both & hopes you will not be sick again Mother. Give our love to Aunt Eliza & Ed & Willie sends a kiss to his Grand Father & Mother. Good night.

Your Loving Son,

Frank

F. A. Clinard to Mr. and Mrs. Livingston N. Clinard

Hickory, N. C.
June 27th 1877

Dear Father & Mother,

I wrote you on a P card that I would write you Sunday, but I was prevented by being Nurse all day. Our Nurse went to a burying & I staid home & played with Willie all day. He is getting very interesting, lays & throws his arms & legs round & laughs & coos. He notices every thing now, is getting so he can use his neck & turn his head round. We are afraid he will have measles, he has had a chance to catch them. Mr. A. L. Shuford's baby has them & Mrs. Shuford & her baby were at our house yesterday evening. We hope he may escape, as he is so young.

Gertie is still very weak. She had another return of dysentery. It seems to be every where. It has been very fatal in Cabaras Co. There has hardly been a person in town but what has had it, more or less. Mr. P. G. H.[38] is very unwell yet. He has had a hard time of it.

We have been very busy all this week taking stock, so you know I have been busy getting up my books. The wheat crop is excellent through this country, flour has fallen $1.00 per sk. in the past two weeks consequently there has been money lost by speculators. Trade is very dull just at this time. Last week we had a big Tobacco sale & expect to have another July 6th. Had a small one today. We have had a big run of Commercial Drummers this season, from two to five, for every day for the past month.

My garden is doing very well, have squashes, cucumbers & beans & hope to have tomatoes before long. I have the finest in town, some very large ones.

I saw Mrs. Clemmons pass here last Saturday. She told me a good deal of Salem news & among the rest, about how Ross Nomack got caught in his own trap, about selling out his goods.

Gertie & Willie send much love to you both & Ed. Mother, we hope you are well again & that your health may continue to improve. Gertie preserved a lot of cherries the other day, they got very nice. Tammie showed our cook how to bake sugar cake right. Good night. Much love to you both. Your Loving Son,
Frank

---

[38] Philo Gaither Hall

A. D. Clinard to Livingston N. Clinard

Newton House
Athens, GA
July 1st 1877

Dear Bro,

I drop you a line after a long delay, and even now have nothing of special interest to write. My health is not very good this summer. My wife is in better health than last year but not entirely well yet. Blanche is well and going to school. Business of all kinds has been very dull here this year. Commencement exercises at the University will begin here the 1st of August, at which time the hotel will be crowded for a few days. Crops of all kinds are fine here this year and better times are expected this fall.

Dear Bro, I enclose a piece cut from a paper concerning an increase of pensions. If it applys to Fathers case, I hope you will secure it for him. I wrote Mother several days ago, have not heard from her for some time. Hope to hear soon. Write soon. Present my love to your wife and children. Mollie & Blanche send much love to all.

As ever,
A. D. Clinard

A. D. Clinard to Livingston N. Clinard

Athens, GA
July 13th 1877

Dear Brother,

I believe you owe me a letter, but I will write anyway, though I have no special news. Myself and family are well and getting along about as usual. I think times will get better here soon. All kinds of crops are very fine and fruit of all sorts very fine and in great abundance. I hope you are all well and doing well.

Does Mother draw a pension since Father's death? I have been told, by persons who appear to be posted in such things that she is entitled to a pension during her life. Look into the matter and if so, see that she gets it. I must close. Mollie and Blanche join in love to all. Write soon.

Yours &c.
A. D. Clinard

F. A. Clinard to Mr. and Mrs. Livingston N. Clinard

Hickory, N. C.
July 22nd 1877

My Dear Father and Mother,

I guess you think I never intend writing you again, but if you knew how I have been run for the past three weeks, you would not have expected a letter from me. I had to take Gertie away from Hickory, so I took her to Mr. Morris', on top of the Blue Ridge & it was too damp up there, so I brought her back to the Valley & left her at Sam Patterson's. I had a letter yesterday & she said she was better. The dysentery came near killing her. I was very uneasy about her for several days & the Doctor said the best thing I could do was to take her to the mountains. I am keeping house myself, doing my own cooking, have been getting along very well so far.

My garden is doing very well since the rain. We have had splendid rains for the past week & things have come out wonderfully. I have been at home nearly all day, have not been well, got a cold. Got wet last Thursday evening & rode till 12 o'clock at night & it made me sick.

Mother, I will tell you what I had for breakfast this morning. Fried Chicken, fried corn, tomatoes in vinegar, pickled cucumbers, fried bacon & scrambled eggs & coffee. I took dinner at Mr. Halls.

Willie is getting along finely, considering his Mother has been so sick. I weighed him two weeks ago & he weighed 14 1/2 #s. He can manage himself now, can raise his head up & turn it when he pleases & I miss him very much, especially at night, for I put him to sleep every night.

Wheat crops are splendid through this country, nearly every body has threshed their wheat. There are two steam threshers in this county, portable engines, they do rapid work. Father, I have been very busy getting up my books & seeing after Gertie that I really have not had time to do any thing. I have written you two Postal cards & sent you a telegram, but have not heard from you in nearly three weeks, not since the 4th Inst. Mother, I hope your health has improved, would like very much to see you & for you to see my boy, but I am afraid it will be impossible for me to get to Salem before next winter or spring. Trade has been very dull up to this time. B. berries have begun to come in, we are paying 4 cents per #. Goodnight. I hope to hear from you soon. Much love to you both.
Your Loving Son,
Frank
P. S. I have not got any pens, so I have written with a pencil.

Blanche Clinard to Mary (Mrs. Livingston) Clinard

Athens
Aug. 9th 1877

Dear Aunt Mary,

I have been thinking for some time lately that I would write to you, but something has prevented all the time. But now I have made up my mind fully and will let nothing interfere. But Athens is so dull now that it will be rather a hard matter for me to make up a letter.

We had a tolerably large crowd Commencement. There were more ladies than there have been here for three or four Commencements. I enjoyed myself exceedingly with them. I only went over to the Chapel twice, there was a large Ball on Wednesday night. I attended it and had a delightful time. I expect we will have quite a lively time here on the 27th of this month, there is to be a Sunday School celebration, about 100 delegates will be sent here from different parts of the state.

Now about the family. Papa and Ma were very much broken down after Commencement, but they have got every thing straight now, and consequently, they feel better. Ma is preserving today, though it is so very warm. I do believe it is the warmest weather I ever felt. When did you hear from Cousin Frank? I am going to write to him as soon as I possibly can. I wrote to Grandma yesterday. When did Uncle Livingston hear from his other brother's families? Why is it, you reckon, that Dora and Alice Butner don't write to me? I wrote to Dora over a year ago and have never received an answer. Is Miss Nela Ackerman and her husband living there now? I would like so much to see them. Aunt Mary, I have had my diploma framed, it is a very large, handsome gilt frame. It looks beautiful hanging up in our room.

There was a very large fire in town the other night. The gentleman who owned the store soon after committed suicide by shooting himself in the neck, insanity the cause. There have been a great many deaths lately, mostly old people. A very old lady was buried last Sunday week. A little boy, while in a large tree, fell out and was not expected to live, but is better now.

Is Cousin Eddie still flying around the girls? Is he at the same store? I would like to see him so much. Tell him I say he must write to me. I would be delighted to receive a letter from him. I do wish I was with you all, but perhaps Papa will send me there to go to school another year before my education is complete. It would be splendid, wouldn't it?

Now Aunt Mary, I have written all that I can think of that would interest you. All of the Family sends a great deal of love to you all. Give my love to

Cousin Eddie and Uncle Livingston, and a large share for your dear self. Remember me to the Butner's and Mr. Ackerman and Mr. Pease, the young man Uncle Livingston gave to me for a sweetheart.
Please write very soon to your affectionate niece.
Blanche Clinard

A. D. Clinard to Livingston N. Clinard

Aug. 10th 1877

Dear Brother,

I have just passed through a very busy week, it having been Commencement week at the University. I made about $400 clear, but being in debt, I have nothing ahead. The Agricultural convention will meet here on the 12th and hold 3 days. I hope to have a full house then. If so, it will set me up all right.

Mr. N. S. Cook of Winston NC, spent a few days with me the first of this month. He said he knew you well and spoke in high terms of you and family. I was very glad to meet him. Dear Bro, I must close as I am very busy. All are tolerably well and send love to you & family. Write soon.
As ever,
A. D. Clinard

F. A. Clinard to Mr. and Mrs. Livingston N. Clinard

Hickory, N. C.
August 10th 1877

Dear Father & Mother,

I received your letter & in reply to your inquiry about my cooking, I would say that I don't ask any odds except bread of course. I cooked the breakfast I wrote you about. I got tired of cooking & have gone to boarding. I didn't have the time to do my own work & keep things clean. Our girl left when Gertie did, she went to see her sister. I am very tired living by myself & intend bringing Gertie home as soon as Dr. will let me. I have had Dr. Scroggs to see her since she has been at Sams. Gertie is well except nursing sore mouth, which is very bad.

My garden is doing splendid, but unfortunately I can't use much of it. I have nice cantaloupes that I know how to use.

Father, I want to get a present for Gertie's birthday, which is the 25th of this month. Would like for you to see Henry Lineback & get him to take a Photo of myself & Gertie, like the ones we gave you framed. He said he would charge 75 cents each without frame. Get frames like yours as cheap as you can & send by Express. Please send by the 25th if possible. Send me bill & I will remit. Henry can frame them. I am going up to see Gertie tomorrow.

The Grand Lodge of I. O. G. Templars meet here next week, will be a large crowd. There are a good many strangers here now & more coming every day. Hickory is right lively.

Mother please send me your recipe for making sweet pickles. I want to have some peaches & muskmelon put up. I was very unwell the first of the week, caught cold in my bowels. Am better now. Give my love to Aunt Eliza & Ed. Much love to you both.

Your Loving Son,
Frank

F. A. Clinard to Mr. and Mrs. Livingston N. Clinard

Hickory, N. C.
Aug. 17th 1877

My Dear Father and Mother,

I received your letter yesterday & was glad to hear from you, but sorry to hear of Mothers bad health. Hope you will improve Mother, as the cold weather comes on. You said you did not know what Nurses sore mouth is. It is a mouth that gets raw all in side & is very painful when any fruit or acids of any kind are eaten. Sis Annie has had her mouth as sore as Gertrude's, but is better. The Doctors say it can't be entirely cured till the child is weaned. I had a letter from Gertie today. She says she is feeling better & wants to come home. She says Willie is just as bright & good as he can be, sleeps all night & is not the least bit of trouble. I am feeling much better since I wrote you last time.

We have had quite a crowd here this week. The Grand Lodge of Good Templars was here. I have had one of them sleeping with me. Mr. Barham from Winston was here as one of the delegates. Hickory is right lively just now. A good many visitors & Trade is looking up right smart. We have had a heavy trade today, sold two wholesale customers good bills, besides a good local trade. We pay 5 cents for berries & 2 cents to 3 cents for dried apples, 5 cents for fresh peaches & 6 to 10 for peeled peaches.

I am much obliged to you for seeing about my pictures, hope they will get here by the 25th inst. Mother, I am much obliged to you for the sweet pickle recipe & hope I will be successful with it.

I was up in the Valley Sunday & I never have seen corn look so well, but rain is needed badly. I had my Irish potatoes dug the other day & they did not turn out anything. I have one of the nicest pigs for his age that I have seen any where.

I had a letter from Blanche a few days ago & she said she had written to you. What has become of Aunt Eliza? You have not mentioned her name in a long, long time. Has she gotten married & left the country? Or is she still flourishing at Mrs. Mickeys? Give her my love & tell her I would like to have some message from her. Tell Ed when I get time I will write him a few lines.

We are having quite a cool spell of weather at present, feels like fall of the year. You spoke of cheap melons. I saw 31 melons sold for 25 cents for all of them & another load today for same. 10 cents is a big price for the largest melons. I have had a good many cantaloupes in my garden, which I enjoy before breakfast in mornings. Much love to you both & I hope next time I hear from you Mother, you will be better.

Your Loving Son,
Frank

F. A. Clinard to Mr. and Mrs. Livingston N. Clinard

Palmyra, N. C.
Aug. 22nd 1877

My Dear Parents,

Gertrude is but very little better today. She has been right quiet all day. She has taken a little food for the first time in three days, which I hope is a sign for the better. She is not out of danger yet, but I hope & pray with good nursing & medical assistance, we will be able to save her. I sat up nearly all of last night with her. 5 o'clock p.m., Sis Annie has just arrived from Hickory to see Gertrude. Dr. Scroggs has come over to spend the night. He has given her some relief since he came, hope she will rally. Dr. says if she could only take nourishment, he thought she would soon improve. Gertrude has all the nursing & attention that any one could possibly have. She sends love to you both. Little Willie is well & bright.

Your Loving Son,
Frank

F. A. Clinard to Mr. and Mrs. Livingston N. Clinard

Palmyra, N. C.
Aug. 29th 1877

Dear Father & Mother,

I am glad to write you that Gertrude is getting better. She is much brighter & looks better, but she is not able to sit up any yet. She has begun to eat a little, so I think she will soon gain strength enough to get up. I hope she will be well enough for me to go to Hickory by Monday.

Willie still improves, he is always in a good humor & laughs & plays. He notices every thing. I wish so much you could see him. I am surprised at not receiving a letter from you before this.

Crops in the Valley are better than they have been for a number of years. Corn looks splendid.

Gertie said give her love to you & said she would write you as soon as she is able. She has fallen off very much, will not weigh more than 70 or 75 #'s. Love to you both,
Your Affectionate Son,
Frank

A. D. Clinard to Livingston N. Clinard

Athens, GA
Aug. 29th 1877

Dear Bro,

I have not received a line from you for months. I feel anxious to hear how you all are. Myself and family are in good health. My business has fallen off considerably this year in consequence of hard times. I have by close economy kept even but have made no money. I expect to keep the hotel next year and hope to make a living which is about all any one can do in any business here unless a great change for the better takes place. This has been the hardest year I have seen since the war. All branches of business have suffered. My friends consider me fortunate that I have been able to keep even and I have only been able to do so by economy and strict personal attention to business. Write soon. Blanche says she is very anxious to go to see you all again. She sends much love to all & a kiss to you & Sister Mary & Eddie.
As Ever,
A. D. Clinard

F. A. Clinard to Mr. and Mrs. Livingston N. Clinard

Palmyra, N. C.
Sept. 2nd 1877

Dear Father & Mother,

I am still with Gertrude, she still improves but slowly. She is not able to get out of bed yet. She sits up by being propped up with pillows. She is getting her appetite again. Drs. S. & C. said she could eat squirrels & fish. I got her some squirrels & yesterday I went to Sam's Mill & in one hour, I caught 51 fish without a hook. I had a black boy to take the fish off the hook & as fast as I would drop my hook in the water, I would draw out a fish. I never saw anything to equal it. I caught as high as 5 fish with one bait, all but one, were large enough to eat. We had a good mess for breakfast.

Dyptheria seems to be raging through this country. There has been three deaths in the last four days. Sam's miller, a Mr. Johnston, lost a boy yesterday & a grown woman & a little girl died down the river at the Witherspoon place. One of Mr. Rufus Lenoir's little girls has it now. I am uneasy about Willie, but hope he will not get it.

Mother, Gertie says tell you she wants you to come up to Hickory this fall & see your Grand-son. She says he is a fine fellow. He certainly is a good boy. He has been away from her two weeks & is just as good & quiet as he can be. He can nearly raise himself up & sit alone. He is not afraid of any body or any thing. He will take hold of a dog or any thing else. I showed him a squirrel & he grabbed hold of it & I believe he would have put it in his mouth if I would have let him. I am very anxious for Gertie to get well enough for me to take her home. I am getting behind very much with my books, will have to work hard to catch up & I don't feel much like it, as I have lost so much sleep in the past two weeks that it has pulled me down considerably. All of Gertrude's kin folks have been very kind to her & give her all the attention they possibly could. Gertie sends love to you & Bro Ed & says Willie sends a kiss to his Grandparents. Coz. Mollie is making shirt dresses for him, he will be 4 mo. old tomorrow. Love to you,
Your Affectionate Son,
Frank

F. A. Clinard to Mr. and Mrs. Livingston N. Clinard

J. G. HALL,   P. C. HALL,

OFFICE OF

HALL BROTHERS,

Successors to HALL & PATTERSON,

Wholesale and Retail

Dealers in General Merchandise,

Hickory, N. C.,

Sept. 13th 1877

My Dear Father and Mother,

I have been terribly run for the past two weeks. I am nearer broken down than I ever was in my life. We have had a heavy trade & my books were behind nearly three weeks, so you know I had some thing to do. I heard from Gertie yesterday & she was still improving, but she wrote me Willie had cold on his bowels, but I hope not serious.

Mother, I dreamed about you last night, thought you came to see me, which I wish was so. Father, you have never sent me bill for those pictures.

Sam Patterson has gone to Raleigh, will return by Salem & if convenient & you are not unwell Mother, I wish you would ask him to take supper with you some evening. He has been so kind to Gertrude & myself that I want you to have him at home for Tea. He can tell you about Willie, as he has had him in his room for the past month.

Father, I bought 10 cords good oak wood, delivered & corded in my yard, for $9.00. How is that for cheap? We have bought an immense amount of fruit this season, & it is nearly all sold at an advance. Much love to you both, & Bro. Ed.

Your Loving Son,

Frank

A. D. Clinard to Livingston N. Clinard

Newton House
Athens, GA
Sept. 16th 1877

Dear Bro,

I drop a line to let you know how we are all getting along. Myself & Family are in usual health and getting on about as usual. My business is gradually improving and I have reason to expect a good travel during the winter. Crops are fine in this section and there appears to be a more hopeful feeling among all classes.

I frequently see persons traveling who know you and Frank. I will name a few. T. W. Dalton of Winston, Thos. B. Long of Salisbury John G. Young of Charlotte These have been here recently.

I hope you and Dear Sister Mary are getting along well. I would be delighted to see you both. How is Eddie doing? I hope is doing well. Do you & he expect to remain another year with your present employers? I hope to hear from you soon. I wrote Mother yesterday and hope to hear from her soon also. I must close. All join in love to you and family. Blanche sends love to those little girls whose acquaintance she made whilst at your house.

Write soon,

Your Bro,   Andrew

F. A. Clinard to Livingston N. Clinard

J. G. HALL,   P. C. HALL,

OFFICE OF

HALL BROTHERS,

Successors to HALL & PATTERSON,

Wholesale and Retail Dealers in General Merchandise,

Hickory, N. C.,

Sept. 17th 1877

My Dear Father and Mother,

I was very sorry indeed to receive your letter about Mothers sickness, hope she is much better by this time. I had a letter from Gertie Saturday &

she said Willie was right sick, had cold on his bowels. She is improving & I hope to be able to bring her home soon.

I have been busier than I ever was in my life. I was nearly broken down Saturday, but feel some better this morning. I slept all day yesterday. We have sold since Aug. 14th to Sept. 14th, $19,571.01 worth, so you can imagine what work I have to do.

Mother, I hope next news I have from you will be good. I am very anxious to go to see you, but I am afraid I can't get off, as I have lost so much time this summer. Much love to you both.

Your Affectionate Son,

Frank

F. A. Clinard to Livingston N. Clinard

J. G. HALL,   P. C. HALL,

OFFICE OF

HALL BROTHERS,

Successors to HALL & PATTERSON,

Wholesale and Retail

Dealers in General Merchandise,

Hickory, N. C.,

Sept. 25th 1877

My Dear Father and Mother,

I received your letter yesterday & was very sorry to hear that Mother was worse. Hope ere this, she may be better. I was up to see Gertie & Willie Sunday, they are improving. I took Gertie out for the first time Sunday, took her to ride, went about one mile. She has lost nearly all her hair & the Doctors say she will lose it all. I am going to try & bring her home next week if she continues to improve, which I hope she will.

I have been preparing for her this summer. I had 20 jars of peaches, 1 Gal. Quince Preserves, Quince jelly, Peach preserves & tomatoes all put up.

There are several cases of Typhoid Fever in town, a young man died last night with it. We will bury him tomorrow with Masonic honors.

We are very busy indeed with the fruit trade. I am nearer broken down than I ever was before in my life. I work late every night & it is impossible for me to keep up my books, as they ought to be.

Dear Mother, I am very sorry indeed you have had such a hard summer of it. I hope next time I hear from you, you will be much improved. Much love to you & a kiss from little Willie. Gertie said when I wrote send her love to you both & Ed. I heard from her today, she is still improving. Good night.

Your Loving Son,

Frank

F. A. Clinard to Mr. and Mrs. Livingston N. Clinard

Hickory, N. C.

Oct. 15th 1877

We received your letter last week & I should have answered it sooner, but am kept so very busy all the time, night & day. We are having the largest trade we ever had & the big fruit shipment we have been making, makes it much larger. Country Merchants are buying their fall stocks. We have shipped about 800,000 lbs. dried fruit & berries, think we will reach 1,000,000 lbs. We have three extra men with us helping. I have really got more than I can well do by myself. The flour trade is getting to be quite an item in Hickory. Last month there was over 20,000 sacks of flour shipped from here & will be that many more this month. I am writing this letter this morning before day. Willie rousted me awhile ago & I have him quiet, so I am writing to you. Gertrude is looking & she says she is better than ever before in her life, Willie is much better. I have a woman to come three times a day & nurse him. He is much better since he has breast milk. I got him a cat Saturday & you just ought to see him wool the cat. He's not afraid of any thing, he is perfectly delighted to see a horse or get on one, will take hold of a horse's mane & pull it & laugh.

Cole's Circus passed here yesterday on their way to Marion, will show here Wednesday, we expect a large crowd here.

You asked about my pig. He is doing very well considering he had no attention this summer. I think I will make a right good piece of pork out of him yet. I have had bad luck with my chickens have lost about 18 or 20 this fall with Cholory.

Mother, we were glad to hear you are improving & that you have good help. Gertrude sends love to you both & Willie, says kiss Grandfather & Mother for him. Tell Ed we heard from him through Miss Annie Bitting.

Give our love to him & Aunt Eliza. I must close, eat my breakfast & go to the store. Let us hear from you as soon as you can.

Your Affectionate Son,

Frank

F. A. Clinard to Mr. and Mrs. Livingston N. Clinard

Hickory, N. C.
Nov. 4th 1877

My Dear Father and Mother,

We received your letter last week & was glad to hear that you are improving. Mother, hope you will continue to improve & get stout & well again. We are both well, but poor little Willie has a dreadful cold & cough. Gertie is making a plaster now to put on his lungs. Dr. B. says he is threatened with bronchitis. He wheezes so we can hear him all over the room. He seems to be some better this evening. Gertie looks better than I ever saw her look before in her life. She is getting gray hairs in her head. Dr. says it comes from her sickness.

Father you asked about the Watauga trade. We have had a larger trade from there this fall than ever before, but all kinds of produce is low down. Cabbage 1 cent per #, chestnuts 60 cents per bu. & butter from 12 1/2 to 16 2/3 cents. We have had a tremendous trade since the 15th of July. We have bought about 900,000 lbs. of Schnitz, will reach 1,000,000 lbs. till the season is over. Most of it is sold & money made on it. My work is double what it was any time before. There is a young man in the store, Mr. Shuford, that helps me some. I work every night, sometimes very late.

Well at last after courting three years, John Bohannon is going to be married, will get married Wednesday morning & come here the same day. His wife's uncle, Mr. Reinhardt, gives him a party. If Willie is well enough Gertie & myself will go to it. John expected Frank yesterday, but he did not come. We have had some fun teasing John, we did not know it till this last week.

I went with Dolph Shuford to his farm today. He has some fine hogs. One will weigh 600 & another 500. You can imagine how he loves to talk about them.

You asked how you got the Press. I pay for it, the Time is not out till next summer some time. I have not received the P. Press lately, hope it may come more regularly.

I wish you would send Ed up to see us Christmas. Mother, I am as anxious to see you & for you to see our boy as you are & wish it was so I could come down, but my expenses have been so heavy this summer & Dr. bills to pay that I can't spare the money, but I am happy to inform you that I am not in debt.

We are not going to have a Fair this fall. Gertie sends love to you both & says she will write you soon again. Give our love to Aunt E. & Ed. Willie sends kisses to his Grandparents. He is sitting up alone now. Gertie is going to put on short dresses on him soon, she is making them now. Cuz Mollie Patterson sent him a beautiful short white dress yesterday. I think she loves Willie as good as Gertie does. We don't think Willie's pictures are good, he has a bright smiling face all the time when he is well.
Love to you both.
Your Loving Son,
Frank

F. A. Clinard to Mr. and Mrs. Livingston N. Clinard

Hickory, N. C.
Nov. 18th 1877

My Dear Father and Mother,

We received your letter last week & was glad to hear from you. I also received Ed's very welcome letter & was glad to hear from him once more. Tell him the little hood he sent Willie suits him splendid, he wore it today. I am glad to write you that he is nearly well again. He & his Mother are having quite a romp just now, he is laughing hartily. Just as soon as I come in the room, he begins to reach out his dear little hands for me & the next thing is to pull off my hat. Next is to pull my hair or beard. Mother, I said to Gertie this evening, if you could only see Willie, you would be perfectly delighted. When well, he is always ready for a romp. I weighed him yesterday & he weighed 18 #'s, he has fallen off in his sickness.

We have had a heavy trade this fall & bids fail to continue & work plenty to do all the time. I am kept very busy all the time. We have had so much fruit to handle that it has kept me busy making out bills & statements for parties bought of & sold to. We have shipped 60 car loads, which will amt. to about 1,200,000 lbs. We are receiving orders daily for all kinds of produce, so it keeps us all moving to keep things up.

Hickory is on the upward tide, several families have moved here recently & more coming. There are several Tobacco Factories to be opened here shortly. There are six or eight new houses being built at present. There was 1900 bags flour shipped from our Depot in one month, which makes 190,000 #'s. A. L. Shuford has put another set of burs in his mill, so he can grind twice as much as he did before.

We have had quite a lot of fun out of John T. Bohannon. He told his Sister In Law good bye & she cried & he cried & took his hand kerchief out & wiped his eyes & said "Sister don't cry. I'll be good to Fannie. She shall come to see you when she wants to. You must come to see us. She shall have what ever she wants & what ever I can get for her, she shall have. Now Sister don't cry. I'll be good to Fannie." So we boys have run him on "Sister don't cry." It is all the truth, he said it all. Gertrude & Willie send love to you both & Willie a kiss for his Dear Grandparents. Love to you both.
Your Son,
F. A. C.

W. A. Butner[39] to Mrs. Livingston N. Clinard

Windfall, Ind.
Nov. 25th 1877

Dear Sister,

You will probably be astonished to see a few lines from me again, it has bin so long since I wrote to you. I have received several letters from you but I always neglected answering them because I hate letter writing so bad. You must excuse me and I will promise that I will answer your letter more promptly hereafter. You probably have not heard from me for some time, so I will tell you that I have bought a farm one and a half miles from Windfall and moved on it. I have a very good farm of 80 acres. 60 acres cleared and in cultivation and a good orchard. Our house is a very poor thing. It is a little old log concern, you would laugh if you would see it. It was built in early times. We are not able to build a new house now, but hope we will be in 1 or 2 years.

My boys and my wife like living on the farm a great deal better than in town. In town I had nothing for my boys to do. Here they have plenty to do.

---

[39] William A. Butner

Me and the boys tended 35 acres of corn this last summer. We are feeding 25 hogs for market, so you see we have plenty work to do.

I paid $40 per acre for this farm 2 years ago. Farming at this time is not very encouraging as most all farm production is very low. Hogs and corn are our main dependence for money and Hogs at this time are only worth $3.75 per hundred live weight. Corn is 30 cents per bunch.

Well Mary, how are you and Sister Eliza getting along? It has been so long since I heard from Eliza. Would like very much to hear from her. Would like to know whether she is married or not and also how brother Ed is getting along and please send me the names of Edwin's[40] children, as I do not know them and my boys frequently ask the names of their cousins in North Carolina.

I believe I have nothing more to write at present. I forgot to state that we are all in good health and hope you are the same. Give my respects to all inquiring friends. Yours truly,
W. A. Butner

Gertrude E. Clinard to Mr. and Mrs. Livingston N. Clinard

Hickory, N. C.
Dec. 2nd 1877

My Dear Father and Mother,

It has been too long a time since I last wrote you, but I have had so much nursing to do since Willie has been sick that I have gotten behind in house-keeping, writing & everything else. Pneumonia left Willie with a bad cough & very nervous & wakeful. He has never been able to sleep well since he had pneumonia & we had to give him medicine to make him sleep for a long time. Dr. Baker says this is frequently the case after having this disease. But I am glad to say that Willie is getting better. I feed him now & he is beginning to eat very heartily & it does him good.

Mr. Bohannan came to see us this evening but didn't bring his wife - said she would not come on Sunday but would come tomorrow. I knew her before she was married & think she is a very nice girl. They are boarding with Mr. Hendrix, the place where we boarded when we were first married.

Mother I am glad to hear that your medicine is benefiting you & hope you may grow strong & well this winter. We are having very cold weather

---

[40] Probably Samuel Edwin Butner, brother of Mary Butner Clinard

now. My health is not as good as it was when I came home but I hope I will grow stronger as Willie gets older & requires less attention.

Frank got a little chair for Willie, which we can put him in & there is no danger of falling out & you ought to see him sit in it & play. He is just like Frank, brim full of mischief & fun & as loving & sweet as a baby can be. It is after supper & time for Willie to be put in his cradle as I must stop & take him. He sends love & kisses to Grandpa & Grandma. Frank joins me in love to you both, also to brother Ed, Aunt Eliza & any friends who may inquire after us.

Your Affectionate Daughter,
Gertrude E. Clinard

F. A. Clinard to Mr. and Mrs. Livingston N. Clinard

Hickory, N. C.
Dec. 16th 1877

Dear Father & Mother,

We received your letter last week & I would have answered it sooner but have been very busy. The trade from the mountains has been very heavy this winter. Apples & all kind of produce are plentiful. We have had a delightful day, it has been so warm we let the fire go down. Willie has been out all day. We have put him in short dresses & he looks so sweet & cunning in them. I have spoilt him about myself, he won't go to sleep at night till I come home, if it is 12 o'clock. I always romp with him & he expects it every night, so he waits for me. I generally put him to sleep.

You asked about my pig. He is doing tolerably well. I won't kill him till the last of January. He is small, would be ashamed for you to see him. So far he has not cost me any thing but what corn I raised. We did not use any roasting ears, so I had my entire crop to get hard.

Miss Em Hamilton is to be married on Tuesday the 18th inst. to John Rosseau of Wilkesboro & on Wednesday, we are to have a grand wedding in Hickory. Miss Florence Hill is going to marry a Mr. Kidder from Wilmington, one of the wealthiest men in the state. They are going to Europe on a bridal tour. We are invited to the wedding & will attend. They did not invite out side of our relatives in town but three families, Dr. Bakers, J. G. Hill's & ourselves. Tell Mr. R. L. Patterson she is to be married, he knows her.

Willie is trying to get me to romp with him now. He is talking & trying to get to me. He is saying "dad, dad, daddy."

I have never heard of Lineback's bill, would like to pay it & get it off my mind. Mother, if you could see Willie, I know you would eat him up, for he is just the sweetest & brightest baby you ever saw. He is not afraid of any body or any thing, generally in a good humor, except when he can't have his own way about any thing. He has some temper, about enough for two babies.

Gertie says give her love to you & says she will write soon again. She says she wishes you a very Merry Christmas. We won't have much Xmas here. We will close the store & go to church & that will be about all we will have. Master Hill is invited to a Xmas tree at Prof. Humphreys, so I guess we will have to take him. I had a letter from Ed this last week, will answer soon. Much love to you both I hope you will enjoy Christmas.

Your Loving Son,

Frank

HALL BROTHERS,

Wholesale and Retail Dealers in

GENERAL MERCHANDISE.

For the Holidays

We have a nice Stock of

FANCY GOODS,

PLAIN AND FANCY CANDIES,

Layer and Valencia Raisins,

BRAZIL NUTS AND ALMONDS,

CHOCOLATE,

Jellies, Sauces, Canned Fruits, Canned
Vegetables, Sardines, Lobster,
Salmon, Oysters, &c., &c.

Goods suited to the Season can be found in our Stock
both useful and ornamental, in all the various lines.

Main Street. Hickory, N. C.

Main Street (Union Square), Hickory, N. C. circa 1906
Photo courtesy Catawba County Historical Association Archives

Personal Letters of L. N. Clinard 1878

F. A. Clinard to Mr. and Mrs. Livingston N. Clinard

Hickory, N. C.
May 27th 1878

Dear Father & Mother,

Yours received last week & we were glad to hear that you are improving Mother. Hope you may continue to. The past month has been hard on me, owing to so much damp weather. Friday & Saturday were both very hot days, but yesterday it was very pleasant. Gertrude is very well, but Willie is not. He has fallen off considerably, hardly looks like the same boy. He was real sick again last week, but better again. Since he has been sick he won't try to walk, but tries hard to talk. I took Gertie & him to ride yesterday evening & he sat up & clucked & hollered to the horse, he held to the lines all the time.

Gertrude wants to go to Salem to see you, but she says she won't go, without I go with her & that is impossible now. We will begin inventory in a week or so. I wanted her to go without me & let Ed meet her in Lexington, but she says she won't go unless I do. I hope to be able to get down this fall. If Ed comes to see us this summer, I think Gertrude would go home with him & then I could come after her. If she does go to Salem can she get any one down there to nurse Willie while she is there? It will cost me less to get a nurse there, than to take one from here.

Our garden is doing finely. We have had some splendid beets & potatoes, my beans are a little backward.

Wednesday will be a big day here. The Judicial convention for this district will meet here.

Farmers are complaining very much about the fly in their wheat, the rust is very light.

The wood work of Mr. Hall's house is nearly finished & I tell you it is a nice job.

We have four Tobacco Factories here now. C. E. Graham of Shuford & Co. went to Winston last week looking for hands to put to work in their Tobacco Factory. There is a good deal of the weed being sold here now, but at low prices.

How is Ed Ackerman getting? Gertrude sends love to you both & says she hopes to see you before next Xmas. Willie sends love & kisses to his dear Grandparents. Father I wish you would send me by Mail, one pair of children's slippers. No. 3 or 3 1/2 for Willie. I want something good but not to cost too much. Also 3 pair of striped cotton stockings to fit with the slippers. If it costs less to send by Express, why send them that way. Much love to you both & tell Aunt Eliza that I have been expecting a box of cake by Express from her for sometime.

Your Affectionate Son,

Frank

Straw enclosed, length of foot.

F. A. Clinard to Livingston N. Clinard

J. G. HALL,   P. C. HALL,

OFFICE OF

HALL BROTHERS,

Successors to HALL & PATTERSON,

Wholesale and Retail Dealers in General Merchandise,

Hickory, N. C.,

.

June 6th 1878

Dear Father,

I wrote you a postal card yesterday stating I had not received package. It came through alright today & the stockings we are much pleased with, also the slippers, but I am sorry to say the slippers are too large & I will have to sell them or keep them till Willie grows to them. I must have missed it in taking his measure. He was asleep in his crib & I suppose I let the straw run too low below his heel. I enclose $2.75, Amt. to pay you $1.75 & $1.00. Please pay my church dues & send me receipt, they dunned me for it a few days ago.

Gertie & Willie are both right well. Willie is cross but that comes from his teeth.

We had our first mess of beans today, have had beets for the past two weeks. Our garden is looking very well. We have nice tomatoes, some as large as a filbert. Willie eat his first beans today & he was fond of them. He is backward about walking. Some days he will walk across the room several times & then again he won't walk at all. He tries to go too fast, is one reason why he can't walk. He tries hard to talk, can say some things very plain.

Last Wednesday there was a large crowd at the convention. A. C. Avery was nominated for Judge & a Mr. Adams from Mitchell for Soliciter.

My Rheumatism is getting better, but I am still troubled with my right wrist & hand. I hope as the summer advances it may get better.

I would like to see Coz. Jennie Shultz. If you see her, give her our love & tell her I said to come to see us. Gertie & Willie send much love to you & mother. Willie sends kisses. Much love to you both.
Your Loving Son,
Frank

F. A. Clinard to Mr. and Mrs. Livingston N. Clinard

J. G. HALL,   P. C. HALL,
OFFICE OF
HALL BROTHERS,
Successors to HALL & PATTERSON,
Wholesale and Retail Dealers in General Merchandise,
Hickory, N. C.,

June 17th 1878

Dear Father & Mother,

I wrote you last Thursday a week ago & enclosed $2.75 to pay you & my church dues & I have not heard from you whether you received it or not.

Yesterday morning at half past one it was discovered that William H. Ellis' store was on fire, so the alarm was made & before it could be checked it consumed two stores, Post Office & Tailor shop. Ellis & Alexander's loss $3300.00, Insurance $2200.00. D. W. Rowe's loss $500 besides house, no insurance. Post office, everything saved except the house, loss $400, Tailor shop loss $200 & Shuford & Graham sustained heavy loss on goods by being removed. It was hard work to keep their house from burning down. It caught several times, but by diligent watching & hard work it was put out. We had the roof of our store covered with wet blankets & kept men on it pouring water all the time.

Gertie & Willie are both quite well & send love to you both. Willie walks a little by himself & you ought to hear him laugh at it. Much love to you both.

No one knows how the fire originated. Nothing at all saved for Ellis & Alexander.
Your Affectionate Son, Frank

F. A. Clinard to Mr. and Mrs. Livingston N. Clinard

Hickory, N. C.
June 30th 1878

Dear Father & Mother,

We received your letter last week & I would have answered it sooner, but have been very busy, we are taking inventory. I began to think you did not intend writing to us any more. I do not understand why you delayed writing so long.

We were very sorry indeed that Ed could not get off to come to see us. We were looking for him for several days till Mr. Roulhac told me he could not get off to come.

Summer visitors are beginning to come in, this week the Press Association of N. C. meets here & the citizens of Hickory are going to give them a reception in the way of a Ball & Supper. We expect a big time. Our trade has been better through May & June than it was last year.

Well at last Willie is toddling around. He can walk where he pleases now, has been walking for nearly two weeks. He is in good health now & is looking well. He sits on my lap every day & eats his dinner. He eats all kinds of vegetables. He tries very hard to talk, says a good many things very plain. Mr. R. L. Patterson sent Willie a carriage last week & by the way, it is a nice one too. Willie is perfectly delighted with it, he likes to ride all the time.

We are living out of our garden now, have got all sorts of vegetables, but tomatoes. Have got plenty of green ones, but they don't seem to ripen. Our potatoes are as fine as I ever saw, they are very large. Mother, I have got peppers as large as goose eggs. We eat beats twice a day, hot for dinner & cold for supper.

Gertie & Willie have gone to bed. Gertie says she is ashamed of herself for not writing to you before this, but she has got her hands full looking after housekeeping & nursing Willie. She sends love to you both & Willie sends kisses to his dear Grandparents. You just ought to see him kiss. He kisses with his dear little mouth open & will lay his arm round your neck as sweet as can be. He calls me Daddy.

Well Mother, I had a good sugar cake today, as good as I ever ate. Aunt Harriett showed the cook how to make them & she succeeded perfectly. I had fried chicken, sugar cake, & fresh pickles for my breakfast this morning, so you can imagine how I did eat. I spoke of my potatoes. I think one of them would do Levin Belo's family for a week & the peeling feed Henry

Meining's chickens the same length of time. Good night with much love to you all.

Your Loving Son,

Frank

How is Ed Ackerman's health now?

F. A. Clinard to Mr. and Mrs. Livingston N. Clinard

J. G. HALL,   P. C. HALL,

OFFICE OF

HALL BROTHERS,

Successors to HALL & PATTERSON,

Wholesale and Retail Dealers in General Merchandise,

Hickory, N. C.,

July 15th 1878

My Dear Parents,

I received your letter last week & was truly glad to hear from you once more. We are all tolerbly well. My wrists are troubling me a great deal. We are having very hot & dry weather. My garden is about burnt up.

We had quite a sad death in town Friday night. It was our next door neighbor Mrs. Wilfong. She was taken sick Wednesday night & died Friday night, had menengetus. She leaves a baby about 18 mo. old. Gertie was there when she died & helped to lay her out.

I have got a lot of work ahead of me. I am behind with my books since June 29th so you can imagine the work I will have to do. Inventory put me back.

Yesterday evening I killed a rattle snake 4 ft. long with eleven rattles. It was quite a curiosity here, it is hanging up at the drug store now. Gertie & Willie send love to you both & Willie sends kisses. I am very busy this morning so I must close.

Your Affectionate Son,

Frank

P. S. I forgot to mention that Byron Spaugh & James Hall staid with us last Saturday & Saturday night. Byron preached & every body that heard him thought he preached a splendid sermon. I went with them to Newton on Sunday & he preached there Sunday night.

F. A. C.

F. A. Clinard to Mr. and Mrs. Livingston N. Clinard

J. G. HALL,   P. C. HALL,

OFFICE OF

HALL BROTHERS,

Successors to HALL & PATTERSON,

Wholesale and Retail Dealers in General Merchandise,

Hickory, N. C.,

July 29th 1878

My Dear Father and Mother,

We received your letter last week & was glad to hear from you, very sorry your health is not improving Mother. We are very well considering the hot dry spell of weather we have had. It has been dry here for over a month till yesterday, we had a good rain. Our garden is entirely ruined, nothing at all we can get out of it, except tomatoes & they are very small. Our corn is dried entirely up. We had four different storms yesterday. The lightning struck Wess Clinard, Fields & Cox livery stable & burnt it to the ground. One horse, one wagon & all their harnesses were burnt up. There was a carriage & hack saved. The lightning also struck a large white oak near the mineral spring. (The balance of C. F. & Co. horses were out).

Saturday was a big day here & a very large crowd here. The candidates wound up their speaking here, they spoke from two o'clock till 6 p.m. We have four candidates for the legislature, one democrat, one republican & two rag tag & bob tail independents. I consider an independent candidate as a dangerous man to vote for, for any office. Let every man show his colors & be a man.

Saturday night the Train ran over a man about 13 miles above here & cut him all to pieces. He was laying across the track, no one knew whether he was put there, or whether he was drunk & laying there of his own accord.

Our trade has opened, we are buying right smart B. Berries, apple crop short, plenty of peaches. The B. Berry crop has been cut short by the dry weather. To show you how hot it has been here, the thermometer has been as high as 96 degrees at my desk. I have one against it. I have suffered very much with heat, as I have been very busy all the time.

You spoke about Mr. Ampler painting Mr. Hall's house. It is about completed & ready for him to move into. He got two painters from Charlotte & they have been at work on it for a month & it is a pretty house. He painted it a French gray & trimmed it with brown.

If I can get off, I want to bring Gertie & Willie to see you this Fall some-time. Willie is toddling round all the time & tries to talk. We are looking for him to take chicken pox, as he has had a chance to get it. I am sorry to hear of Ed Ackerman's low condition, give him my best regards. Gertie joins me in love to you & Willie sends kisses.

Your Affectionate Son,

Frank

P. S. I would like to have my church receipt.

F. A. Clinard to Mr. and Mrs. Livingston N. Clinard

J. G. HALL,   P. C. HALL,

OFFICE OF

HALL BROTHERS,

Successors to HALL & PATTERSON,

Wholesale and Retail

Dealers in General Merchandise,

Hickory, N. C.,

Aug. 12th 1878

Dear Father & Mother

I would have written to you yesterday but I was very unwell all day, had severe attack of diarrhea, so I was in bed the greater part of the day. Willie has had quite a hard time for the past week, has cut two teeth & two more nearly through. He has had running off of the bowels & been throwing up a great deal.

We are very busy in the store at this time buying lots of berries, have bought about 150,000 #s up to this time, have sold 4 car loads.

Gertie's health is improving, she has been doing our own cooking for about two weeks till Willie got sick & I had to get a cook. Willie is trying hard to talk, he says a good many things.

Father, there will be a present from Gertie & myself to you for your 50th birthday, come to you by Express from New York. Hope you will be pleased with it. I am very busy, pushed all the time. Gertie & Willie send love to you both. Mother, I hope you are still improving. Willie sends kisses to his dear Grandparents.

Your Affectionate Son,

Frank

F. A. Clinard to Mr. and Mrs. Livingston N. Clinard

J. G. HALL,   P. C. HALL,

OFFICE OF

HALL BROTHERS,

Successors to HALL & PATTERSON,

Wholesale and Retail Dealers in General Merchandise,

Hickory, N. C.,

August 26th 1878

My Dear Father and Mother,

We received your letter & card, sorry to hear you are suffering so much Mother, hope your fingers are better by this time. I was not at all surprised to hear of Ed A's death, as you had written me, & I saw Charles Bahnson on Tuesday last & he told me all about his sickness. You wrote me Gus Butner was elected to Legislature & Charles B. says Frank Johnston is elected.

Gertie had her 21st birthday yesterday. She is right well, but Willie is very fretful. I was up till 3 o'clock this morning with him. He is growing very rapidly, both in size & meanness.

Father, I will have to do something about that Cold Spring debt & I want your advise. Shall I sell Gertrude's part & what is it worth? Would like to have your opinion & advise. I never will be able to make money enough to pay it off. I wish you would please write me at once what you think best. We are having a heavy trade & I am very busy. Gertie & Willie send love to you both & hope Mother will soon recover.

Your Affectionate Son,

F. A. Clinard

G. E. Clinard to Mr. and Mrs. Livingston N. Clinard

Hickory, N. C.
Sep. 5th 1878

My Dear Father and Mother,

It has been a long time since I wrote a letter to any body, but I think it is high time for me to answer some of my letters, so I will begin by writing to you. I was sorry to hear of the risings on your fingers Mother. They must be very painful. What do you think could have caused them?

202

Frank tells me that tomorrow is your birthday Father. I hope you will have a happy one & live to see many returns.

I hope you will like the photographs, which we will send of Willie. We think it very good. It was hard work for me to get him still long enough to have it taken. He runs every where now & is beginning to say a good many words, this to say, every thing he hears any body else say.

For several weeks past, I have been canning & preserving fruit for the winter. I believe I have gotten through with it all now.

A few days ago we were alarmed by the report that Sis Annie's little Alex had Dyptheria, but it proved he had only a severe dry throat.

Our garden was almost entirely burnt up during the long dry spell, so we have to buy most of our vegetables now. I hope you had better luck with your garden. It does not pay to make a garden & then have to buy vegetables.

There is no news in our town, or at least I do not know of any. I stay very closely at home. Willie is very slow about cutting teeth, have only six yet, but I am glad he does not cut them during this warm weather. He & Frank are well, send love & will write soon. With much love to all.
Your Affectionate Daughter,
G. E. Clinard

F. A. Clinard to Mr. and Mrs. Livingston N. Clinard

J. G. HALL,   P. C. HALL,
OFFICE OF
HALL BROTHERS,
Successors to HALL & PATTERSON,
Wholesale and Retail
Dealers in General Merchandise,
Hickory, N. C.,

Sept. 23rd 1878

Dear Father & Mother,

We are all well at present, but I am very busy. Gaither has gone to N. Y., so it keeps me busy all the time to keep up the correspondence & my books. We are very busy now selling goods, have opened a Wholesale establishment in Shuford's Brick Store.

Secrest, the man that murdered his wife & step child was convicted of murder & his sentence is to hang on the 9th of Nov.

We want to come see you next month, provided I can get off, & do so. We are having the heaviest trade we ever have had. I have to work every night, sometimes very late.

I have two very nice pigs fattening. Gertie & Willie send love & kisses to Grandmother. Much love to all of you. I am very busy, or I would write more.

Your Loving Son,
Frank

F. A. Clinard to Mr. and Mrs. Livingston N. Clinard

J. G. HALL,   P. C. HALL,

OFFICE OF

HALL BROTHERS,

Successors to HALL & PATTERSON,

Wholesale and Retail Dealers in General Merchandise,

Hickory, N. C.,

Oct. 9th 1878

My Dear Parents,

I ought to have written to you sooner, but I have, & am still, pressed with work. We are having a heavy trade & I am kept very busy. It is now 11 o'clock p.m. & I am not through yet.

Last Thursday night, Bro Rondthaler stayed with us. Gertie & myself were much pleased with him. He went from here to Asheville.

Last night was an eventful night at my house. To begin with, Willie fell on the rockers of a chair & hurt his head very badly & just before he went to bed he got carbolic acid on his legs, which took all the skin off & left him in a bad fix. Then this morning, before day, my cook waked us up screaming & calling me & I run out to her house & found she had smothered her baby to death. So Gertie has had her hands full today, nursing & cooking.

She is sewing hard every day to get ready to go to see you, which we hope to do sometime this month. I will notify you a few days before we start.

Mr. J. G. Hall returned from N. Y. on last Saturday & he has bought a large stock of goods. I know one thing very well, that he has got more work to do than one Book Keeper can, or ought to do. I feel tired all the time & my breast has been hurting me for the past month.

Dr. Bahnson & family left for home today, he was very successful in his operation on A. L. Shuford's baby. Gertie & Willie send love to you both. So do I.

Your Loving Son,

Frank

P. S. Mother, how are you getting on raising bees? I understand you had turned your throat into a bee gum.

F. A. Clinard to Livingston N. Clinard

J. G. HALL,   P. C. HALL,

OFFICE OF

HALL BROTHERS,

Successors to HALL & PATTERSON,

Wholesale and Retail Dealers in General Merchandise,

Hickory, N. C.,

Oct. 29th 1878 (Telegraph me at once)

My Dear Father,

This morning our new Book Keeper broke out with Variola, or rather a slight case of small pox & I have been with him all the time. Do you think it advisable for me to come to Salem? If so, Telegraph me at once. If I get sick here, no one will nurse me except Gertie & I don't want to expose them (Willie & her) to it. I don't think I will take it, as he left as soon as he found it out. It is a slight case, but every body in town is panic stricken, they even run from me when they see me coming. Don't say any thing to any one in Salem, for it will spread, for every one would be afraid of me if I do come.

Your Son,

Frank

P. S. We are ready to come Friday, if you say so. Dr. Baker advises us to go

F. A. Clinard to Mr. and Mrs. Livingston N. Clinard

J. G. HALL,   P. C. HALL,

OFFICE OF

HALL BROTHERS,

Successors to HALL & PATTERSON,

Wholesale and Retail Dealers in General Merchandise,

Hickory, N. C.,

Nov. 4th 1878

My Dear Parents,

I am still kicking. I received your Telegram & letter. Your Telegram was just in time to save me. We were packed & dressed, ready to start. Had told a Negro to get my trunks. Willie was impatient & talking about the Train all the time. We were very much disappointed about not getting off. We have postponed this is the 4th time.

Well, every body here is acting like a set of fools, in my estimation. Lots of them run from me. I keep myself close all the time. The young man that had the Small Pox is getting well. I thank you for offering to send me a nurse if I get sick. Don't pay him too much, 50 or less cents a day & board, or less if you can get one, for it is not hard work.

My friend, A. C. Shuford, that stays with us in the store, said to ask you to send him a nurse if I Telegraph for one (expenses paid). He slept with the young man several nights & they both slept in our office. I had Willie vaccinated & am going to have myself & Gertie vaccinated again. I understand the usual time for taking Small Pox is 21 days, hence it will be about two weeks yet till I get it, if I get it at all. Gertie was very much disappointed at not getting to make her trip, for she has been working hard making Willie & herself clothing & had every thing fixed to go. Even had her chicken fried & her lunch fixed up. My letter must have been delayed a day some where, as I mailed it on Wednesday. I hope it will all pass off & we may get home by Ed's 21st Birthday, which is the 27th of this month. We all send love & Willie sends many kisses for his dear Grand Parents.

Your Affectionate Son,

Frank

F. A. Clinard to Livingston N. Clinard

J. G. HALL,   P. C. HALL,
OFFICE OF
HALL BROTHERS,
Successors to HALL & PATTERSON,
Wholesale and Retail Dealers in General Merchandise,
Hickory, N. C.,
Nov. 29th 1878

My Dear Father,

I just received your letter about 8 o'clock last night. Had been out on a collecting expedition & did not get home till that time. I am very sorry indeed that we can not come this week, but Mr. Hall will not let me off. I am to start to Watauga in the morning, provided it is not raining too hard. I am getting about half mad & Gertie is full mad that I am put off from time to time. It is about two months now that we have been starting every week. There will be a fuss in the family soon if he does not let me off. I have gone to right smart expense to get us all ready to come to see you & I have disappointed you & Mother several times & I am tired of such work & I know you are too, but it can't be helped. Gertie & Willie are both well, except colds. I will let you know by Telegraph when we will start if at all. I am almost determined to go any way, if I lose my place. Don't you & Mother trouble about fixing for us any more, till you know for certain we are coming. I had a letter from Uncle Andy yesterday. He says he is having a good run of customers. Gertie & Willie send love to you both.
Your Affectionate Son,
Frank

G. E. Clinard to Mr. and Mrs. Livingston N. Clinard

Hickory, N. C.
Dec. 26th 1878

Dear Father & Mother,

I was most pleasantly surprised to receive the beautiful shawl Xmas Eve, & I am very much obliged to you both for it. It is something like the one I sold, except that was red. I like the white better. I wish I had something nice to send you. Hickory is a poor place to get Xmas presents & I have not had time to make any thing since we came home. I hope you all had a pleasant

Xmas. I had a very quiet day. Frank was invited to Mr. P. Hall's to dinner & said he eat so much it made him sick. Xmas night we were invited to Mrs. Halls to an eggnog party. I had no one to leave Willie with, so I could not go & Frank was too sick to stay only a very short time.

You would have been amused & astonished if you had seen Willie the day before Xmas. I told him all about Santa Claus & drove a nail where I told him he must hang his stocking so that Santa Claus would fill it with good things for him. He understood it all perfectly, for everybody that came in that day he would take them to the nail & say "nail, tockie, Santa Taws, chimmey." It was the first thing he thought of next morning & he was delighted to find his stocking & toys. His arm does not seem to trouble him at all now, so we hope it is all right.

Mother, I was so sorry to hear that your cough was troubling you again & hope it will not do so all the winter. Frank does not complain of Rheumatism much - his health is a great deal better than it was last winter. He is at home earlier than usual tonight & joins me in love to you all.

We killed our hog last week & I will be very busy packing tomorrow & the next day, as we will move on Monday. I think we will have a very comfortable home. Tell Brother Ed I hope he got to see Bessie Xmas. It is nearly ten o'clock at night, so I reckon it is time for me to stop writing. Hope to hear from you soon.

Your Affectionate Daughter,

G. E. Clinard

Francis A. (Frank) Clinard on his 55th birthday

Nora Shuford, Wm. L. Clinard and Lulu Powers, December 1894
Photo courtesy of The Hickory Landmarks Society

Personal Letters of L. N. Clinard 1879

F. A. Clinard to Mr. and Mrs. Livingston N. Clinard

Hickory, N. C.
January 5th 1879

Dear Father & Mother,

We wish you both a Happy New Year, if it is late. We expected a letter from you this last week, but were disappointed. Gertrude wrote you right after she received your Xmas present. She wore it New Years eve to a party given by Thomas H. Hardin. We had quite a gay time here Xmas & New Years. There was several parties, dances & oyster suppers given. Christmas day I took dinner at Philo Halls & got it between 3 & 4 o'clock & I was so hungry that I eat too much, it made me sick the balance of the evening. The Masons gave an Oyster Supper for the benefit of the Orphans & we made quite a success of it.

Well now about the weather. We have had & still have the coldest weather I ever felt. The mountains are all white & have been for several weeks. There is still a good deal of snow here & looks this evening like we are going to have more.

We moved last Monday, had a cold time for it, but we certainly have made a good change, have got comfortable rooms & more rooms in the house, have got 6 & a pantry room on our back porch. This house is plastered all over & good fire places. We have got a large pile of good dry wood & it cut up & at our back door. I have succeeded in getting away with a good deal of it today. Gertie says I am trying to run her out of the house with my big fires.

All the Ice houses in town are full of ice 4 in. thick.

Willie is using his arm again, as good as ever. He is now sitting cross legged, reading a newspaper with his Mamma. He has begun to call her Mamma at last & now he calls me Pappie & talks about Uncle Ed, Pa, & tries to say Grandma, but can't quite fix it up right. He calls Ed & Pa nearly every day & goes to the window & looks for them. He is talking a great deal more than he did. He rides his horse & calls him Ed. His play things are a great deal of pass time for him. He makes trains & hauls his baby, blows his whistle & makes all sorts of noises. He sees the train pass every day, right in front of our house & it pleases him mightily. You ought to have heard him talking about Claus, stakins & chimneys. At Xmas he hung up his stocking & we fixed it up for him. He was the proudest little fellow you ever saw. His Uncle Gaither gave him a large reindeer & slay with a laplander driving, he was proud of it, called it "my billy goat." He is begging for a pemmie now, he wants to write like me. He has a piece of paper & marking on it. We had several vows here at Christmas & the parties concerned got rid of several dollars, which went in the Town Treasury.

We sent a Negro to the Rail Road to work yesterday evening. He stole a pair of shoes from our store & Craig Shuford & myself went after him & caught him, got the shoes, brought him back, tried him & sent him to work on the Lenoir R. R. He started to run when we over took him, but we soon stopped him & he begged like a good fellow.

Trade has been dull since Xmas, owing to the very cold weather, the mountain wagons are frozen up. We sold a nice lot of Butter the other day at 18 cents. I thought of you & your butter. We have had very good luck so far with butter, have been selling at 15 cents for some time, but we ship mostly on orders.

I had a letter from Uncle Andy this week & Mollie & Blanche still join him in love.

Mother, I ate some of your souse for supper & have got a nice piece yet, but let me remark here, all the peppers are gone, to my sorrow. Eat the last yesterday.

I would have written to you sooner, but have been very busy, have been collecting & making out statements of accts. ever since I have been home. Gertie says tell you she is anxious to hear from you & to tell you she has been busy fixing up our new home. We were fooled awfully bad when we went to move. We thought we had about two loads goods & had five, besides what we carried by hand. Willie sends kisses to his dear Grandparents & Uncle Ed. Gertie & myself send love to you all.
Your Loving Son,
Frank

Blanche Clinard to Eddie (E. C.) Clinard

Athens
Jan. 15th 1879

Dear Cousin Eddie,

Your letter reached its destination safely last week and I assure you, it was very highly appreciated, your letters always are. Well, it has been two or three weeks since Christmas, but that won't keep me from writing something about it, it passed off very quietly, with the exception of a few fireworks and they had fantasies. I received a great many handsome presents, there were several very sad deaths, and there is still a good deal of sickness in Athens.

The weather is beautiful now, I hope it will stay so a long time, we have had a very little sleet or snow either, have you all had much? I have had a very severe cold for several weeks and have somewhat gotten over it now, but have a very bad sore throat, which you know is not very pleasant.

I haven't heard from Grandma for several weeks, Papa and I wrote to her, several days before Christmas and haven't received a reply to it yet, hope she is not sick. Neither have we heard from Cousin Frank in a long time. Cousin Eddie, you are very fortunate, your sweetheart being so near to you. I think mine is several hundred miles away from me. Oh! He is the nicest young man I nearly ever saw in my life, "except you."

Have you ever seen, or heard anything of "Eddison's Phonograph"? There are two gentlemen stopping at the Hotel now that are going around with it, they give entertainments in the different cities. I expect it is very interesting. I don't know though when they will give an entertainment in Athens.

There will soon be a concert given at Denprel's Hall, all the musical talent of Athens, composed of a great many gentlemen and ladies have joined it and have formed a Society called "Hayden Society." I expect it will be excellent, 50 cents admission. I am very glad, for Athens is the dullest place for young people to enjoy themselves, I ever saw in my life. Why, all of my correspondents nearly, are always writing to me about going to weddings and parties and all "sick like" and I don't get to go anywhere hardly, only to Prayer Meeting. Well, that is a splendid place to go to. I visit very little, I hardly ever have time for I am always working nearly.

Cousin Eddie, I wish you would have your picture taken and send it to me. I would prize it so much. Tell Alice Butner I think she is treating me right unkindly, not writing to me. Give my love to Uncle Livingston & Aunt

Mary, I hope she is well of her cold by now. Papa suffers more here lately, with dispepsia and headache than I ever knew him to. He blistered his forehead yesterday with some medicine he gets from the Drug Store, it relieved him somewhat, but not entirely. Ma is very well. Excuse my bad writing if you please, my pen is not a good one at all. I was just thinking of going to the Book Store to get me a good one. Remember me to Mr. Ackerman. What has become of Mr. Robert Pease, I met at your house? Is he still in Salem? You never say anything about him. I reckon you think I am never going to stop writing, but I love to write letters so much that when I get at it, I scarcely ever know when to quit, especially when I am writing to "you." I don't know of any more news now to write, so I will have to close. Write very soon and frequently, to your devoted cousin.
Blanche Clinard

F. A. Clinard to Mr. and Mrs. Livingston N. Clinard

Hickory, N. C.
Jany. 18th 1879

Dear Father & Mother,

We received your letter last week & it found us all well. I have been gone ever since Wednesday morning till last night. I had a terrible rough trip, went all over Caldwell Co. & found lots of ice & mud, the roads are nearly impassible. Cabbage has advanced to $2.65 per hundred #'s & butter 16 2/3, but few wagons running. Tom Coffey & Henry Taylor are about the only men that will venture out this weather. It is terrible cold here tonight, has been getting colder all day. There are a few ponds in this country that there has been scating on for a few days over four weeks.

Trade is dead, but I have had good luck collecting. I collected a debt this week of over $80.00 that has been standing nearly four years.

This evening Willie called "Grandpa" & "Uncle Ed" & then said "mew cow." He talks about the "mew cow" nearly every night & it is the only thing he is afraid of. He is talking a great deal. I am going to write a sentence now, like he says it. "Dive my ove to Grand mamma and a tiss. Grand Pa I ove you and Uncle Ed. I wide my hoss and have pun." He said all the above, just as I have got it down. He is looking at pictures now, can tell a mule from a horse.

We are going to get back the white woman that was cooking for us when you were up here Father. She came to see us the other day & wanted to come back so we hired her. Will come to us the first of Feby. I will feel safer when away from home, when she is here with Gertie. Gertie is looking better than I ever saw her look. She has gotten rid of those sores on her face & her complexion is clearer. She sends her love to you & says she will write to you soon again. She has been writing this evening to some of her Aunts.

You asked me if we have put up Shoats. I sold my sow & pigs for $5.00 & have not bought any yet. I want to put up two & see if I can't raise some big hogs this year. Your large hog weighed right well considering he would not eat well. Mother, I am fond of pickles & souse & wish I had some more. We will have a richer garden this year than we had before & hope to have better luck than last year.

Love to you all,
Frank A. Clinard

Katharine Willock to L. N. Clinard

OFFICE OF DR. SAMUEL S. FITCH
DR. H. T. WILLOCK - PHYSICIAN IN CHARGE
No. 49 East 29th Street,
Late of 714 Broadway
New York

February 1st 1879
Mr. L. N. Clinard

Dear Sir,

This is to notify you of the sad and unexpected death, on January 28th, 1879, from Typhoid Pneumonia, of our Brother, Samuel Sheldon Fitch, M. D., only son of our Father, the late Dr. Samuel Sheldon Fitch, who died December 25th, 1876, and to say that our Brother left all his affairs and practice to be conducted under his name as heretofore; also, that we have retained our Cousin, Dr. Henry T. Willock, a regular graduate in medicine from the same College as our late Brother, in the Medical Department, (in which he has been an assistant to our late Father and Brother for over sixteen years;) the said department now to be entirely under his care and sole management from this date. Our Father and Brother having always found him faithful and competent alike to their interest and to the best welfare of the numerous patients left under his charge during those years. He has, of course, a full and thorough knowledge and understanding of their system and mode of practice, as well as the virtues, action and application of the

215

various remedies made use of by them, and himself for them, in the successful treatment of Throat Diseases, Consumption, Asthma, Heart Disease, Liver Complaints, &c., &c .

And, in retaining him in the Medical Department, we feel confident that he will, as heretofore, devote his time and give his best energy and skill for the benefit of the sick, so that we cheerfully recommend him to the entire confidence and trust of our late Father and Brother's Patients, and others who may need and wish to avail themselves of his professional services.

Patients and all others who may write for consultation or advice, or for medicines, will please address Dr. Samuel S. Fitch, No. 49 East 29th Street, New York.-inside to Dr. H. T. Willock-

All medicines will be made according to the original Recipes, with the assistance of competent assistants, as heretofore. We are now in sole possession of all rights and title to manufacture all the Remedies made use of in the practice and for sale to Druggists and others.

We are now also the only ones representing our late Brother, and the only ones who have any legal right to practice and for sale to Druggists and others. We are now also the only ones representing our late Brother, and the only ones who have any legal right to collect moneys due him, to receive and open letters, sign checks, &c., addressed to or made payable in his name or the name of the late firm of Drs. S. S. Fitch & Son, which was retained by him after his Father's death.

Hoping that this will prove satisfactory to you, we remain,
Respectfully yours,
Katharine Willock Alexander n'ee Fitch
Emmeline Willock Fitch. Admy.

F. A. Clinard to Mr. and Mrs. Livingston N. Clinard

J. G. HALL,   P. C. HALL,

OFFICE OF

HALL BROTHERS,

Successors to HALL & PATTERSON,

Wholesale and Retail Dealers in General Merchandise,

Hickory, N. C.,

Feby 12th 1879

My Dear Father and Mother,

I received Bro Ed's letter this evening & was sorry to hear you are both sick, hope by this time you are better. We thought something was the matter, as we did not get a letter yesterday, our regular day. We are all well & getting along finely, have got our old cook back & we feel alright. She helps Gertrude a great deal with her sewing & is so much company for her.

We are having a cold rain tonight & I think it will turn to sleet, which I am in hopes it will, in order to put up price of Eggs. I have been, and am yet, in the Eggs speculation, have made some money & hope to make some more. A. C. Shuford, our Book Keeper, is my partner & we bought most of our Eggs from the firm. Hall Bro's encourage us in it.

Gaither had another boy born at his house Sunday, he weighed 9 #'s. Philo had one at his house about two weeks ago. Willie is still growing & talks all the time. He says any thing he wants to.

Ed writes me he will be married in May. We want him to come to see us, but I advised him to wait till June, for if nothing happens, as Jim Mickey use to say, Ed will be Uncle again.

Trade is rather dull just now, but I am kept busy collecting & keeping up correspondence. I have had splendid luck collecting, have collected some right large debts, that was made in 1875.

Gertie & Willie send love to you both. I had a letter from Aunt Carrie & she sent her love to you both & said she wanted to hear from you & see you all once more. She said she received an Almanac from you Father, which she was much obliged for. Good night.

Your Loving Son,

Francis

Aunt Carrie says she intends to write to you before long.

J. G. Hall to L. N. Clinard

J. G. HALL,
HALL BROTHERS, Hickory N. C.

P. C. HALL,
J. G. & P. C. HALL, Wilkesboro, N. C.

OFFICE OF
HALL BROTHERS
(Successors to HALL & PATTERSON)
Wholesale and Retail Dealers in General Merchandise

Feb. 20th 1879
Mr. L. N. Clinard

My Dear Sir,

Your letter of date the 6th inst. was duly received and should have been replied to at once, but its coming was just on the eve of my leaving home for a week and hence reply was deferred. Since my return home I have been exceedingly busy.

Now I propose to write briefly and frankly as to Frank & his prospects. This I have not said to Frank, nor will I say a word to him of it, but his habits have not been such as they ought to have been. Not that he has been to say discipated, but that he has drank he will not deny. That he has occupied no unimportant position in our business, one worthy of the highest degree of confidence and one that none other than the best of men could occupy, ought to have inspired him to guard all his actions. He has been faithful in the performance of his duties - he has been honest - only forgetting himself in the face of temptation, and allowing love of drink, to now & then get the best of him.

Has kept liquer concealed on the premises, & offered it secretly to younger boys about the store. In other aspects, his conduct has been unexceptional. These are facts I have never spoken to him of and yet he is aware that I know all & not two days ago, he addressed me a letter, asking me to forgive him and promising, God being his helper, never to in the least be led astray. I do truly forgive him.

He also begged in his letter that I would say nothing to him or anyone of it - that his cup was running over - and begging me also to let the past be forgotten, and to watch his future. I will not grieve him by saying a word, and would that you will not write to him upon this subject. Let him alone. He is now living as well as he could. I have no fear but that he will do well.

His idea of going into business for himself, it was not suggested by me, though he spoke to me of it. If I do not keep him it will be because the profits of our business will not justify it. Nothing has been spoken between us to mess our special relationship and intercourse, besides, we are "bound together - by stronger ties" - ask Ed Ackerman if I could claim the special use of these words and do him an injustice.

Very Truly Yours,

J. G. Hall

Tell George Rufe I will write him a long letter soon. Ask any Mason if these last words of mine are not the best I could find. My fourth child -a boy, was born on the 9th inst. at 9 o'clock & weighed 9 lbs, was then full 9 month old, a regular nine spot bouncing young fellow. Mother and child getting on as nicely as any indeed. His name it is thought, will be Joseph Gaither Hall. If he can stand it I can.

Gertrude E. to Mr. and Mrs. Livingston N. Clinard

Sunday

Hickory, N. C.

Feb. 23rd 1879

Dear Father & Mother,

We were sorry to hear that you were both sick again & hope as the warm weather comes on that your health may improve. We have very cold, disagreeable weather the first of last week, with snow & sleet, but it rained yesterday & is right warm today.

Frank is at church this morning. I did not feel well enough to walk so far, as the church is some distance from our home. We are going to lose our Pastor, Mr. Joiner. He has had a call to a different part of the state & this is his last Sunday here. He was a great favorite in all his congregation & we hate very much to give him up, especially as there is no one to take his place at present.

I am very thankful to write you that Frank is not drinking near so much as he did last winter & in fact, he has scarcely touched liquor for some time past. As I trust in the mercy of God, I pray most earnestly that my dear husband may be enabled to conquer this terrible habit forever. I have spoken to him about it & he seems truly anxious to do so.

Willie has just waked up & sends love & kisses to Grandpa & Grandma & Uncle Ed. He is quite well & growing larger all the time. Please give much love to all for Frank & me. Hoping to hear soon that you are well. I am as ever,

Your Affectionate Daughter, Gertrude E. Clinard

F. A. Clinard to Mr. and Mrs. Livingston N. Clinard

Hickory, N. C.
Mar. 9th 1879

My Dear Father and Mother,

Your letter received last week & we were glad to hear from you. I have had the pleasure of attending Court nearly all last week, Judge Greaves presiding. He only held court 1/2 days, owing to sickness, he was in bed balance of the time. I managed to get my case tried & the Negro I was witness against was sent to work on the R. Road.

Willie is writing a letter to you, he often talks about you & Uncle Ed, says you are on the Train. When I get a letter, he always says "letter from Grand Pa." He has been sick with a severe cold for several days, was threatened with croup a few nights ago. I have been unwell about a week with sore throat & a cold in my head. Last Sunday, I was in bed nearly all day & my eyes felt like they would go out & I was so deaf, I could hardly hear. I forgot to tell you about Willie singing a song every night when he gets sleepy. It is "By Baby Bunting, Daddy gone a hunting, to catch a rabbit skin, to wrap baby in."

We have had nice weather for the past week & need rain very much. We have not made any garden yet, are going to commence in the morning, would have made it last week if I had been at home.

We are having quite a good trade at present, but produce is awfull high. Cabbage is worth 3 cents, apples 1.00 per Bu., butter 10 to 12 1/2, bacon 7 1/4 hog round.

They are at work on the C. & N. Y. R. R. about 3 miles from Hickory, have got up the stockade 3 miles from here & about 70 hands at work.

Gertie is tolerbly well & says she will write you soon again. She is now singing to Willie at his request. We had quite a struggle with him, giving him a dose of Castor Oil.

Tell Ed to write to us again. We are anxious to hear from him. Please do not forget those receipts I wrote you for.

There has been a good deal of influenza in town in the past month. Nearly every body has had it. Gertrude has escaped so far & I am very much in hopes she will not get it. Willie sends love to his dear Grand parents & Uncle Ed. Gertie & myself send love to you all. Good night. Your Loving Son,
Frank

G. E. Clinard to Mr. and Mrs. Livingston N. Clinard

Hickory, N. C.
March 23rd 1879

My Dear Parents,

I intended writing to you last week, but was prevented from doing so. I was much distressed to hear of Mother's poor health, but trust she may regain her strength in time.

I suppose Brother Ed enjoyed his visit to his sweetheart very much. We want them to come to see us in the summer. We also would be delighted to have you & Mother pay us a visit. I think a change would help Mother. It would rest her for house-keeping is a great deal of trouble, especially when one does not feel well.

Willie takes a long walk with his Papa every Sunday & he enjoys it so much. They have been to walk this morning & are now both asleep. I wish you could hear Willie sing. He sings "Bye baby bunton," "Little Bopeep," & "Rock a bye baby in the tree top" so sweetly & pronounces all the words very distinctly. He can say almost anything he wants to now. He sometimes calls himself "Papa's dumage," (meaning Dutchman) & sometimes "Widdie Tinard." Everybody says he is a smart child.

Numie Clinard, youngest son of Wesley Clinard, was buried last Wednesday. He died of consumption.

We made our garden two weeks ago & all the early vegetables are up. I suppose Mother is getting on finely with her gardening. Frank has waked up & gone to work with Mr. Beard. Willie is still asleep. Give much love to all for us.

Your Affectionate Daughter,
G. E. Clinard

F. A. Clinard to Mr. and Mrs. Livingston N. Clinard

Hickory, N. C.
Mar. 24th 1879

I went out to see the N Gauge R. R. yesterday evening. They have it graded within 1 1/2 miles of Hickory. We got in a car load B. F. Averys Plows about two weeks ago and I have been advertising them by circular. I have sent out over a thousand besides a lot of papers Avery sent us.

I am very sorry to hear of Mother's ill health. She had better come up and stay with us this summer. It will do her good and we will be so glad to have her. From our house she can feast her eyes on mountains for hundreds of miles around. Tell Ed to communicate with us his proposed intentions.
Your son Frank

A. D. Clinard to Livingston N. Clinard

Newton House
Athens, GA
March 30th 1879

Dear Bro,

I drop a line to let you know how we all are. Myself and family are in usual health, but in great distress on account of the death of Mr. Wharton, my wife's Father, which took place on Friday last. I am totally at a loss what I shall do now. It may be that I will take charge of the Hotel, if I can make suitable arrangements with the owners of the property. I have no means at all to commence any business. I am temporarily managing the house, and will know in a few days what I will do, and will write you.
Yours as ever,
A. D. Clinard

F. A. Clinard to Mr. and Mrs. Livingston N. Clinard

J. G. HALL,   P. C. HALL,

OFFICE OF

HALL BROTHERS,

Successors to HALL & PATTERSON,

Wholesale and Retail Dealers in General Merchandise,

Hickory, N. C.,

April 8th 1879

Dear Father & Mother,

Since writing you last week we have all been sick & are suffering yet. Willie has been real bad off with a cold & he has the soarest mouth & nose you nearly ever saw. Gertrude has been sick with a cold also & is still suffering. I was in bed all yesterday evening suffering with my head & lungs, have been at work today & feel considerbly better.

Since we wrote you last we have weaned Willie from his bottle, or rather he weaned himself. He let his bottle drop & cut his hand & he said he would not have his old bottle any more. He said "nasty thing cut my hand, won't hab it." He has not had it for nearly two weeks, he still keeps growing.

Well, I guess dried fruit will be worth some thing this year, everything visible in this country has been killed. Wheat has been injured for the past week. The mountains have been covered with snow & we have had the full benefit of it. We are having quite a good trade this spring, have increased our wholesale trade a great deal, have taken out state license & will keep some one traveling nearly all the time. We issue a weekly circular every Monday morning & send to our customers. We are working up a big trade on Avery Plows. We have distributed a thousand papers , "Home & Farm," besides several hundred catalogues & large posters. It cost some postage & some work. I got up the names, which was quite a job. We have sold about $1000 worth of goods today.

Mother, I hope your health is still improving & as it gets warmer you will get better & stronger. Gertie & Willie send love to you both. Good night. Your Affectionate Son,

Frank

P. S. I enclose samples of circulars we change every week & we find it money well spent. The plow circular we issue only to good merchants.

G. E. Clinard to Mr. and Mrs. Livingston N. Clinard

April 20th 1879

Dear Father & Mother,

As Willie is away with Frank, I will take this opportunity to write to you. I never can write when Willie is with me because he is so restless. We had a good deal of rain during the past week & our garden is looking better. How is it with you?

Last week two children living about a mile from this place were badly bitten by a mad dog. The Dr. burnt them with a hot iron & so far they are all right, but I suppose the parents will feel a great uneasiness until the ninth day has passed.

This morning Willie took a long walk with his Papa & Dr. Baker. He got so tired coming home that he went to sleep & Frank had to carry him most of the way. He said it wore him out, for Willie is a right heavy load. He is growing larger all the time but getting taller & not so fleshy. He is entirely weaned from his bottle.

Tell Brother Ed he must not back out of coming to see us some time this summer. I told Willie he was coming & nearly every day he says "Uncle Ed tum on & see Willie." I don't think he has forgotten any of you. Every time Frank brings a letter home he says "etter from dan-pa" & listens while I read it. Give love to all for us, & accept much from
Your Affectionate Daughter,
G. E. Clinard

F. A. Clinard to Mr. and Mrs. Livingston N. Clinard

Hickory, NC
April 30 1879

My Dear Father and Mother,

I am am happy to inform you that we had a daughter born today at 3 o'clock P.M. She is very large & weighed 8 1/2 pounds. She has a full head of black hair, looks like Will. Willie has not seen it yet. I expect he will fight it. Gertie is doing well so far & sends love to you.

I write in a great hurry.
Your loving son,
F. A. Clinard

J. G. HALL,   P. C. HALL.

OFFICE OF

Hall Brothers,

SUCCESSORS TO HALL & PATTERSON,

WHOLESALE AND RETAIL DEALERS IN GENERAL MERCHANDISE,

Hickory, N. C., 30th April 1879.

My Dear Father & Mother,

I am happy to inform you that we had a daughter born to day at 3 o'clock P.M. She is very large & weighed 8½ lb, She has a full head of black hair, looks like Will. Willie has not seen it yet, I expect he will fight it. Gertie is doing well so far & sends love to you,

I write in a great hurry.

Your loving Son

J. A. Clinard

F. A. Clinard to Mr. and Mrs. Livingston N. Clinard

Hickory, N. C.
May 4th 1879

Dear Father & Mother,

I wrote you on Wednesday last telling you of the birth of our daughter. Well now you know we are happy with our two babys. The little lady is doing finely & I am glad to say Gertrude is getting along splendid so far & she says she intends to take care of her self. Willie is the best pleased little fellow you ever saw, has had several fights for "my ittle sister" as he calls her. Dr. B. told him he was going to take her off & Will took the broom & let in on him & said "you shant have my little sister." At first he did not know what to make of it & kept telling Mamma to get up. He says he is Papa's baby & ittle sister is Mamma's baby.

Well our baby has a full head of black hair & favors Will, has got a head exactly shaped like his. She has been a good baby so far, has not cried any hardly. She sleeps & eats. Gertie has a great deal of milk, has to have her breasts drawn two or three times a day. She had full a half gallon drawn at one time today, you never saw the like. Gertie has named her Estelle Lenoir, her own middle name & her Mother's middle name. I named Will, so she named this one. We will call her Estelle.

Well we had a success of our Grand Opening, sold lots of goods, between 5 & 6000 dollars worth & had a good many merchants to visit us, made several new customers. We certainly were kept busy.

Thursday night we had a heavy frost & damaged beans & potatoes. I have not received those Tomato plants you wrote me you would mail. If you have not sent them, send by Express in a box. I will pay at this end of line, they will come so much safer.

Mad Dog excitement has been running high here for the past two weeks. There were several parties bitten & a number of dogs, there has been six or seven dogs run mad from the bites. There has been a general war on dogs through this country. Every dog that is caught in our streets is shot down. I have shot two. There was a young woman that has just been married about 4 mo., was attacked in the road and bitten in the breast & face. I have heard that she went mad & died, but I do not know it to be the truth. I saw the woman a few days after she was bitten. There were two boys near town that were bitten, but they are alright.

Gertrude & Willie join me in love to you both & Ed. Estelle would send you a message, but she is asleep. Your Loving Son, Frank

A. D. Clinard to Eddie (E. C.). Clinard

Newton House
Athens, GA
May 7th 1879

Dear Eddie,

It occurs to me that I owe you a letter, but if not I feel it my duty to write you any way. I have learned through letters to Blanche that you are to be married on the 14th inst. This will be to you the most important event of your life and one which incurs great responsibility. I think you are right to marry and I doubt not you have made a wise selection for a companion. Permit me to advise you to ever be mindful of your wife's comfort & happiness. Let home be the happiest place on earth. Be sober, industrious & economical. I doubt not but you will be all this, but a hint from me can do no harm and may make an impression upon your mind, which may result in good. I often see drummers who know you and all speak very highly of you.

I received a letter from Frank today. He states he had a daughter born on the 30th of April. I am glad all are doing well. He states that your Father and Mother are in bad health, this is sad indeed that both are sick at the same time. Present my love to them. I hope they may soon recover health. My wife & Blanche join in love to you and them. Write me as soon as you can after your Marriage, and as soon as convenient send us a likeness of yourself & wife. We are all in usual health.

Your Uncle Andrew

F. A. Clinard to Mr. and Mrs. Livingston N. Clinard

J. G. HALL,   P. C. HALL,
OFFICE OF
HALL BROTHERS,
Successors to HALL & PATTERSON,
Wholesale and Retail Dealers in General Merchandise,
Hickory, N. C.,

May 8th 1879

My Dear Parents,

I am very much grieved to hear you are both in such bad health now. You take my advise, after Ed is married let them keep house for you & you come up & spend a month or so with us. It will rest you both & recruit you up.

The change will be the very best thing you possibly could do & we would be delighted to have you with us. The good mountain air & change of life & scenes will do you more good than any thing you can possibly do. If you could not leave a month, stay two weeks or as long as you can. Write me what you think of it.

Well Gertie & Will, I mean Estelle, are getting along splendid so far & I am in hopes they will continue. Baby is the best little thing so far I ever saw. She never cries. She is a bright, sweet little creature. I wish so much you could see her.

We are all aglow with Rail Roads at present. The Narrow Gauge is being finished here today & several gentlemen started out this morning to get the right of way between here & Lincolnton for the Carolina Central R. R. They are going to work on it at once. Then we will have three roads running here.

We are having a big trade so far & we hope it will continue. Gertie sends love & Will kisses. Will don't like to go bare footed, he says rocks hurt his feet. Love to you both.

Your Loving Son,

Frank

P. S. I received plants ok & set them out. They look alright so far, please accept thanks.

F. A. Clinard to Mr. and Mrs. Livingston N. Clinard

J. G. HALL,   P. C. HALL,

OFFICE OF

HALL BROTHERS,

Successors to HALL & PATTERSON,

Wholesale and Retail

Dealers in General Merchandise,

Hickory, N. C.,

May 20th 1879

Dear Father & Mother,

We are very much surprised that we have not received a letter from you or Ed. We thought certain one of you would write us. Gertie & Estelle are getting along finely. Gertie is up & going about & is much stronger than when Willie was born. The baby has been remarkably good so far. She is getting as fat as a butter ball.

I noticed last week that Patterson & Co. had dissolved. Why did you not write me? I saw it in a paper the same day got your letter. Do you intend to stay with Mr. Fries Father?

Our garden is looking well, considering the dry weather we had on it, but the little striped bugs & cut worms are playing havoc with my plants, have cut down three tomato plants for me.

We have had a big Tobacco trade for the past week. Our general trade holds up better than we expected. We all send love & baby & Will kisses for their dear grand parents.

Your Loving Son,
Frank A. Clinard

Robert F. Williams to L. N. Clinard

Robert F. Williams & Co. Importers and Wholesale Grocers
Richmond, VA

July 23rd 1879
L. N. Clinard, Esq.
Salem, N. C.

Dear Sir,

We are in receipt of yours of the 21st inst., and in reply would say that there is no Physician who makes a specialty of such diseases. Drs. F. D. Cunningham, R. J. Coleman, John G. Skelton and J. H. McCarn are about the most skilled practitioners in our city.

Yours very truly,
Robert F. Williams & Co.

E. Burke Haywood to L. N. Clinard

Raleigh, N. C.
July 23rd 1879
Mr. L. N. Clinard
Salem N.C.

Dear Sir,

I prefer that you should bring your wife to Raleigh. I can then examine her thoroughly and advise you what to do. I am of the opinion that it would not be necessary for her to remain in the city longer than one to two days. You will please stop at some hotel and report to me on arrival.
Yours respectfully,
E. Burke Haywood M. D.

F. A. Clinard to Mr. and Mrs. Livingston N. Clinard

J. G. HALL,   P. C. HALL,
OFFICE OF
HALL BROTHERS,
Successors to HALL & PATTERSON,
Wholesale and Retail Dealers in General Merchandise,
Hickory, N. C.,

July 29th 1879

My Dear Father and Mother,

I ought to have written to you sooner, but have been very busy. Mr. Shuford, my help in the office, has been gone for the past week, so I have been unusually busy, worked late every night.

I am sorry to say that Gertrude does not improve very fast. She is very weak & suffers every few days with severe headaches. She has had quite a number of severe sores to contend with. Willie was quite sick last week cutting his stomach teeth, but is about well again. I don't think I can take him to Salem. I am afraid that it would make him sick & be too much for you Mother. He is a tearre, is on the trot & talk all day.

Sis Annie still has our baby & she is the brightest, sweetest little thing you ever saw. She is prettier than Willie. I have a wet nurse for her, the one that nursed Willie. She is a convenient darkey.

We are having fine rains & every thing is looking well. I have got the finest lot of Tomatoes you ever saw & more different kinds. There are some large yellow ones that I think is the finest flavored tomato I have ever seen. Our cow is doing splendid, is getting fat & gives a gallon & a half at a time. She is a rich red with dark muzzle & legs, thin neck & small tail. Will be a beauty when she gets right fat.

Our old cook has gone home to get married & we have in her stead, Susan Bradford, Cratons daughter. We like her very well so far. Gertie & Willie sends much love to you both, also to Uncle Ed & Aunt Bessie. Tell Ed to write to me, he owes us a letter. Love to you all. I must get to work, as the month is nearly gone & my work not done.

Your Loving Son,
F. A. Clinard

F. A. Clinard to Mrs. Livingston N. Clinard

HICKORY BOARD OF TRADE
Secretary's Office
Hickory, N. C.

August 25th 1879

My Dear Mother,
You can not imagine how delighted we were to get your kind letter yesterday. If some one had sent me $100,000, I could not have been more surprised. Your advise is very good & I thank you for it. I wish so much you were able to come to see us all. It would do you good, as well as us.

Well I am happy to write you that Gertie has improved wonderfully in the past two days. She sat up a short while today for the first time & she is cheerful & thinks she will improve. Dr. Baker is very attentive to her & does all he can to relieve her. I think Dr. Scroggs will be here this week & I will call him in. G's womb trouble is much better, but her kidneys are affected with some disease like "diobetis" or some such a name. She is not allowed to eat sweet things, or any thing that contains any sugar. I am in hopes, by close nursing & careful watching, Gertrude will soon be up & going about.

For the last 40 days & nights, we have had rain & every thing is so damp that I am fearful it will cause sickness. Diptheria has been in several families near town, but not fatal.

We hear from Willie every few days. He is much better & is enjoying himself finely. I saw Tommy Lenoir Saturday from up there & he says Sam & every body up there takes his time playing with him. He is boss of the whole house. I expect he will be hard to get to come home again. Estelle is growing finely & is very bright. She has had some cold for the past few days, I wish so much you could see her.

Well Mother, Hickory has been, & is still, crowded with visitors, both Hotels are over run. I have not been to a single party or dance this summer, have been very busy at work & trouble so much that I have not felt like doing any thing. Gertie has been so very low several times this summer that we thought she could not live. I am glad to hear you think you are better, hope you will continue to improve, be prudent.

There has been an excursion passed here every few days for the past three months. I saw all the Clemmonsville boys a few weeks ago up here on an excursion. I showed them through our store, & they say we beat Pfohl & Stockton, which I recon Ed would not admit. We are buying all the berries through W. N. C. & giving from 4 to 5 cents per #.

Gertrude is 23 years old today. Today 2 years ago was the time she was at her lowest, in the Valley. She sends much love to you & says she wishes so much she could see you. Give our love to Father. Love to you from
Your Affectionate Son,
Frank A. Clinard

F. A. Clinard to Mr. and Mrs. Livingston N. Clinard

J. G. HALL,   P. C. HALL,
OFFICE OF
HALL BROTHERS,
Successors to HALL & PATTERSON,
Wholesale and Retail Dealers in General Merchandise,
Hickory, N. C.,

Sept. 16th 1879

My Dear Father and Mother,
    I have landed back home again after having a pleasant trip to Georgia. I staid in Atlanta two days & saw the city, had a very pleasant time, done some business. Went over to Athens & spent 2 nights & one day & was very cordially welcomed by Uncle Andrew's family. Blanche took a duck fit over me. Aunt Mollie is a beautiful woman & was just as clever & kind to me as any one possibly could be. They begged & plead with me to stay longer, but I could not, as I was uneasy about Gertrude. I left her with Sis Annie while I was gone, she does not improve very much.

233

Atlanta is a pretty city. I like it better than Philadelphia. Athens is also a pretty place & lots of business done there. I think Uncle A. is doing a good business. He had good arrivals every day. I looked over his register, the Hotel is right well furnished. Blanche has a new piano & plays well on it. Uncle Andrew has some fine hogs, he can come up to you.

I am in hopes you are better Mother by this time & as the cold weather comes on you will grow stronger. We are very busy just now getting in some new goods & buying dried fruits. We are up to 7 cents on B. Berries now. The biggest thing I saw while gone was making Ice. It certainly is a strange process. I was 50 ft. down in Ice & it looked all round me like a crystal palace. The proprietor showed me through & I asked him price of Ice & he said 25 cents per 100 #'s. Think of it. We pay 2 & 2 1/2 here, where nature makes it for nothing.

I think I will go to see Willie on Saturday. We hear from him every few days, he is getting along finely. Our baby has been quite unwell for the past week. We all send love.
Your Affectionate Son,
Frank A. Clinard

F. A. Clinard to Mr. and Mrs. Livingston N. Clinard

J. G. HALL,   P. C. HALL,
OFFICE OF
HALL BROTHERS,
Successors to HALL & PATTERSON,
Wholesale and Retail Dealers in General Merchandise,
Hickory, N. C.,

Sept. 23rd 1879

My Dear Father and Mother,
Your letter received, glad to hear you are improving Mother, hope you will continue. I am sorry to have to write you that our baby is very sick, has not slept for two days & nights & Dr. says if she does not soon sleep, she can't last much longer. I hardly think she will live 24 hours. She looks now like a corpse. It is making Gertrude worse, as she stays by her all the time & it is more than she can stand.

I went up to see Willie Saturday night. He is doing finely, has improved very much, has grown & got fatter & his color is much better. He is well contented with his Aunt Mollie, as he calls her, & she is perfectly devoted to him. He seems to be boss of the whole house hold & does as he pleases but he is obedient & as mannerly a child for his age as I ever saw. Every body that sees him remarks that he has the best table manners of any child his age they ever saw. He is one of the cleanest children you ever saw, keeps his clothing nice & his hands & face clean.

Our dear little baby has Cholera Infantum. There are several cases of Typhoid Fever in town, has been one death. Will write soon again.
Your Son,
Frank A. Clinard

M. E. Vogler to Joe

SALEM FEMALE ACADEMY
Founded 1802
Rev. J. T. ZORN, Principal
SALEM, N. C.

Sept 23rd 1879

Dear Joe,

It was my intention to write to you on Sunday, but as I had not seen the children in two days, I thought I would better wait until I could go over. I was over yesterday evening. I went by Martha's & took Mamie with me, as I had promised Emma I would bring her down some evening she went with me once before and when we left Emma said she wanted "that girl" to stay & play with her, so I promised to bring her some other time. It was seven o'clock when we got there. Anna was teaching Henry his grammar lesson; Emma & Mr. were playing, & wife Mary was sitting in the kitchen stringing beans for pickling. She had about three pecks in the basket.

Emma says her sores are well and she was very lively.

When we got through with the lessons, we all helped Mary string beans. I wished you could see us all crowded around the basket we talked of you being in Bethlahem & probably just talking to your brothers. Mary thinks Emma a very smart, bright little thing; you ought to have seen Emma hug & kiss her & the old lady returning it with interest. I think it pleases her very much that Emma takes to her and it is so much better for the child, for then she won't get impatient with her. She says the boys are doing well too.

Miss Fogle gave me quite a favorable report of Henry's progress in school a few days ago. She says he can spell better now than Frank Miller.

Anna did not take Emma to Lovefeast on Sunday, as she thought it too damp to walk in slippers; the boys went with Mr. Miller's.

Miss Mary is getting a good many cucumbers. She said you did not tell her to pickle any in salt brine for Winter and said there was a slave there she could use for the purpose; I told her she would better use it after filling all the jars. Do you want her to put grape leaves in, or only brine?

Although it was a raw, drizzly, cloudy day on Sunday, the services were all well attended. Mother went down morning & afternoon. It did one good to hear dear Mr. Rondthaler's voice again. The church was very prettily decorated. Mr. Schweinitz was not able to come down, but he sent a message to the congregation, which Mr. Rondthaler delivered in the Lovefeast.

Yesterday Mary & I called to see Mrs. Leibert. She told Mary, Ed & his wife were very comfortably located in the Castle. She heard them say they were expecting company.

What day will you go up to Nazereth? And when to Mauch Chunk? I wish I knew so I could be with you in spirit. When you go to Anoko Glen be sure when you get to the top where that parting is, to walk on farther until you get a view of the other valley. Nobody told us before we went up, & so we missed that and they say the view is very fine. To climb up that rugged glen is hard work and I am afraid Willie can't do it with his lame foot. Please give my love to Mrs. Oerter, Mr. de Schweinitz's, Helen especially, and all enquiring friends, also your brothers and their wives. I fear you will not find Miss Ruderman in Bethlahem. I hope you will enjoy your stay in Bethlehem very much. Don't be uneasy about home, everything is going right there. All send love to you both.

Very Affectionately, your loving sis,

M. E. Vogler

F. A. Clinard to Mr. and Mrs. Livingston N. Clinard

J. G. HALL,   P. C. HALL,
OFFICE OF
HALL BROTHERS,
Successors to HALL & PATTERSON,
Wholesale and Retail Dealers in General Merchandise,
Hickory, N. C.,

Sept. 29th 1879

My Dear Father and Mother,

I am sorry to have to write you that our dear little Babe is in a very critical condition. I hardly think she will survive this attack, although she may. She has all the attention any one possible could have. I have a splendid wet nurse for her & she gets all the nourishment she will take. She may survive, but it will be miraculous if she does. She has been brighter for several days, till last night, she was taken worse. Has not slept any today till late this evening she went to sleep. She was as stout a child as Willie was till she got sick. Now she is one of the poorest looking objects you ever saw. Gertie is some better & would improve right away, but for the care of baby. We have moved her home. She has been at Sister Annie's ever since she was six weeks old till last Thursday.

There is a good deal of Typhoid fever in town now, have been two deaths in the past week. There are four cases near my house. I have had my premeses thougherly cleaned & hope to escape. I am skinnier than I have been for 3 years past, have been hard worked, troubled, & sat up a great deal with Gertie & baby.

Tell Ed, I think he or Sister Bessie might write to us. We are situated so we can't be punctual writing you as I would like to be, but some times it is impossible for me to be. I am sorry to hear you have lost your good health, for we were so in hopes you would improve this fall.

Mother, we often think & talk of you, wish so much we lived closer so we could see each other oftener. Mother, my peppers turned out alright this year & I have a nice lot of them put up. We have a splendid cow. She is getting fat & is a perfect beauty. She is a nearly Thougherbred Devon.

I sent Willie's shoes to him, but have not heard from them yet. I do hope they will fit him, they are the nicest I have seen any where. We all send love & hope to be able to send a more favorable report from baby in a few days.
Your Loving Son,
Frank A. Clinard

Livingston L. Clinard to Mrs. Livingston N. Clinard

H. W. Fries,
Dealer in General Merchandise,
And Buyer of Country Produce.
Salem N. C.

October 21, 1879

My darling, Mrs. Barrow asked me on yesterday to ask you for your Ehrichs Fashion book. I forgot to ask you yesterday or this morning. Will you please send it over?
Lovingly & truly, Livingston

Gertrude Clinard to Mrs. Livingston N. Clinard

Dec. 15th 1879
My Dear Mother,

At last your Ottoman is finished & I trust you will like it. It is entirely a Hickory production, so you may judge from it what sort of work we can get done here. Please tell Father I received his letter & am glad he liked the handkerchiefs.

We had a dreadful rainy Sunday, but it is clear & cold today. How are you getting on now? I hope your health may be better through the winter than it was in the warm weather. My own health is somewhat better, but I have a dreadful bad cold at present, & the baby too is sick with cold. The Dr. told me not to keep her too closely confined to the house, but to take her out into the fresh open air. I took her visiting today a little while & everybody said she looked beautiful in her new cloak & hood. I am afraid the visiting didn't do her much good, for she hasn't closed her eyes today, & won't go to sleep tonight. She is crying now & the nurse shakes the room so in her efforts to keep her quiet that I am afraid you can't read this scratching. I am nearly crazy to see Willie. Please give much love to Father, brother Ed & Sister Bessie & Aunt Eliza. Frank also sends love. Accept much love for yourself from
Your loving daughter,
Gertrude
P. S. We would have had a cord put around the top, but could not get color to match. I wish you & Father a very happy Xmas, wish we could be together. Love to all of you.
Your Son, Francis. Ottoman goes by today's Express.

World's Dispensary Medical Association to Mary E. Clinard

Dec. 24, 1879
Mary E. Clinard,
Salem, N.C.

Dear Madam

We have carefully read your esteemed letter, and feel confident that we can restore your health. We have made a special study of pulmonary diseases, and are able to cure most forms of colds, catarrh, hoarseness, affections of the throat, coughs, and chronic bronchitis. The symptoms you so accurately describe are associated with increasing debility, loss of vigor, energy and flesh with palpitation, difficulty of breathing, dizziness, nervousness, copious perspiration after slight exertion, crawling, chilly sensations followed by hot flushes; with irritation in the throat, and lungs, and sometimes loss of blood through the mouth, or again with constriction, nausea, and vomiting, pain in the chest, dyspepsia, derangement of the bowels, and general functional disturbance, until the patient becomes very much emaciated; is tormented by an unceasing cough, exhausting sweats, or diarrhea, and rapidly sinks. Although you do not have, at present, all these symptoms, they will soon follow, if your complaint is not arrested. Your case being a complicated one, it requires specially-prepared medicines that are adapted to the conditions present. If unable to visit us in person, we feel confident that we can treat you successfully at your home, by preparing the necessary medicines and sending them by express or mail. Our treatment will remove the cause of the disease, counteract its effects, and substitute healthy for morbid actions and conditions. They purify and enrich the blood, carry off all the irritating and poisonous products of abnormal forces, compose the nerves, ameliorate the cough, difficulty of breathing, and palpitation of the heart, and improve the general health. We advise you to exercise in the open air, as much as your strength will permit. Eat plentifully of good, nutritious food, and observe the directions for the general management of health, to be found in the "Common Sense Medical Adviser." Sincerely Yours, World's Dispensary Medical Association.

P. S. Our terms will be $20.00 for first month's treatment, and $10.00 per month thereafter, including all necessary meds.

HYGIENIC RULES.

The following Rules should be observed by all who are afflicted with any Chronic, or Lingering, Disease:

RULE 1st.—Use no alcoholic drinks or tobacco. Warm drink taken with the meals is preferable to cold, but tea and coffee should be used sparingly, and not be made strong.

RULE 2d.—Let your diet consist of wholesome food, properly prepared, such as well-baked bread, lean meats, thoroughly-cooked vegetables, and also berries and other fruits. Eat at regular intervals, and partake of nothing between meals.

RULE 3d.—Let your supper be of plain food, which will digest easily. Rich pastries, sweetmeats, and highly-seasoned viands, are contra-indicated and not allowable. Let the conversation at the table be lively and entertaining, for good cheer is a promoter of good digestion.

RULE 4th.—In order that the sleep be refreshing and restorative, let it be obtained in a pure atmosphere. The room should be large and well ventilated. Retire early, and get as much sleep as is required.

RULE 5th.—A bath should be taken every day. Cold baths should be taken in a room where the air is comfortably warm. A bathing-tub is not essential to a good bath. A hand or sponge bath can be made available by the use of an ordinary wash-basin or bowl. Use cool, soft water, and follow by brisk friction with a coarse towel or flesh-brush. Salt put in the bathing water two or three times a week materially aids in the cure of chronic diseases. If a *bath* be not taken daily, rub the entire surface of the body every morning with a flesh-brush or coarse towel, until the skin is in a perfect glow. A warm bath should be taken twice a week, in the evening.

RULE 6th.—Freely inhale the fresh air, in order that the blood in the lungs may be purified, and what you have eaten be transformed into blood, muscle, and bone. Outdoor exercise is necessary, provided the invalid be able to take it, either on foot, horseback, or in a carriage. Some light, pleasant employment is beneficial in the cure of most chronic diseases. It must not, however, be indulged in so as to produce fatigue. If the invalid be too weak to exercise, he should, in warm weather, sit in the open air and sunshine. Sunshine is as necessary to the growth and health of animal life as to vegetable existence. The human being, like the plant, sickens and grows weak and tender if constantly kept in the shade.

RULE 7th.—Cultivate the genial sentiments of social and domestic life. Do not fret over "spilled milk," but turn over a new leaf and resolve to live a different life. Exercise your will in the right direction.

RULE 8th.—Observe the above hygienic rules, take the medicines as directed, and you will enjoy the great satisfaction, as thousands of others have done. of seeing and feeling the bloom of health return. Do your duty well. and, after having done it, you may safely leave the rest to Him "who doeth all things well."

BUFFALO, N. Y.   **WORLD'S DISPENSARY MEDICAL ASSOCIATION.**

Note.—Further hygienic advice is given in "THE PEOPLE'S COMMON SENSE MEDICAL ADVISER." Price, $1.50 (post-paid).

Personal Letters of L. N. Clinard 1880

World's Dispensary Medical Association to Mary E. Clinard

W. D. M. A.

WORLD'S DISPENSARY MEDICAL ASSOCIATION BUFFALO AND LONDON

Consultation Rooms at Invalids' Hotel

For The Treatment Of All

CHRONIC DISEASES

Of Either Sex,

Particularly Those Of A

Delicate, Obscure, Complicated, or Obstinate Character

Buffalo, N. Y.

Jan 6th 1880
Mrs. L. N. Clinard

Your favor, containing $20.00, received. After a careful consideration of your case, medicine has been prepared, with full instructions, and expressed this day to Salem N. C. Hoping that you will take it as directed, deriving the utmost benefit therefrom, and report the result when all taken,
We are, very respectfully,
WORLD'S DISPENSARY MEDICAL ASSOCIATION.

DIRECTIONS.

For *Mrs. L. N. Clinard*

As many patients prefer not to have labels on the bottles or packages containing medicines prescribed for their use, we adopt the plan of labeling each bottle or package simply with the name of the medicine contained therein, and

IN THIS ENVELOPE

will be found corresponding labels to those on bottles or packages, giving directions for each medicine.

WORLD'S DISPENSARY MEDICAL ASSOCIATION,
BUFFALO, N. Y., and LONDON, Eng.

A. D. Clinard to Livingston N. Clinard

Clinard House
Athens, GA
Jan. 26th 1880

Dear Brother,

I have neglected writing you longer than I ought, but I have been in a strain for a month moving & fixing up. I have been doing a fine business since I moved to my new place. My old customers have followed me beyond my expectations. Nearly all the citizens of the town are in sympathy with me. I am doing fully 5/6 of the business in my line though I have not got a regular Hotel building. I have a residence and some rooms over stores. 14 in all, and carpeted. We are in usual health except colds. I heard from Frank a few days ago. They were getting along very well.

Your friend J. W. Harrison, of Richmond, has been stopping with me since Saturday, will leave tomorrow. He thinks a great deal of you. He and Blanche are taking on considerably. I must close. All join in love to all. Write soon. I hope your dear wife is improving in health. Blanche & I often speak of her kind attention to us when at your house. We would be delighted to see you all again.
Yours as ever,
A. D. Clinard

F. A. Clinard to Mr. and Mrs. Livingston N. Clinard

J. G. HALL,   R. L. PATTERSON
Office of HALL BROTHERS,
WHOLESALE AND RETAIL DEALERS IN
General Merchandise.
HIGHEST MARKET PRICE PAID FOR ALL COUNTRY PRODUCE
Hickory, N. C.,

Feby 11th 1880

Dear Father & Mother,

Your letter received today, glad to hear you are both better. We are all tolerbly well & our babies are growing finely.

You spoke of Butner selling his Hotel. I have it from good authority that W. F. Blackwell & Co. of Durham are going to buy Butner's Hotel & the old

Zevely house & turn the latter into a Tobacco factory. If such be the case it will help out Salem very much. Our Tobacco interests here look very bright at present. I am striving to make my business a success. If I do, I will make some money. I have a substantial man & a good judge of Tobacco for my partner. We are going to sell Guano, which will pay us a commission of 15% over and above freights & Co. I wrote my first advertisement, which you will see in this weeks Press. You said in your letter that you were not aware that I intended going into the Tobacco business. Neither was I, or any one else, 24 hours before I did. I saw a good chance & made for it at once. The snow favored me in helping me make the trade I did. I have been on the lookout for some time past for some sort of business to embark in. You were aware of that, for I wrote you several times. I have found out one thing, & that is, if a man expects to make any money or a name for himself, he must go in business & not work on a salary. Today there are not ten saleried men in North Carolina that are making any thing besides their bread & meat & clothing. I must look ahead. I have some children that I expect to try & give good educations, for I know what it is to be without education.

I hope you will be able to come to see us this summer. I know it will do you good.

Our children are both very sprightly. Will has got the best memory I ever saw. He can memorize any thing very quickly & he never repeats any thing till he can say it all. He will sit perfectly still & listen & when he knows it, will say he does & always does. I do not want him to crowd his brain while so young. Gertie, Willie & Estelle send love to Grand pa & Grand ma & want to see them very much.

Your Loving Son,
Francis A. Clinard

HALL & DANIEL,
—— TOBACCO MANUFACTURERS, ——

HICKORY, N. C.

HALL BROTHERS, GENERAL AGENTS,

Offer to the Trade the following Brands:

Brand.	Size.	Plugs to ℔.
Waverly,	11 inch,	4
Gold Coin	11 "	5
" "	10 "	6
Little Katie	10 "	6
Marble Hall	10 "	6
Swannanoa	10 "	6
Game Cock	11 "	5
Sparkling Catawba	11 "	5
Hancock Twist	6 "	12 Caddies
English "	6 "	16 "
Campaign "	10 "	9
Choice o' the Club Twist	10 "	8
Hall's Medeira (Plug)	6 "	8 Caddies.

These Tobaccos, without doubt, are as honest and reliable in quality as can be bought elsewhere. Write for prices and terms.

HALL & DANIEL.

Hall's
Warehouse
For the Sale of Leaf Tobacco.
HICKORY, N. C.

"We take great pleasure in bringing our TOBACCO WARE HOUSE more prominently to your attention.

You have doubtless noticed ere this, that in this long cherished enterprise of ours, we at last have a competitor for your patronage. In this we feel gratified, and especially so since we can cheerfully say that we have gentlemen to compete with, who are "worthy of our steel." Mesa Whey & Mcryen who now enter the list with us in asking the encouragement and patronage of all TOBACCO PLANTERS are thus helping us to realize the long cherished hope of

A Tobacco Market at Hickory

Firmly and Surely Established.

And now that our efforts are so far crowned with success, we can with confidence come before the PUBLIC and assert truthfully, that to the past, through our efforts, all tobacco had shipped here has in its average price brought more money to the planter, than same leaf would have brought in any market far or near.

If such be the case may we not soon hope that greater success will follow our efforts in the future?

With competition in the sale of Leaf Tobacco, we accept the truth that

Competition is the Life of Trade,

With five factories, and possibly two more ready to go to work, as soon as the weather opens suitable for working, and all desiring to secure their Leaf here. This of itself gives

COMPETITION

among buyers, which should attract the attention of all Tobacco Growers, who are in search of

A GOOD MARKET.

Leaf Dealers everywhere, are ready to flock here so soon as they know that we have good leaf and plenty of it to offer.

The Senior of our firm is himself managing partner of the largest Tobacco Factory in N, C., West of Winston, and is ready to pay

CASH FOR
500,000 POUNDS
Good Leaf

In this market. To this end he will attend all sales in either of the WARE HOUSES at this place.

We may yet have to meet argument, and questions as to the truth of our ability to get the full value for all Tobacco brought to us, so we will proceed here to

ANSWER THEM IN ADVANCE.

Q. What is tobacco worth in your market?

A. All good, well handled tobacco is worth its full value upon any market and STOCK such as is suited to the uses of our manufacturers is worth more here than elsewhere, for the reason that our manufacturers must have it, and will pay higher for it rather than seek it in older markets, at a greater expense for buying, freight charges &c.

Q. Will fine tobacco sell well in YOUR MARKET?

A. We guarantee satisfactory sale of Fine Tobacco, in that we will prize and ship else where, without charge, any lot of tobacco, with the prices of which the planter is not satisfied, and we say this in good faith.

Q. Are your buyers able to pay cash for any and all purchases?

A. We guarantee the cash on all sales as soon as made, and that to any amount brought us.

Q. Are there any Rings or Combinations against the planter on your market?

A. We know our interests too well, to allow such to exist around us. All success in this country must be built up by encouraging the various industries of the country. Both common honesty and common policy and interest, would frown down any combination against the planter.

Excuse us for saying that our record is before you. No industry of the country has ever been brought to our notice, that we have not zealously tried to give it strength.

Let all who have tobacco to sell, consider what we say intelligently and without prejudice and we fear not the result of your conclusions will be

TO PATRONIZE US.

We beg to say in conclusion that our facilities for handling Tobacco properly will be surpassed by none. We have a commodious WARE HOUSE soon to be remodelled, with SKY LIGHTS and all necessary Trucks, Scales, &c. Wagon yard and shelter for wagons. Stables for horses, and a comfortable room for

WAGONERS.

We have a first class AUCTIONEER, polite and accommodating, whole souled and clever Tongued, whom we re-introduce as, HAL FETTER.

Very Respectfully,

Nov. 17th, 1879.   **HALL BROTHERS,**

PIEDMONT PRESS PRINT.

F. A. Clinard to Mr. and Mrs. Livingston N. Clinard

J. G. HALL,   R. L. PATTERSON

Office of HALL BROTHERS,
WHOLESALE AND RETAIL DEALERS IN
General Merchandise.
HIGHEST MARKET PRICE PAID FOR ALL COUNTRY PRODUCE
Hickory, N. C.,

March 15th 1880

My Dear Father and Mother,

It has been some time since I wrote you, so I will take that pleasure to-night. We are all well except colds & I am suffering with rheumatism in my legs. We have had a very severe spell of disagreeable weather for some time, had a regular thunderstorm tonight. All the water courses are up very much, so it interferes with trade.

Gertrude has been doing her own cooking for the past two weeks & she succeeds splendidly. She has made some as good light bread as I ever saw anywhere. She is very proud of it & takes great delight in her undertaking. I am afraid she will not be able to stand it.

Our baby is growing and is as fat as a pig. She is trying to talk & begins pulling up by chairs. She is one of the best little things you ever saw. She will sit on the floor & play by the hour. Willie keeps growing & has begun to beg me to get him some pants like I wear. You asked for their Photographs. We will send them some time this spring. Our artist is now absent.

Well, I will tell you about my new business. So far we have succeeded better than we expected, have sold more Tobacco & got better prices than we anticipated. We had good sales last week & on Friday sold between 4 & 5000 #'s. If we can only continue the balance of the year, as well as we have begun, we will make some money, which will be more than we expected this year. I think by another year that it will pay handsomly, as there is large crops going to put out this year & I think we will get our share of it to sell. We have bought several hundred pounds of Leaf & made two shipments, but have not yet heard from it. I hope to make some money in that way, as we buy only five wrappers & smokers. We do not buy common stock at all.

The children send love & kisses to their dear Grandparents & Willie often talks of you & says he is going on the big train to see his Grand pa & Ma. Gertie & myself send much love to you both & hope to see you up this summer.

Your Loving Son,

F. A. Clinard

A. D. Clinard to Livingston N. Clinard

Athens, GA
March 15th 1880

Dear Brother,

I will write a line to say all are well, and doing well, and to ask you to write soon. I enclose a notice (cut from an Atlanta paper) of my house, which will give you a fare idea of how I stand with the public.
All join in love to all,
A. D. Clinard

Clinard House.

Among the best and most hospitable hotels in Georgia is the Clinard House, at Athens, presided over by that popular veteran of the hotel business, A. D. Clinard, Esq.

Clinard's table cannot be surpassed for the substantials or elegance by any house in the State, which fact is always cheering news to the traveling community—especially to drummers, for whose especial accommodation he has large, well-lighted rooms with plenty of sample-tables. Success to our friend, and may he live long to welcome his many friends.

H. W. Barrow to L. N. Clinard

Dunham, Buckley & Co.
340 Broadway,

P. O. Box 147   New York

April 8th 1880
Mr. L. N. Clinard

Dear Sir,

I was glad to receive your letter this morning. I have purchased the Black Drop Lining. I am about through here & want to go over to Baltimore to-night on the fast train & want to get through with my purchases at that place & start home Saturday morning. I have not bought as many prints as we thought & have been advised to hold off for the present, as it is the gen-

eral impression they will come down soon. Cotton is a shade lower. The weather is clear & cold here. I hope it most pleasant in our County. Glad to hear you have had a good trade. My kindest regards to all,
Yours truly,
H. W. Barrow

A. D. Clinard to Livingston N. Clinard

Clinard House
Athens, GA
April 24th 1880

Dear Brother,
    I drop a line to say we are all well as usual and getting along tolerably well. If I only had a good hotel building, I could do all the business in my line. I have doubts whether a new one will be built. The man who keeps the old hotel I used to keep, is doing very little. He and the owner of the property are in low already. He is the most unpopular man I ever saw but it helps me. The Grand Lodge Knights of Honor have been in session here this week. I entertained 38 of them. My house was headquarters as you will see from enclosed programme. Next week Ford's Theatrical of 20 persons will be with me two days. I must close.
All join in love to you & family.
A. D. Clinard

G. E. Clinard to Mr. and Mrs. Livingston N. Clinard

Hickory, N. C.
April 28th 1880

Dear Father & Mother,
    Frank has been away on business for several days, got back yesterday. I intended to write while he was gone, but felt so lonesome I kept very busy so that I might not get blue. We were sorry to hear that Mother's plants were killed - ours are doing well.
    We feel right anxious about our baby. She has not been at all well for several weeks & is falling off every day. I am afraid she is going to be sickly during the warm weather. Willie is well & still plays with the animals

Mr. Bush came down from Lenoir last Saturday & gave us a sermon on Sunday.

Brother Ed's letter came to Frank while he was away & I was glad he wrote, for he is awful mean about writing & Frank has been real hurt with him for not answering his letters before now. How is Sister Bessie's health now? Please give much love to them & all our other relatives & friends. I hope you will excuse a short letter this time, for I haven't enough ink to finish writing. Frank & the children send love. Frank is very busy.
Your Affectionate Daughter,
G. E. Clinard

F. A. Clinard to Mr. and Mrs. Livingston N. Clinard

J. G. HALL,   R. L. PATTERSON
Office of HALL BROTHERS,
WHOLESALE AND RETAIL DEALERS IN
General Merchandise.
HIGHEST MARKET PRICE PAID FOR ALL COUNTRY PRODUCE
Hickory, N. C.,

May 10th 1880

My Dear Father and Mother,

It has been some time since I wrote you and the reason for it is, I have been very busy, have had a good many settlements of large accts. to make & have done a good deal of hard, long riding. Since the last of March, I have made three long trips. One in the South Mountains, one to Tennessee, & the last one to the Northern part of Wilkes. I saw Lige Blair & he told me he had seen you Father.

We are getting along with our Tobacco business very well, in fact have sold more than we expected to. The preparation through this country is large for the coming crop & most people say they have fine plants, several have set out. We have sold a good lot of Guano.

Hickory is improving rapidly & I think we will have a town yet of no small pretentions.

I had three propositions made me last week, to sell my interest in my warehouse but I refused. I think I have got hold of the thing to make some money out of. I have done a power of hard work to try & build up a trade & I think another year I will reap the harvest.

Our garden is looking finely, but we are beginning to need rain. We sent our Wet Nurse off Saturday. Weaned Estelle & she is doing very well. Gertrude is doing her own nursing now. Willie is a great big fellow for his age & he has been after his Mama to let him wear pants & coat like Papa. Gertie made him some new dresses & he said he did not want them.

I am very busy, have got the Books all on my hands. Our Book keeper has gone off on a trip to Virginia for himself. I have bought in my rounds five head of horses, & have made some good trades. Made $50.00 on a pair of mules.

Gertie & the children send love to you both. Willie often talks about you. He tells me he will take me to see you if I want to go. My love & I hope you will both enjoy good health this summer.
Your Loving Son,
Frank A. Clinard

F. A. Clinard to Mr. and Mrs. Livingston N. Clinard

J. G. HALL,   R. L. PATTERSON
Office of HALL BROTHERS,
WHOLESALE AND RETAIL DEALERS IN
General Merchandise.
HIGHEST MARKET PRICE PAID FOR ALL COUNTRY PRODUCE
Hickory, N. C.,

June 8th 1880

My Dear Father and Mother,

Doubtless you have been looking for a letter from me sooner. I am very busy these days, collecting apc's, preparitory to taking inventory. We are all tolerbly well. Estelle was very sick last week with Cholera Infantum, but is better. I got her a Nanny goat last week & we have been feeding her on goats milk, which seems to agree with her splendid. Willie was very well the last we heard from him. I am going after him Sunday, if nothing prevents. I miss him a great deal, especially on Sundays.

Well Mother, we have something to eat now, such as snaps, potatoes, beets, cucumbers, etc. Our cabbage will soon do to eat. It is heading nicely & our tomatoes are as large as the top of a tumbler. Our potatoes are fine. I believe I have the finest garden in town & thanks to you for part of it. We have plenty of fruit on our lot. Gertie has sold several bushels of May Apples (had dumplings for dinner). We have cherries, raspberries & plenty of peaches & apples, also plums. You speak of your young cow. We will soon have a fresh cow at our house. My cow is nearly throughbred Devon. She is a beautiful red, & a good rich milker.

Father, I am of the opinion you are, about the Pfaff matter, & I will ask you to account for me in the matter. I am sorry you were busy & could not show Mr. Joyner more attention, for he is one of the best friends I ever had, if he is a preacher. He married us, & baptised Will & was always my personal friend.

Hickory is moving onward & upward. Lots of building going on & lots of Tobacco being manufactured. The growing Tobacco round through this country is looking finely & there is a large crop planted. I hope to handle large quantities next season. We have sold near 50,000 pounds so far, which far exceeds what we expected. Gertie sends love to you both & Estelle kisses. Much love to you both.
Your Loving Son,
Frank A. Clinard

G. E. & F. A. Clinard to Mr. and Mrs. Livingston N. Clinard

Hickory, N. C.
June 24th 1880

Dear Father & Mother,

I should have written sooner, but have been so busy lately sewing, putting up fruit &c. I canned & pressured cherries & yesterday put up one bushel of blackberries. Later I will have to put up tomatoes & peaches.

We were so glad to hear of the birth of our little niece. I have written to them, but have heard nothing since you wrote, hope they are getting on all right.

Frank did not get off for Willie until last Sunday. They came back on Monday. Willie has been very well & contented since his return, says he wants to stay at home now. He & the baby have fine times with the kid. It is very playful & is company for the children. The baby is well except for a cold.

We are needing rain badly & the garden does not look as flourishing as it did some time back. Our cow has a fine young calf & I am in hopes we will have plenty of milk now, but I am afraid our woman does not understand milking properly.

Frank is very much interested in his tobacco business.

Lindsay came down from the Valley yesterday, will return today.

Our new Episcopal minister preached for us the first time last Sunday. We are much pleased with him. Frank & the children send love. Please give my love to all.

Your Affectionate Daughter,

G. E. Clinard

P. S.

Father, our Bookkeeper, Mr. Shuford, will be in Salem Saturday & will call on you. He leaves today for Kernersville. He is interested in the Washing Machine business. Show him what attention you can, as he is a particular friend of mine & we are together all the time in the office.

I have had a very bad cold for two weeks & it don't seem to improve much. Ed is a strange boy, he has not written a word about his folks, did not write about the birth of his baby. Mother, I hope you are better & will take care of yourself & not go & over heat yourself canning fruits &c. We are having dry hot weather & our garden is suffering badly. Much love to you both.

Your Loving Son,

Frank

F. A. Clinard to Mr. and Mrs. Livingston N. Clinard

J. G. HALL,   R. L. PATTERSON

Office of HALL BROTHERS,

WHOLESALE AND RETAIL DEALERS IN

General Merchandise.

HIGHEST MARKET PRICE PAID FOR ALL COUNTRY PRODUCE

Hickory, N. C.,

July 8th 1880

My Dear Father and Mother,

We are all tolerbly well except Estelle, who had the misfortune yesterday to get a severe fall. Our nurse let her fall over the banisters of our front porch & bruised her head badly, also her left hip & back. The Dr. says he fears she is internally hurt. She can't stand up today, but she is bright & playful, was playing with Willie when I went to supper.

Well, we have had some Winston people here this week. Mr. & Mrs. Stockton & Frank Bohannon. They came Monday night & left last night, except Frank B., who is still here. Gertie, myself & the children called on Mrs. Stockton Tuesday. Mr. Stockton went to the Valley to see Sam Patterson. They seem to be enjoying their trip very much. I met them at the train Monday night & saw them off last night. Mr. Stockton seems to be well pleased with Hickory. Mrs. Stockton can tell you about our children.

We have had several good rains lately, which has helped vegetation very much & especially our garden. We have had tomatoes nearly two weeks, also cabbage & corn. Tobacco through this country looks finely & the general prospect is we will have a large crop. Mr. Wiley is now in Rutherford Co. prospecting. We are going to begin work early, & work hard to build us up a large trade. We have sold Tobacco within the last week from Eagle Mills, Iredell Co., so you know we are beginning to work up a trade from a distance. Our trade is rather dull at present. Black Berries have opened at 5 cents, but I think will go higher soon.

Craig Shuford was very much pleased with his trip to Salem & Winston. He told me Ed showed him round & was very kind to him.

Gertrude received a letter today from Sister Bessie. We are glad to hear she & the baby are getting along so finely. Ed never has written a word to us yet. He is a strange creature, can't understand him. Willie continues to beg me for "big pants, vest, coat, suspenders & a great big shirt like I wear." He says sister is my Gal baby & he is my little man. Our neighbor, Capt. John Walker, has a little girl, a little larger than Willie, who plays with him every day, they are great friends. Gertie sends much love to you both & the children kisses. Love to you all.
Your Loving Son,
Frank A. Clinard

C. Vogler to L. N. Clinard

Eagle Hotel
Asheville, N . C.

July 10th 1880
Mr. L. N. Clinard

Dear Friend,

I was very glad indeed to get your letter & to know that Bro Pfohl is better & that you are getting along so nicely. So far I have had just a delightful trip & have enjoyed myself very much. I am feeling a great deal better, & have not been sick any at all since I left home. I am now at Alexander's, 10 miles from Asheville, on my way to Warm Springs. We will remain here over Sunday as it is such a pleasant place. I am glad you had the good luck to sell a Rake & I immediately took your advice by Thomas Atkins, of Davenport who is up here for a while.

I saw Mr. Hall when I passed Hickory & he said Frank & family were well as usual. I want to stop over a day when I return if I can. I guess I will be home by next Wednesday a week. Cuz Carrie Stoffer wants me to wait until then for her, as Hy Fries will stop at Palmyra. I hope Mrs. Clinard's health is better & that you may be able to keep up. Give my kindest regards to Mr. Barrow, Pfohl & Johnnie.

Your Friend,
C. Vogler

R. A. Jinkins to L. N. Clinard

Washington City, Virginia Midland
& Great Southern Railroad
General Office
Greensboro, N. C.

July 30, 1880
Mr. Clinard

Dear Sir,

The ticket is $26, will only be good till 15 of August going & 1st of Nov. coming back. This is best that can be done & I think the % to be sold at this price is limited, but don't know at what amount of any charge should take place & the tickets be extended till 1st of Sept. going & will let you know at once.

Most Respectfully,
R. A. Jinkens
Mr. McAdoo's ticket are the same as Charlotte.

F. A. Clinard to Mr. and Mrs. Livingston N. Clinard

J. G. HALL,   R. L. PATTERSON

Office of HALL BROTHERS,
WHOLESALE AND RETAIL DEALERS IN
General Merchandise.
HIGHEST MARKET PRICE PAID FOR ALL COUNTRY PRODUCE
Hickory, N. C.,

August 5th 1880

My Dear Father and Mother,

Your's received last week & was very glad to hear from you and especially to get your note Mother. Your writing is good for sore eyes. I have been exceedingly busy for the past week, have had more to do than I could well get through with.

Gertrude is complaining again with her old disease & Willie has been real sick with some sort of fever. I think it came from eating to many peaches. He has been in the habit of going out to the trees & helping himself. We are having a cool rainy spell, both were needed very much.

Mother, I did not intend bringing Gertrude with me if I go to Salem. She will hardly be able and you can rest assured, no one has fibbed on me, we look for it on Father's birthday.

I was at a wedding reception last night of Miss Hattie Hardin & Berry Binford. Miss Hardin is a daughter of Maj. Tom Hardin, the shoe man. We had quite a pleasant time.

This section & the mountains beyond here are crowded with visitors. I have never seen the like. Everything in town is full up with boarders. Tobacco is looking splendid all through this section, a large crop expected & I hope to handle my share of it. I am glad to see Ed has embarked in the business. We sold some Tobacco today from Cabarus Co., which you know is a long ways from here. Gertrude sends much love to you both & the children send kisses. Love to you both.

Your Affectionate Son,

Frank A. Clinard

E. C. Clinard to Mr. and Mrs. Livingston N. Clinard

August 15th 1880

Dear Father,

I thought I would write you a letter this evening. I hope you and Mother had a nice trip and that you arrived in New York all right. I went down to Church this morning, Aunt Liza was there, she said everything was going on all right at home. She sends love. I am feeling a good deal better than I did when you left, my breast is not hurting me at all. I have not had any more headache for the last few days.

Byrin Spaugh is very low, they don't think he will live. Dr. Bynun was buried Saturday, there was quite a large crowd at the funeral. Old Mr. Cloud, Mr. Willis Father in Law, died yesterday, was buried this evening at 4 o'clock. I did not hear what was the matter with him.

We have not changed the price of Berries yet, but I think they will go to 5 1/2 or 6 cents in a few days. I will let your folks know it as soon as we change the price. We had a right good trade Saturday. I saw Mr. Barrow this morning. He did not say how trade was with them. I think it will be right lively this week, it has cleared up nice, so the people can get to Town once more.

I received a letter from Bessie this morning, she sends Love to you and Mother. She says the baby is getting on fine, it is growing fast and getting right fat.

I am going to move our things from the Hotel tomorrow, so I will have every evening during the week to fix up. Bessie will be home on Saturday.

Henry Siddall was in Durham on Saturday out of his head, they say he had a sun stroke, he had a whiskey stroke I expect, he came home last night on the train. I have not heard how he is, since he is at home.

I hope your trip will do you and Mother both a heap of good. I received a letter from Frank yesterday, they are all well, he said he thought he would come down this fall and bring Willie. I wish he would, I want to see Willie. I wrote a letter to Uncle Andy, I know he will be surprised to get one from me, it has been so long since I wrote to him. Give my love to Mother and accept the same for yourself.

Your Affectionate Son,

E. C. Clinard P. S. I received your letter this morning (Monday) was glad to hear that you arrived safe.

E. C. C.

G. E. Clinard to Mr. and Mrs. Livingston N. Clinard

Hickory, N. C.
Aug. 28th 1880

Dear Father & Mother,

We received your welcome letter several days ago & the children's presents came safely to hand this morning. We are very much obliged for them. The sack is beautiful & is exceedingly becoming to Estelle, although she is so fair. The goods for Willie's suit is handsome, & just came in the nick of time for I was wishing for something of the kind to make him a nice Sunday suit. It is enough material to make him two full suits. He is the craziest child for pants you ever saw & was so proud when we told him you had sent the cloth for his pants. I asked him what I should tell you & he said "Tell Grand-pa & Grand-ma it is very well indeed."

We were so glad to hear you enjoyed your trip & that Mother was benefited by it. I earnestly hope she may continue to improve. Estelle has had a severe cold for several days but otherwise is well & gets fatter every day. She is walking alone now & trys very hard to talk. She shows the girl in her love of dolls, but she soon breaks them up. Sis Annie got one of these painted leather dolls for her little girl here. I tried also to get one, but were all gone before I knew of it. So Estelle has taken the elephant for her baby. It is as much as she can do to carry it & I wish you could see her rock & sing to it. Willie is a perfect boy & begs for pants, whips, wagons, wheel barrows &c.

We have had fine tomatoes all summer & I have canned a good many. We also had a fine chance of peaches on our lot, which I used to can & made preserves & sweet pickles, also made some nice sweet pickle of the citron melon. Frank joins in love to all.

Your Affectionate Daughter,

G. E. Clinard

F. A. Clinard to Mr. and Mrs. Livingston N. Clinard

J. G. Hall,   P. C. Hall
Hall Brothers,
Wholesale and Retail Merchants,
Hickory, N. C.

Sept. 9th 1880

Dear Father & Mother,

I am glad to inform you that all is well & that we have another Daughter at our house, was born today at 1 1/2 o'clock & her name is Mary Charlotte. You ought to have seen Estelle taking on over her. Willie is at Sis Annie's, don't know what he will say. Gertrude is doing very well & sends love to you both. Will keep you posted as to Gertrude's condition. Of course you know who we named the baby for. For you Mother, & my own Mother. Love to you both.

F. A. Clinard

Father, she is a birthday present for you. We were in hopes she would be born on your birthday, but she missed it 3 days.

P. S. The berry trade has been rather slim, have only ship'd 8 or 10 car loads, but apples, the whole face of the earth is covered with them & low prices.

F. A. Clinard to Mr. and Mrs. Livingston N. Clinard

J. G. Hall,

P. C. Hall

Hall Brothers,
Wholesale and Retail Merchants,
Hickory, N. C.

Sept. 24th 1880

Dear Father & Mother,

Your letter received yesterday & we were glad to hear from you. Very sorry to hear you both are unwell, hope you may get better very soon.

Well, we have had quite a busy week, have had something to do every night. Tuesday night I enjoyed myself, more than I ever did in one night in my life. I heard the Elocutionist Willoughby Reade, he is the best I ever heard. Wednesday, the Circus & we shut up & all went in the day time. Willie can tell all about it, was perfectly delighted. He got away from me & started under the rope to see the animals, was going right up to the cage & I caught him. He tells all the different names of the animals. Last night the Democratic Candidates spoke. Worth, Jarvis, Leach, all spoke in our warehouse & had a large crowd.

Well, Gertrude is getting along finely, also the Baby. She is growing fat. I can hardly tell you who she looks like. I think she will be a brunett. Estelle is a beautiful blonde now & I think she will not change. I hope not, for she is a beauty & has the prettiest eyes I nearly ever saw. They are light, what would be called a gray eye. She is cutting her jaw teeth & it makes her a little fretful at times. Gertie is trying to take care of herself this time. She is prudent in her diet & she only stays up part of the day. I do hope she will get better, for I have been sore afflicted with Doctors bills, till I git out of heart some times, but I look on the bright side & keep cheerful, which I find far better than to get low spirited. Gertrude is not troubled with her milk so much this time as before, & she thinks she will be able to nurse Baby all the time. She sends much love to you both & will write you as soon as she is able. The children send kisses to their dear Grand Parents.
Your Loving Son,
Frank

G. E. Clinard to Mr. and Mrs. Livingston N. Clinard

Hickory, N. C.
Nov. 1880

Dear Father & Mother,

I am afraid you think me a poor correspondent, but I really find it hard work to find time to write with so many little children around me. It is late at night now & they are all asleep. Frank has told us all about his visit to you & I wish so much we could take all the children to see you. Last Tuesday, the baby was two months old & I had her & the other children weighed. Willie weighed 39 pounds, Estelle 28 & Charlotte 16. Don't you think that will do pretty well? Yesterday a week ago we had the baby baptized. She behaved as well as possible, sat up & looked all about the church & everybody said she was a little beauty.

Well Mother, Estelle is happy now since she has her baby doll. I wish you could have seen her delight when the box was first opened. She hugs & kisses & rocks the baby & sings to it. She has examined all its clothes & I believe the shoes please her more than anything else, for when anyone comes in to see us, "my babie's oes" are the first things she shows. I asked her if I must send Grand-ma a kiss for her & she said "no," for that is what she always says when she means yes.

We are expecting to get a white cook from Lenoir this week, Corrinna McNeal by name. She is said to be an excellent girl, so I hope she will suit me.

I could write more, but it is so late I really must close. Please give my love to Aunt Eliza & to Ed & Bessie when you see them. Frank is away later than usual tonight. I hope you both may continue to improve in health. Hoping to hear from you soon,
I am Your Affectionate Daughter,
G. E. Clinard

Memoir of Sister Charlotte Elisabeth Clinard

Memoir of the married Sister Charlotte Elisabeth Clinard, m. n. Shultz.

Our departed sister was born on Sept 6th 1834. The parents were Br. Jacob Shultz, and his wife Johanna Eleanore, m. n. Vierling, who resided near Salem.

They dedicated this their daughter, the youngest of a family of nine children, to the Lord, in Holy Baptism, on Oct 5th 1834. Her childhood and youth were spent at home and in this place, and as a member of the congregation here at Salem, she enjoyed the privileges of our church, becoming a full communicant member by the rite of Confirmation, on Palm Sunday, April 13th 1851, and partaking for the first time of the Lord's Supper on the following Maundy Thursday.

On June 8th 1853 she was united in the bonds of Holy Matrimony to Br. Livingston Nath'l Clinard, to whom she has approved herself as a faithful Christian wife.

She was endowed with a strong constitution and always enjoyed good health. The privilege of being brought up in the nurture and admonition of the Lord, was not without its beneficial effect upon the formation of her character, and the development of those qualities of mind and heart which for her were the esteem and friendship of her acquaintances, and endeared her to her now bereaved husband and children. To them she endeavored to discharge her duty faithfully as an affectionate wife and mother, and her memory will be blessed and precious to them, while they hold in fond remembrance her efforts for their happiness and welfare. In the family-circle, amongst her friends and neighbors, and as a member of the Christian Church, she commended herself to the esteem and love of all. The means of grace were appreciated and enjoyed by her, and she endeavored to walk worthy of the vocation wherewith she was called.

That she derived benefit from her religious privileges, and was prepared by them, through the grace of God, to leave this world in peace, and become a happy member of the church triumphant, was abundantly manifested during her last sickness, even to the end. Some weeks ago, she was attacked by the fever which had now proved fatal. Although her illness was severe indeed, her mind remained perfectly clear, and she was fully conscious to the last. Not only did the Lord spare her in this respect, but gave her great peace in her soul. No doubts or fears distressed her, nothing was suffered to disturb the calm repose of her soul upon the mercy and love of

261

her God and Savior. She was quite resigned to his will, and although she would gladly have remained with her dear family, especially when, in the early part of last week there seemed to be some prospect of her recovery, yet when there was again a change for the worse, it caused her no uneasiness or disquietude. She evidently enjoyed that "peace of God that passeth all understanding," and felt assured that nothing could separate her from His love.

On last Tuesday morning it became evident that all hope of her recovery must be relinquished. Towards evening we gathered at her bedside, and united in singing and prayers on her behalf, and although no longer able to speak distinctly, she signified upon being asked, the pleasure and comfort it had afforded her.

Yesterday morning (July 28th) the last blessing of the Church was imparted to her, and about an hour after, she peacefully breathed her last.

> "Blest soul! How sweetly doth she rest
> From every toil and care
> Enjoying now on Jesus' breast
> Bliss far beyond compare"

Her age was 34 years, 10 months, and 22 days.

Her husband and family desires to return thanks to the many kind friends who rendered assistance during her illness.

Memoir of Sister Mary Emmeline Clinard

The memoir of our departed Sister Mary Emmeline Butner is drawn up according to her modest request.

She was the daughter of John Christian and Mahala Butner, and was born at Bethabara Oct 15th 1837. She was baptised in her infancy and was confirmed as a member of the Moravian Church at Salem, on April 1st 1855. On August 31st 1870 she was united with Br L. N. Clinard. She entered into rest on Tuesday morning, Feb 11th 1890 at the age of 52 years, 3 months and 26 days.

Livingston N. Clinard Obituary

Union Republican   March 26, 1896

SUDDEN DEATH OF MR. LIVINGSTON N. CLINARD

One by one our friends and acquaintances of long standing are laying down life's burdens and entering into their eternal rest.

This week it is our painful duty to chronicle the death of Mr. Livingston N. Clinard, which occurred in Salem, Saturday evening, at the age of 67 years.

After a busy day in the store of H. A. Giersh, where he was a valued employee, he started home for supper about 6:30, o'clock. As he was going down the cross street that intersects Main and Liberty Streets, at Shaffner's Drug Store, the summons came. Parties passing came at once to his aid and he was carried into the Drug Store and medical assistance given, but to no avail, for the vital spark of life had fled. The deceased had been in feeble health for some time, suffering from pulmonary trouble, but his sudden death was unexpected and a shock to both relatives and friends.

Mr. Clinard was born in the Abbott's Creek section of Davidson county and came to Salem early in life as a clerk in the store of Boner & Crist. He was possessed of exceptional business tact and qualifications and twice engaged in mercantile pursuits, once under the firm name of Boner & Clinard and again, later, as Clinard & Brooks. The intervening time was given to positions as salesman in several of our local firms of the past and present. For many years he was Secretary and Treasurer of the town of Salem.

In the family circle two sons survive, Mr. Frank Clinard, of Hickory and Mr. Ed Clinard, of this city. He was twice married, his second wife preceding him a few years since. Since that time he has been living with his son in this city, and to whose home he had started for supper, when the fatal messenger came.

We have known the deceased since our boyhood and will miss his familiar face and almost daily greeting. He was a staunch patron and constant reader of THE REPUBLICAN. He has entered into rest. Peace to his ashes.

The departed was a member of Calvary Moravian Church and Bishop Rondthaler and Rev. A. D. Theeler conducted the funeral services Tuesday morning after which the remains were interred in the Moravian Graveyard.

Family of Livingston N. Clinard

Livingston Nathanael CLINARD; b: Sep 6, 1828; d: Mar 21, 1896

+Charlotte Elisabeth SHULTZ; b: Sep 6, 1834; d: Jul 28, 1869; m: May 25, 1853, Salem, NC

— Francis (Frank) Augustus CLINARD; b: Mar 8, 1854; d: May 10, 1934

  +Gertrude Estelle JONES; b: Aug 25, 1857; d: Sep 17, 1932; m: Jun 7, 1876, Catawba Co., NC

    — William Livingston CLINARD; b: May 3, 1877; d: Dec 27, 1961

      +Lucille MONTAGUE; m:

      +Lillian Charlotte DELLOW; b: Feb 22, 1887; d: Sep 20, 1961; m: Oct 15, 1918

        — infant son CLINARD; d: Dec 25, 1922

        — Lillian Charlotte CLINARD; b: Jun 14, 1924; d: Jun 20, 1924

    — Estelle Lenoir CLINARD; b: 1879; d: 1926

      +Horace Beard HAYES; b: 1878; m: est 1901

    — Mary Charlotte CLINARD; b: Sep 9, 1880; d: Oct 9, 1900

    — Francis (Frank) A. CLINARD; b: Nov 6, 1882; d: Mar 2, 1885

    — Edward Clifton CLINARD; b: Nov 9, 1885; d: Feb 7, 1914

    — Annie Edith CLINARD; b: Dec 17, 1889; d: Jul 17, 1890

    — Jones "J." Weston CLINARD; b: Jan 20, 1892; d: Apr 11, 1971

      +Mary Sue BELL; m:

      +Hazel Minter EARP; m:

      +Rosa COLLINS; b: May 20, 1897; d: Dec 30, 1955; m: Jun 5, 1920

    — Bahnson W. CLINARD; b: Oct 16, 1899; d: 1899

— Edward Clifton CLINARD; b: Nov 27, 1857, Salem, Forsyth Co., NC; d: Sep 8, 1927, Dobbs, NC

  +Bessie BROWN; b: 1862; m: May 14, 1879

    — unknown CLINARD; b: 1880; d: bef 1900

    — Mary P. CLINARD; b: 1883

      +Brantley H. FINCH; b: 1880; m: bet 1900 and 1910

+Mary Emmeline BUTNER; b: Oct 26, 1837; d: Feb 11, 1890, Salem, NC; m: Aug 31, 1870

Memoir of Bro. L. N. Clinard

Brother Livingston Nathaniel Clinard was born September 6th, 1828, in Davidson County. At about 18 years of age he began to clerk at the store of Hamilton Lindsay, at Friendship, in Guilford County. Moving to Salem in 1851 he entered the employ of Boner and Crist, merchants. After one of his business changes in Salem, he became book-keeper for the R. L. Patterson factory in Caldwell County, at Patterson. Moving back to Salem in 1868 he remained here in business until his departure from this life.

On January 25th, 1852, he had joined the Moravian Church at this Salem, being received by the rite of adult baptism. He partook of the Holy Communion for the first time on Feb. 1st, 1852.

On June 8th, 1853, he was married to Charlotte Elizabeth Shultz, of Salem. Two children blessed their wedded life, Francis Augustus and Edward Clifton, both of whom survive him and their mother. On July 28th, 1869, Bro Clinard was left to mourn the death of his wife, who had been by his side for 16 years.

On August 31st, 1870, he was again married to Mary Emmaline Butner. Twenty years later, Feb 11th, 1890, he was again bereft by the hand of death, of his wife, after a long and lingering illness, and he has since then been living at the home of his son Edward, when in the spring of 1892 this circle of Moravian membership was formed. Bro Clinard, believing that it would be for the advancement of the Maker's cause, gladly put down his name as one of the 30 who voluntarily withdrew from Home Church connection, to form the nucleus of the Calvary Congregation. Since then he has most zealously and earnestly labored in every way to support the work at this place, being one of the most loyal and true brethren that a church could ever have. He served a term as member of the Calvary Committee, and has for about two years been a faithful teacher in the Sunday School. Latterly his failing health occasionally forbade his attendance in God's house, but he never ceased in his petitions to the throne of grace for a bountiful blessing upon the church and congregation he loved, and also upon his pastors. The joy that he took in everything that concerned the Lord's service has, in recent months particularly, been one of his happy characteristics. Latterly, also, the noon-day prayer meeting in Salem has been one of his most loved spheres of activity.

For about a year he has never been quite well, and sometimes he would speak of his end and hope that it might not be preceded by a long, slow illness. The Lord answered this desire, for the call came to him with startling

265

suddenness. Seemingly in as good health as usual, he attended to all his duties last Saturday, March 21st, 1896, but as he was coming home to supper that evening the swift summons came to him "Come to the better house." When friends reached his side, it was already almost over, and easily, peacefully, he passed on beyond, to be forever with his savior, whom, having not ever, he loved. His age was 67 years, 6 months and 15 days.

Gertrude E. Clinard Obituary

Hickory Daily Record   Saturday, September 17, 1932

MRS. CLINARD DIES OF HEART AILMENT HERE

Prominent Resident; Funeral Set For Sunday

Mrs. Gertrude E. Clinard, 75, wife of Frank A. Clinard and a member of a prominent western North Carolina family, died at her home on Thirteenth street at 8:50 o'clock this morning, following an extended illness.

Mrs. Clinard had been in failing health the past fifteen months and for the past eleven days her condition had grown critical. She had been suffering from heart trouble.

The funeral will be conducted at the Church of the Ascension, Episcopal, Sunday afternoon at 4 o'clock by the rector, Rev. Sam S. Stroup, assisted by Rev. E. deF. Heald and Rev. E. N. Joyner. Burial will follow in Oakwood cemetery.

Active pallbearers will include T. M. Johnston, T. A. Mott, J. L. Cilley, J. L. Friday, R. E. Martin and J. C. Martin. The honorary pallbearers will be H. A. Wise, E. W. Walton, Jim Burns, M. H. Yount, J. H. Patrick and Ervin Yount.

Rev. Mr. Joyner performed the ceremony that united Mr. and Mrs. Clinard in marriage on June 7, 1876 in the old German Reformed church on Ninth avenue. The wedding of Mr. and Mrs. Clinard was the first to be solemnized in a Hickory church.

Mrs. Clinard was the daughter of the late Captain and Mrs. William F. Jones. She was born in Hendersonville but came to Hickory in 1875. Her father was the first man to take a company from Caldwell county to the War Between the States. He was captain of the troop and a lawyer by profession.

Surviving Mrs. Clinard are the husband, Frank A. Clinard, two sons, William L. Clinard and J. Weston Clinard, of Hickory, and two granddaughters, Mrs. Graham S. Ridgen of Portland, Oregon, and Miss Charlotte C. Hayes of El Paso, Texas.

Six children preceded their mother to the grave. They were; Mrs. Horace B. Hayes, El Paso, Texas, Miss Mary Charlotte Clinard, Frank A. Clinard, Jr., Edward C. Clinard, Annie E. Clinard, all of Hickory.

Hickory Daily Record   Monday, September 19, 1932

MRS. CLINARD FUNERAL HELD

Rites Conducted Sunday At Episcopal Church Here

The Church of the Ascension, Episcopal, was filled to overflowing for the funeral services conducted for Mrs. Frank A. Clinard, 75, Sunday afternoon. The services were held in charge of the rector, Rev. Sam B. Stroup, assisted by Rev. E. deF. Heald and Rev. E. N. Joyner.

Active pallbearers were T. M. Johnston, T. A. Mott, J. L. Cilley, J. L. Friday, R. E. Martin, and J. C. Martin. The honorary pallbearers were H. A. Wise, E. W. Walton, Jim Burns, M. H. Yount, J. H. Patrick and Ervin Yount.

Burial took place in Oakwood Cemetery, the grave being mantled over with beautiful flowers.

The death of Mrs. Clinard occurred Saturday morning following an illness for fifteen months of heart trouble. For the past eleven days Mrs. Clinard's condition had grown critical. She is survived by the husband, Frank A. Clinard, and two sons, William L. Clinard and Weston Clinard, all of Hickory. Six children preceded their mother to the grave.

Mrs. F. A. Clinard, 75, who died at her home here this morning, was the first woman married in a Hickory church. The above picture shows Mrs. Clinard as a young bride.

Frank A. Clinard Obituary

Hickory Daily Record   May 10, 1934

FRANK CLINARD, PIONEER LOCAL RESIDENT, DIES

Illness Proves Fatal To Well Known Citizen

Frank A. Clinard, age 80, one of the best known citizens of Hickory and a pioneer in local business and fraternal circles, died this morning at 4:50 o'clock, at the home of his son, W. L. Clinard, North Thirteenth street.

The funeral will be held Friday afternoon at four o'clock from the Episcopal church. The burial will be at Oakwood cemetery here, with the Masonic lodge led by Knights Templar escort, in charge.

Active pallbearers named, all members of the Masonic lodge, are: E. L., Dr. J. B. Little, W. R. McDonald, P. J. Suttlemyre, V. B. Cashio and W. L. Boatright.

Honorary pallbearers named are: L. A. Wise, J. H. Patrick, T. M. Johnston, J. C. Martin, A. J. Bradshaw, Mayor M. H. Yount, J. L. Cilley and Major T. A. Mott.

Mr. Clinard had been in failing health since the death of his wife, at whose bedside he watched devotedly. A few months ago he became critically ill and it was thought he could not possibly survive. However, a few days he rallied and for some weeks he had been able to be around the city almost daily, chatting with his friends and enjoying his old-time cronies.

Mr. Clinard, who was born March 8, 1854, in Forsyth county, had enjoyed a crowded, active life. He had looked forward with much anticipation to reaching his eightieth milestone, and this had been pushed by two months and two days when the end came.

Mr. Clinard had been one of the outstanding figures in Hickory for many years. He came here on September 3, 1873, from Winston-Salem, and with the exception of a few years had made his home in Hickory for the past sixty years.

He and his wife, the late Mrs. Gertrude Jones Clinard, were the first couple to be married in a church at Hickory. The ceremony was performed in the old Germany Reformed church on Ninth avenue, on June 7, 1876, by Rev. E. N. Joyner, Episcopal minister, who now lives in Hickory. Will Clinard, a son of the couple, was the first baby to be baptized in a church in Hickory. The ceremony took place at the present Episcopal church.

269

Frank A. Clinard, age 80, shown above, pioneer in Hickory business and fraternal circles, died this morning at 4:50. The above picture shows Mr. Clinard about the time of his marriage in 1876 to Miss Gertrude Jones, who preceded him to the grave. They held the distinction of being the first couple to have a church wedding in Hickory.

At the time of his death Mr. Clinard was the oldest Mason from point of membership in Catawba county. When he joined the lodge Mr. Clinard realized an ambition he had cherished since early boyhood. He was active in Masonry and took his third degree work on St. John's Day, June 24, 1876, in Hickory.

When Mr. Clinard first came to Hickory in 1873, the town was little more than a village, not anywhere nearing its thousand population mark. Some years ago Mr. Clinard helped to lay out the present city limits of Hickory, which is a circle forming it's center on the smokestack of the freight depot.

The first work that Mr. Clinard engaged in after coming to Hickory was as bookkeeper for Hall and Patterson, one of the largest general mercantile establishments in this section of the state. He remained as bookkeeper for Hall Brothers successor to Hall and Patterson, and later went into the tobacco warehouse business, for which Hickory was once noted.

In 1883 Mr. Clinard started with the Piedmont Wagon and Manufacturing company as traveling salesman with all southern states south of Maryland, and east of the Mississippi river, as his territory. For a time he left the road and went into the insurance business, but resigned to go back with the Piedmont Wagon and Manufacturing company until he retired some years ago and removed to his farm in the Happy Valley. Later, he returned to Hickory and continued to make his residence here, where he had grown to be a part of the very heart of the city.

Mr. Clinard was a genial figure and numbered his friends by his acquaintances. He was one of the staunchest Democrats the party ever had locally, and delighted in the campaigns made in local, state and national elections. Winter or summer, Mr. Clinard was never seen without a flower in his buttonhole, nor was he ever seen without his famous smile and cheery greeting to every person he met.

Two sons survive Mr. Clinard. Will Clinard and Weston Clinard, both of Hickory. Other children and Mrs. Clinard preceded him to the grave.

A Tale of Corn, Hogs and a Large Stick[41]

"Among the intimate sketches concerning the early population of Hickory given by Major Latta are the following:...Back in the days of 'auld lang syne,' hogs, cows, sheep and other stock were permitted to run at large, the cultivated fields alone being enclosed by fences. At that time it was not at all unusual for what is now called Union Square to be thronged with hogs and cows. Hall Brothers operated the largest store in town, and handled considerable country produce. The late F. A. Clinard was bookkeeper for the store. The late Daniel Whisnant lived in a large log house, built on the spot where C. H. Geitner's stone residence now stands. Mr. Whisnant had many hogs that made daily trips to town. On a certain day, Hall Brothers had bought a load of corn, some of which spilled on the ground and on the store floor. The hogs followed the trail of scattered corn, until possibly a dozen hogs were in the store. The bookkeeper mentioned above had gotten tired of driving the hogs out through the front door, and it occurred to him as being a good time to teach the hogs an object lesson. The back door of the store was ten or 12 feet above the ground. The bookkeeper quickly closed the front door of the store, and at once began pounding the hogs with a large stick, forcing them to make their exit through the back door. Upon striking the ground some of them were killed outright, some escaped with broken legs, others crippled otherwise. About this time Mr. Whisnant was informed as to what happened up to that time and began gathering up the dead and crippled hogs, and immediately a contest in modified profanity ensued, which old timers say reverberated for several hours after the contest, but no further damage was done...."

---

[41] The compilers believe this story,which is not mentioned in the letters, would be of interest to the reader. From "A History of Catawba County", compiled and published by Catawba Historical Association, Inc., 1954, page 450

Index

Index

Index

Index

Index